SMART

IN EVERYTHING

... EXCEPT

SCHOOL

By
G. N. Getman, O.D., D.O.S., Sc.D.

VisionExtension

Printed in the United States of America

Managing Editor: Sally Marshall Corngold
Illustrations: Susan Neas
Cover Design: Carolyn Davis Design

Published by VisionExtension, Inc.
2912 South Daimler Stret
Santa Ana, CA 92705-5811

Library of Congress Cataloging-in-Publication Data
Getman, Gerald N.
    Smart in everything—except school / by G.N. Getman.
        p.   cm.
    Includes bibliographical references.
    ISBN 0-929780-03-5 :
    1. Visual learning. 2. Child development. 3. Learning disabilities.
    I. Title.
    LB1067.G48 1991
    370.15'23--dc20   92-3089
                                                          CIP

CONTENTS

Preface

The first draft of this book was written more than 15 years ago and for various reasons has rested in the bottom drawer of a file cabinet since then. It all came about in the first place because of a deep and troubling concern about the academic failures of too many children who, no matter how evaluated, should not have been failing. At the end of many months of struggle with that first draft, there seemed to be some significant changes emerging in the curricula being offered in our educational system, as well as a definite change in attitudes toward the child who was not performing as well as everyone thought he should in the classroom. It looked, at that moment, as if a book of this sort was no longer necessary, that there was a new and more positive interest in the learner, and that changes would certainly come about to make the classroom a more affirmative and productive experience for every child. Now, 15 years later, the realization that this book is 15 years too late for thousands of youngsters demands that the manuscript be finished as quickly as possible.

Unfortunately, the hoped-for changes have not come about, and now almost every daily paper carries headlines like: *The Nation Still at Risk; Schools Still Less Than Mediocre; and Educational Research Found to be Inadequate.* Almost every magazine and every television news program, along with the currently popular talk show hosts, present desperately negative stories about the failures of our educational system. Special reports predict that by the year 2000, one out of every three young adults will be illiterate, and that 700,000 young adults will graduate from high school each year without the reading skills needed to survive in the business world. These stories run the gamut in pointing the finger of blame. They pile statistic on top of statistic to prove how serious the situation really is and how deeply it puts our nation at risk in the very issue of its international survival. It is not necessary to review all of these criticisms, condemnations, and statistical horrors here. There is enough of that done elsewhere, so that by now everyone should be fully aware of the magnitude of the problem and all of its catastrophic implications.

The amazing aspect of all of the commentary is that most of it is directed at the educational *system*, its administrators, its teachers, its economics, its curricula and/or its disciplinary problems. No matter how many of these articles one reads, nor how frequently one listens to commentators, one finds but minuscule references to the *learner* the student who is supposed to be the beneficiary of our educational system. Oh, yes, there is much discussion of students' problems, but all this attention is consistently and repeatedly drawn to the end products of the contemporary educational programs: facts "learned" to achieve better test scores on standardized tests. Only in rare and infrequent instances are there any references to the *process* by which the student learns, or how he succeeds in making use of the knowledge gained. It is almost entirely a concern with the *academic product*, with almost no consideration of the *learning process*.

In these critical times, the valid and viable information on human development and how individual development is influenced by the learning process characteristic of genus homo is not being applied to the educational problems we are facing. The tremendously important book *Principles of Mental Development*, by R. H. Wheeler and F. T. Perkins,[1] has been lost in the depths of the library stacks because of the preoccupation with test scores. We have been pouring information into children as young as 2 or 3 years of age, whether or not they have any practical use for it, as if they were little sponges that would then retain these abstract data until needed sometime in the distant future. There has been an all but total ignoring of the fact that the human *only learns that which is needed for performance at the moment*. For example, very few of us undertook to learn the Russian language in the days when it might have been needed for military or space purposes. Only if a sightseeing tour of that country were imminent, did we make some effort to pick up a smattering of conversational Russian. Yet, children are given computer training by the age of 2 or 3 so that they will be "computer-literate" when they reach the mechanized world of adulthood. Sixth grade children in America are taught Greco-Roman history; yet these same students cannot locate major cities on a map of the United States.

The wealth of information on human development and the learning process which clearly exists, both prenatally and postnatally, is being overlooked and even ignored because there is too little exposure to developmental concepts in teacher education. In addition to including these concepts in teacher training, there must be a serious effort to bring changes in parental attitudes and beliefs about the learning process in every child regardless of the denigrating labels attached to too many children. Further, parents must become much better informed about the programs offered by "children's universities" and "early learning centers," and whether these are really little more than day-care facilities with fancy labels. Parents have too frequently been subtly convinced that their preschool child can be totally prepared for the primary grades by starting "readin', 'ritin' and 'rithmetic" lessons when they have scarcely left the cradle. These children have too often become pint-sized achievers under adult-sized pressures. Parents who are more fully informed on the developmental and learning processes that are innate and indisputable will know better what to demand and what to expect from these preschool academies. Thus, the claims of the preschool entrepreneurs can be more realistically examined for more assured benefits for all children.

Now, some 15 years after it was begun, this book must be finished as an attempt to protect and more fully serve all those children who are *Smart in Everything ... Except School.* It is no longer possible to wait until our distraught educational system can change, as was expected when this book was begun. Some attempt has to be made to bring full attention to how a child learns, and how all adults can monitor and guide the developmental procedures in order that comfortable success may replace the damaging frustrations of the failure so epidemic among those children whose obvious potentials are not being reached. There will be no further condemnations and criticisms here. There will be critical analyses of the situations that need inspection and evaluation, and at times this may seem to be critical just to be critical. There will be a diligent attempt to find all of the positives existing in every child instead of detailing the negatives that have been used as excuses for, and causes of, the failures now being documented every day.

G. N. Getman, O.D., D.O.S., Sc.D.

Prologue

A recurring dream with several nightmarish characteristics revolves around a conference of several hundred people gathered to discuss "The Progress of Man." This meeting is held in a mammoth convention center, and the arguments echo back and forth across the scantily filled auditorium. Two very distinct points of view are vociferously expressed. One group holds that man has gained in longevity, intelligence, creativity, and social amenities in his cultural rise. The contrasting discussants insist that man has lost most of his important survival skills and many of his self-sufficiency abilities in this process of becoming civilized. The emphatic arguments on both sides of the auditorium are both logical and believable.

As this discussion progresses, there is a modicum of agreement over all that man has been pressed to accomplish, both as a member of the human race and as an individual. There is mutual recognition of the fact that man has literally been forced to raise himself by his own cleverness and his own innate drives. There is general agreement that some of the gains might have been worth the cost of the self-inflicted traumas suffered in the adaptation process. This line of conversation finally brings the participants to the conclusion that man spent literally millions of years preparing himself for the impact of the invention of the printing press with all of its advantages and disadvantages. Those who have been holding that man has sacrificed more than he has received in the rise to the present cultural levels have difficulty defending their position when the breadth and power of the printed word is acknowledged. A level of tentative agreement is fully reached, and the dream becomes more comfortable, when all present at this conference more carefully examine the printing press and what it offers, or "imposes," as a few of the holdouts still insist.

A dream like this has to be evaluated in the waking moments that follow, and because it continues to occur. The need for man to communicate with others is a characteristic taken too much for granted without fully considering how this human ability has been accomplished. This is the first question the context of this dream raises. Reflecting thereon brings the realization that man has spent hundreds of generations developing a spoken language. It is interesting to ponder on all of the discussions that must have taken place among wise men and priests, among kings and commoners, about labels and descriptions; the agreement and disagreements over which words should be used; about which words would be acceptable to others, and about all that each word might mean. This discussion has never ceased after all these generations, and after all of the efforts and studies of the semanticists who have spent their lifetimes searching for the true meanings of words. And this discussion should undoubtedly persist forever.

This line of thinking leads to the next consideration of the thousands of years man has spent in the exploration and use of pictures in his need to master time—to find the drawing that would leave a concise message for someone who might pass by a day or a month later. One can almost feel the excitement of the person who discovered there was a way to tell someone else where the best food supply could be found; of what might be expected to happen in days to come—all with scrawled pictographs on the cave wall. It is quite apparent that when man found he could encapsulate time in pictures and scrawled hieroglyphics, he had already cast a die for himself and all his descendants. He had also cast the die for all of genus homo with his simple systems of symbols, symbols that would not only determine the culture into which he was moving, but would also determine a further erosion of the independency that survival and self-sufficiency had produced up until this time.

It is now most interesting to consider that what took man hundreds of thousands of years to invent, develop, and expand has now become one of the major problems overwhelming a shocking number of the inhabitants of our contemporary culture. The ability to design and use symbols is undoubtedly one of man's greatest inventions and, seemingly, one of the most natural results of the intellectual potentials God gave to man. Why, then, are these symbol systems the greatest stumbling block now hindering the progress of so many thousands who should have been its beneficiaries instead of its victims? Why, when spoken and written words are so significantly a part of an individual's need to progress in his own development, are these such overwhelming deterrents? In every other area of human development, all the abilities for mastery of the environment are achieved and extended because of their importance to the individual. Why do the skills for mastering these culturally significant symbolic systems elude so many?

Several of the reasons for this dilemma are becoming more and more obvious to those clinicians who spend a part of almost every day observing and appraising individuals with unquestioned intellectual potential. The clinical evidence brings two inescapable conclusions: First, there has been such an eagerness for *early* results that we have overlooked the individual's developmental *readiness* for the symbolic tasks laid before him, and, secondly, the methods of symbol presentation have been more mechanical than developmental. We have made the gross mistake of thinking that mere exposure and repetition would accomplish the end, instead of realizing that the activity had to be compatible with the learning systems and the learning strategies each individual has achieved.

To be more specific, the most essential manual, visual, auditory, and language skills are not being achieved by a large number of the children arriving at the first grade classroom door. There can be no doubt about the heavy load now put on the visual systems of the primary grade child when 80% of the classroom day is spent on constricting visual tasks of spiritmaster or photocopied sheets and workbooks. Further, the other 20% of the school day is spent on tasks where vision is the primary support system to audition and touch in the manual tasks. Very few children start school with the preparation and skills needed. The visual skills of detail inspection and discrimination have not been achieved by the majority of these youngsters. (There will be extensive discussions on the great differences between *sight* and *vision* in later chapters.) The ability to maintain efficient visual discriminations at reading and writing distances has not been acquired, and, as a direct result, the fatigue and frustration that arise deter basic comprehensions that must come out of these tasks if the child is to succeed in the "learning to learn" process. Similar auditory and language skills are not present in the majority of these children, and the fatigue and frustrations can be just as great in "listening" tasks. Also, for a number of reasons, too many children arrive in the primary milieu without the hand dexterities they must have if writing is to become the method of expression it is supposed to be. Thus, the overloads on these immature learning systems not only interfere with their development, these stresses actually prevent the organizations and integrations with other learning systems so essential to any degree of classroom achievement.

The methods used to present current symbolic complexities to the learner are the next reason for the increasingly common difficulty so many children are demonstrating. If one explores this criticism, and if methods being used are carefully evaluated with an open mind, the horrific qualities of the original nightmare can become a "daymare" in the waking moments as one begins to realize we may have injured and hindered more beginning learners than we have assisted and benefited. It becomes apparent we must carefully and patiently review all of the inherent learning processes that have supported mankind in his progress through the ages and take a more careful look at the acquisition of these systems for the mastery of symbols back in the dawn of history.

A better understanding of the required visual skills and the intimately related inherent learning systems of audition and manual exploration could well give us the clues to assisting today's learner. Children are not finding the mastery of these abilities in the presently popular educational programs that are substituting electronics for evolution. It never need be a case of attempting to turn history back to the first ages of man. It need only be a sensitive attempt to overcome our preoccupations on the end product—scorable reading levels according to the national norms—with intelligent scrutiny of the available learning processes that lie in every infant and young child. Further, there must be unobstructed recognition that moving back to the basics must be much more than earlier impositions of academic subjects and already unproven procedures that seem to be labeled basic just because they were successful for the grandparents of today's children.

If we can be intelligent enough to accomplish this, the human individual's need for time- and energy-saving symbols will become the reading teacher. If all of the learning systems are allowed to achieve the skillful maturity they are coded to achieve, there could be generations of "spontaneous" learners and readers who go successfully sailing past all attempts to *teach* them the academic routines. Let us make a serious attempt to discover how to get out of the learner's way, to remove the many hurdles we are unwittingly designing, to eliminate the diversionary procedures now included in so many classroom programs, to recognize and provide supports and enhancements the learning systems can have—and let "nature take its course." There is now every reason to believe there would be multitudes of successes we are not presently witnessing.

About This Book ...

This book is not written as a scientific treatise. It will not contain pages of statistical data and extensive reports of carefully controlled research. Instead, it will be an expression of my increasingly firm conviction that there is a need for a book especially written to assist parents, teachers, and the open-minded clinician toward a greater understanding of the learning problems more and more thousands of children and young adults are manifesting in the late 20th century. This book is produced expressly for all those who have the desire to assist individuals who are having learning problems they should not be having, regardless of the "scientific" explanations offered. To accomplish this, we must draw as much attention as possible to the dynamics of human development, the processes of the universally present learning sequences, and the realization that the panaceas are only *within* the learner. It is time we devote all time and effort to an understanding of these developmental characteristics instead of the electronic shortcuts that may provide some answers but no understanding of the questions.

The responses to this book can be predicted and will be most interesting. The armchair statisticians will ask for scientific proof gathered in carefully controlled research, much of it on animals that have none of the same reasons for learning that humans have. Other statisticians will demand research that completely ignores individual differences, individual interests, and individual motivations. My convictions, after more than 40 years of observing and studying children, are that we must completely consider the individual child and his individual characteristics rather than almost any consideration of how he fits into generalizations drawn out of group averages. There is now a critical need to compare every child with himself rather than to plot him somewhere on the percentile curve of the multitude. This has been most appropriately stated by Dudley White, M.D., a highly respected heart specialist and student of the purposes of the human heart. Dr. White said, "I am much more interested in how a person's heart is critically related to his gall bladder, his lungs, his general muscle tone, his digestive system, and his attitudes than I am to how this heart compares with 10,000 other hearts." These types of individualized data are difficult to put into group statistics, but it gives the thoughtful clinician the information needed to approach the problems of the individual and the solutions that must be found for the desperately needed guidance and assistance.

The teachers' responses to this book, especially the responses of teachers who are now so completely trained in teaching methods and prepackaged, problem-directed materials, will also be interesting. Many of these "methodists" will be uncomfortable with the lack of cookbook-type routines to be applied at a given hour within a given curriculum for a given group of children. There will be the lament that the contents of this book have not been presented to fit the diagnostic categories so popular today. This lament will come even though these popular categories do not assist in the design of a program for so-identified learners. The special educator, who has been loaded with special programs that include detailed and selective attacks upon specially pinpointed "handicaps" usually identified by easily mouthed initials, may very well be uncomfortable with my conviction that there is more of the "normal" than there is of the "abnormal" in every child, regardless of labels or categorizations.

There will probably be a response from the classical optometric clinicians that clinical validations are lacking here. Actually, such a wealth of his validation lies beneath all presented here it would fill dozens of books this size. Every clinician who is primarily concerned with each patient's progress and performance will probably agree that the validations all come in the successes of the patient whether or not specific cause and effect relationships can ever be detailed. The increasingly publicized recognitions regarding patients' attitudes and their personal beliefs that they *can* improve themselves in both health and performance give strong support to the position that the important point is the improvements, even though we may not fully understand them or the reasons they occur. The present recognition that the placebo effect is frequently more significant than either drugs or surgery makes all other efforts to assist the patient to physical and mental performance successes more valid than ever.

It has long been recognized by numerous clinicians that if a clinical procedure can be replicated by others in unrelated and completely disconnected circumstances, and if the procedure and its results are consistently repeatable, it has validity beyond the level of chance or doubt. The procedure may be criticized and reviewed. It can be explored and modified, but if the basic clinical concept and approach is maintained, the results will be consistent and valid. Further, if a procedure is to be "tested" by others, the procedural design must be carefully duplicated because any variation in the original design automatically brings variables the original procedure did not contain. These are the factors of clinical validity upon which every patient-oriented professional relies. Many criticisms of clinical procedures have come from studies that varied enough in basic design that the same questions were not asked. In spite of such variations, the researcher condemned another's research without admitting the variations. This is what has provoked the recent statements that "40% of educational research should have been rejected outright, and another 41% accepted only with revisions."[2]

Further, the consistent evidence that "it works" is now changing many attitudes about the clinical care for patients and the acceptability of the procedures. One of the greatest examples of this is the burgeoning awareness of the importance of nutrition and exercise and the influence of proper diet on classroom and occupational performance at all ages. There are still many, many questions about the physiological and biochemical reasons for all this, but the obvious benefits have opened minds so that patients can now receive the primary considerations they have so long deserved.

Just to be certain there are no misunderstandings, let it be recognized that I am fully cognizant that what follows is totally and completely the product of *my* interpretations and conclusions. These have been greatly influenced by a number of wise individuals from numerous occupations and disciplines. Both personal acquaintance and intimate research associations have brought information unavailable in any book yet written. Likewise, hundreds of books and papers have been explored for the information personal contacts could not provide. One large fact remains—what is presented here can only be credited to *me*, just as nothing written here can be blamed on anyone else.

It is sincerely hoped that this book can give every reader some added insight and understanding about children and the problems they face in their need to succeed in a culture that is becoming increasingly more abstract and complex. This book is not written for any specific discipline or group. It is offered for any person—regardless of bias—as another view of children and the responsibilities we all face in the care and guidance they deserve. I do not ask the reader to accept and agree with everything presented here. I ask only that it be read with an open mind and the desire to be of greater service to children. Further, although the emphasis is constantly directed at children, I know that much of the contents can be almost equally applied to adults. After all, the adult is only the product of childhood with camouflaging sophistications laid on like frosting on a cake.

This book has three points to make. First, sight and vision, about which you will be reading a lot, are two totally non-synonymous words. They have completely different meanings and must be understood much better than they are now. Sight is nothing more than the actions of the physioneurological parts of the eyes that act upon light and light contrasts to send a series of neural blips to the brain. Sight involves nothing more than the eyes and the neural pathways to the proper brain centers. In high contrast, vision involves the entire person and is wholly dependent on personal experiences and learning. Thus these two words cannot be used interchangeably as if they identified the same aspect of human behavior.

Secondly, this book will, to the best of my ability, explore and present the dominant role that vision plays in every aspect of human behavior with greatest emphases on the role it plays in the learning process related to academic success.

Finally, the point will be made that the failures of hundreds of thousands of youngsters to reach their intellectual potential must not be ignored one moment longer. This book will direct all possible attention to the innate developmental processes that can be so guided that the vast majority of these youngsters will become successful in their culture instead of continuing through life as wasted individuals never having reached the potential God gave to every one of them.

About the Title ...

The past 50-plus years of optometric clinical practice, consultancies, and classroom observations of literally thousands of children have all brought me into close contact with many devoted teachers and parents. The most frequently offered descriptive phrase heard from these dedicated persons has been: "I cannot really understand this child .... He (or She) is smart in everything—except schoolwork!" This phrase has been so often expressed during the years of close, office-based practice that it became the catch-phrase for most of the children being cared for in that practice. Parents would use this phrase when making the original appointment or at the start of the first conference. Teachers used this phrase in almost every description of children about whom we were having a conversation. It so completely identifies the child about whom this book has been written that it seemed most appropriate as the title. It is not intended to be cute or catchy. It pointedly describes the situation that exists.

The title has been chosen for another reason. There was a time just a few years ago when it was generally thought that if a child was clumsy, there would automatically be some learning problems. In this vein, it was also thought that every child with a learning problem had to be clumsy. The realization that clumsiness and academic problems were not so closely related came when a child having classroom problems would perform in a superior manner on the playground. It also became evident that the child who could perform extremely well in what has evolved as "perceptual-motor training" could not necessarily overcome his academic problems. Each time we return to inspect the problems, it becomes apparent that these are the children who are "smart in everything ... except school." Under this title, we will endeavor to carefully explore some of the more promising solutions these children need.

About the Author ...

G.N. Getman, O.D., D.O.S.

I am quite well known to many readers because of previous publications and various discussions of my work with children and my philosophies on how to assist them. A previous book, *How to Develop Your Child's Intelligence*,[3] has been surprisingly popular as a college text and as a reference book used by many developmental optometrists. In addition, there have been numerous references to, and critiques of, my work by other authors. It is especially interesting to find several of these criticisms stating that I put too much emphasis on the visual system and the visual aspects of the learning process. Since the mid-1930s I have been a developmentally-oriented optometrist. (The term behavioral optometry or behavioral optometrist is an umbrella term which encompasses *developmental* and *functional* optometry. Behavioral optometry and behavioral optometrists treat visual problems wholistically, seeking the causes of visual problems rather than symptoms. Henceforth in this book the term *behavioral optometrist* will be used.) Although research and study have taken me into many fields of interest and relevance, most of my time and effort has been spent in attempting to understand vision and visually-directed performance in the human, which has fostered a deep appreciation of the close relationships that exist between vision and all the other information processing systems present in the human. This research and study has brought close contacts with top authorities in every other discipline who are now searching for a better understanding of children and their needs. Much time has been spent with education and all the branches of education that deal with children's performance as something more important than the parrot-like mastery of methods and materials. Much time has been spent with experimental and developmentally oriented psychologists in the attempt to comprehend that the functions of human information systems are often above and beyond the limits of their anatomical structures. The old and well documented "law" that "function will determine final structure more than the structure will determine the final function" has made this research of great interest. This is especially true since I am an optometrist who repeatedly notes that optical measurements of the two eyes and the performance of the visual system are most often very contradictory. Much time has also been spent with pediatricians who have a greater interest in children's abilities and cultural performance than they do in childhood pathologies. These are the pediatricians who also recognize that a child's potentials are not fully expressed by a simple state of wellness.

As will be presented in the following pages, there is now more and more evidence that vision is a dominating factor in the performance of every individual who must compete in our overweighted symbolic culture. There is also the growing evidence that vision is closely related to several other information processing systems that must also play a significant role in successful performance. The role of vision, and its supporting systems of manual manipulation, audition, and language, is now recognized as tremendously important to the earliest sequences of development and the child's mastery of his immediate environment. This has led me to a bias for which there is no apology. If one is to explore all the possibilities that must be faced in this search for the needed information, even a degree of prejudice is essential, and there will be no apology for this either.

It would seem that criticizing an optometrist for too much emphasis on vision is comparable to criticism of a lawyer for too much emphasis on legalities, or criticism of an educator for too much emphasis on academics. Vision, its development and its enhancements, has been my interest and driving force for more than 50 years. Why should there be any dampening of the accumulated information to avoid the criticisms of speaking too much like an optometrist? Herbert G. Birch, M.D., a developmental pediatrician, about whom you will read later, stated: "The elaboration and choice of a research strategy stems not only from the analysis of what may be an important set of mechanisms in the development of a disturbed pattern of behavior, but also from the background of experience of the investigator. The scientist's personal history functions to determine the kinds of thoughts he may have about the problems and the techniques he can begin to use to approach it."[4] This is obviously as true of the developmental optometrist as it is of any other investigator. Thus, the emphasis on vision in this book should not be a surprise.

The information now available to everyone who can honestly look at children as visually-directed and visually-dominated humans will be presented here as it is especially pertinent to the total welfare of children and young adults. The consideration given to this information by many hundreds of educators, clinicians, and parents who have participated in workshops and seminars I have conducted around the world gives support to the posture that this information can be helpful in the guidance of children—especially those who are failing unnecessarily in the multitude of visual tasks that exist in the modern classroom.

There is really only one goal here!! This is the greater support and more positive assistance to children in spite of, or maybe because of, biases and prejudices any of us may have.

And, of Greater Importance, About You, the Reader ...

No book is of any value if it is never opened and read. The fact that you have picked up this book indicates you have an interest in the same children who have attracted me for so many years. Thus, there is the assumption that you, too, are seeking additional information about how to help these children. Some of what you read here may be familiar to you. Some of what you read will be in direct contradiction to the familiar. The result is sure to be some confusion. Arnold Gesell, M.D.,[5] often said that confusion is the most dynamic stage in the entire developmental process because the clarifications of the confusion always bring new knowledge, and there would be no effort to achieve new knowledge without the stimulus of confusion.

There is only one request being made of you. If you are confused by what you read here, and if some of the discussion seems to be contradictory, do not close your mind until you have checked it out by observing some children in activities relevant to the discussion. All that is presented here is based on carefully repeated observations of children, and the conclusions have come when either the task, or the environment, is manipulated to see how children respond and perform. You will find some of the discussion inconclusive simply because all of the evidence is not yet available. You will make a splendid contribution to the total search by your observations, and by the results you will have when you explore some of the suggestions presented. Some of the final reasons for the performances observed may not be any more available to you than they have been to someone else. In spite of the fact that conclusive reasons are not determinable, do not hesitate to create situations that might bring new results. The fuller understanding of the performance and its neurological, psychological and/or physiological reasons may come later. When the stated goals of this book are reached, the fuller understandings will be the fringe benefits we all seek for the children we serve.

Those of you who have read and used the book How to Develop Your Child's Intelligence will remember that a man by the name of Fenelon was quoted in its introduction. That same quotation is presented here because it is even more appropriate in the "19- nows" than it was 30 years ago: "If I were asked what single qualification was necessary for one who has the care of children, I should say patience ... patience with their tempers; with their understandings; with their progress. It is not brilliant parts or great acquirements which are necessary for parents and teachers, but the patience to go over first principles again and again; steadily to add a little every day; never to be irritated by willful or accidental hindrances." What Fenelon describes here is the developmental process this book will explore.

Hopefully, this prologue will have set some attitudes of interest and some expectancies for what the following pages will offer. This has been done with the intent that you, the reader, will find this book to be one you will return to as you find yourself becoming a more astute and insightful observer of the developmental sequences in all individuals regardless of age, and of the basic abilities each individual has acquired. As all of this occurs, it is sincerely hoped you will find yourself looking at your own abilities with new understandings, and this will then lead you, too, on to more successful mastery of our complex, increasingly abstract culture.

Very Special Appreciation to ...

Mrs. Virginia Burch, whose superb editing, typing, and composing skills have produced this splendidly finished manuscript in spite of all of the additions, deletions, and revisions handed to her at inconvenient moments.

Homer H. Hendrickson, O.D., D.O.S., whose unique abilities to eliminate the errors and confusions that would have seriously altered the meaning of my statements and whose clinical editing skills are completely unmatched within our profession.

There never are the really suitable words needed when one attempts to express the gratitude one feels for friends such as these two wonderful individuals. My deepest thanks go to each of them.

G. N. Getman, O.D., D.O.S., Sc.D.

Chapter I—The Dynamics of the Developmental Sequence From a Behavioral Perspective

Before moving into this discussion, the two words *developmental* and *behavioral* need some defining so all will know how and why they are being used here. *Developmental* as used in this context, describes the process by which the human moves from conception through all the time, use, and practice of those abilities inherent in being a member of genus homo, to the ultimate performance skills the well individual should achieve in these abilities. This is a never-ending process (until death occurs) of discovering and extending all of those potentials innate to the human as he moves to the fullest awareness, and the fullest possible mastery, of the environment and its contents.

The word *behavioral,* as used here, is the term which describes the result of all development—how effectively the individual performs in meeting the challenges the problems the environment presents.

Development is the covert internal organization of self in "getting there," and behavior is the overt external effectiveness and efficiency of the individual "after getting there." At the top of all this is *intelligence,* which is then judged by how successfully the individual copes with, and solves, the problems the culture brings.

Thus, the developmental sequence to be considered here is that sequence of actions and responses the individual experiences and organizes in becoming an effective person. The behavioral perspective is simply the vantage point from which the individual is observed and judged as he demonstrates the uses and applications of all that development produced. In this chapter the developmental sequence will be presented as the "how-with- all," and the behavioral perspective will be presented as the "what-with-all," as demonstrated by intelligent performance in relevant activities.

The Immediate Problem

The comic pages and cartoons that appear in the daily newspapers repeatedly give a more cogent and realistic view of our culture and our foibles than any other part of the ubiquitous communications media. A favorite cartoon strip that has been used to close dozens of lectures to parents and teachers comes to mind. It is a strip of "Broom Hilda." In the first panel the little maestro walks onto the stage with his conductor's baton in hand. In the second panel he taps on the music stand to get the attention of the orchestra. The third panel shows him leading his musicians into the overture. The major panel shows the music coming out of the trees, the flowers, the grass and weeds, and the rocks. The little maestro quips: "It is always there—you just have to know how to get it out." This lovely cartoon so completely illustrates the thrust of this book that it is called to the readers' attention early on. It succinctly expresses the message that will be expressed here, and the hope of the author is that this same message can reach every reader. Paraphrasing the little maestro: "Every child, regardless of the diagnostic labels and clinical insults so given, has abilities that are lying in wait for the right maestro." We, the maestros, "just have to know how to get them out."

Hopefully, every reader will have become more and more aware of the need for a more positive and dynamic approach to the problems so many children are demonstrating in the contemporary classroom. The evidence now available strongly suggests that our present culture, and the present levels of "civilization," may be contributing more problems, and fewer solutions, than ever before. It becomes more and more apparent to almost anyone observing children's total development that a large majority of the youngsters entering the primary classroom have arrived there without many of the basic learning skills the contemporary classroom demands. As stated in the introductory comments, it seemed this situation was being reversed by the interests and concerns of young parents who had gained an awareness of some of the problems their children were demonstrating. These parents were not being lulled by someone who smilingly said: "Oh, not to worry— he will outgrow it," or "Just give him a little more time—he is just immature," or "Yes, there does seem to be a problem but he will take care of it in our special program here at our preschool." Too frequently the child's problem was exacerbated while the parents thought it was being ameliorated.

Back in 1975 the federal legislature passed the Education for All Handicapped Children Act (see Appendix A for details), which mandated the provision of free appropriate public education in the least restrictive environment to all handicapped children. This act, now known as Public Law 94-142,[6] holds that education must meet the individual needs of children as determined and implemented through individual educational programs (IEP). Every state now has elaborated and extended this original national law. In many instances there have been deteriorations in the programs intended for these children, and there have been increases in the terms and phrases used, bringing further misinterpretations of the problems children have acquired. Although the IEP brought parents and teachers closer together in their efforts to find solutions, the actual program was too frequently a program of substitutions instead of the direct approaches and solutions the youngsters needed. This made all adults more comfortable, but no substantive gains were observed in the child. Although these sentences may sound very much like more of the criticisms to be avoided here, these are facts which must not be overlooked if we are to avert even greater, and more numerous, learning problems among larger populations of school children.

Learning Disabilities or Academic Problems?

The first, and major, issue to be faced here is the label now widely used to categorize the youngsters who are "smart in everything ... except school." Undoubtedly, the greatest single trauma done to literally hundreds of thousands of children is the label "learning disabled." One cannot help but wonder just what the innovators of this phrase had in mind when it was proposed back in the mid-60s. One also wonders if these same phrase makers would have accepted this label so quickly if they had been the recipients.

That was a time when most of the children failing in the usual classroom for no obvious reason were being identified as "minimally brain injured." This phrase was acknowledged to be very negative, and no clinical syndrome could be found to prove there was any evidence of trauma to the brain. As a direct result, the phrase "learning disabled" was coined, and it has now become so official that it appears in all sorts of laws and regulations. With the usual clarity of hindsight, one cannot help but ponder what definition of the word *disabled* was being used as this phrase became so acceptable. What does one think of when the phrase "disabled veteran" is used? What does one think of when the phrase "physically disabled" is used? In most instances, these uses of the word *disabled* suggest a situation in which a person is actually missing an extremity, or has such damage to the body that there is very little help or hope for any "normal" performance. In such situations, either some sort of prosthesis is sought, or there is an attempt to find a kind of substitutive or circumventive way to keep the individual active.

It is not difficult to reach the conclusion that these common inter-pretations of the words "disabled" and "disability" have so influenced general attitudes that if an individual is so labeled, there is the immediate assumption that there is very little help for him, and some sort of a program must be designed to ignore or avoid the area of difficulty. Thus, such an individual is frequently discarded as being beyond help, the learning abilities present and available to this person are ignored, and from then on he is actually prevented from develop-ing those abilities that *are* in fact present.

Study and research, consultations and project supervisions, seminars and workshops, along with hundreds of classroom visits have never produced evidence of a child who could *not* learn, one who was really *disabled* in learning. These same thousands of observations of children have revealed many children who were not learning what some adults thought they should be learning, but there has never been a child who could not learn something. There need be but one qualification to such a dogmatic statement. Children observed in state institutions, who would be classified as "basket cases," might be categorized as "learning disabled." One is constantly struck even in these surroundings with those children who seem little more than barely alive who have achieved some of those abilities that had to be learned in some manner. If these children learned any of the usual movement patterns, any of the simplest communication abilities, any of the self-support abilities, then they had learned much. If they had progressed to any degree of self-care, toilet patterns, speech patterns used appropriately, or even the simplest patterns of play, then we must agree there must have been *some* achievement in learning. Thus, even these are not disabled in the dictionary definition of the word. True, these may be the children or adults for whom no academic programs can be planned, but we cannot use the same semantics to describe children who are merely failing in the classroom, describing them with this same word.

The very word *disability* is so demeaning and so destructive that it has negatively influenced all of the design and implementation of programs promoted to help children in the classroom. Children so labeled have been approached by many adults as if the problem were inherent, and thus insoluble. An "Oscar" winner once commented during an interview that she was "learning disabled" and so could not read any of the scripts given her. She went on in detail to report how she could learn any script read to her if she could listen to it a few times. Part of the interview revealed the trauma she had experienced because of her "learning disability" and it was evident the entire conversation was difficult for her. Further, she added that her daughter was also "learning disabled," almost as if the daughter had inherited the problem from her mother. The very idea of inheritance has added more problems to the search for some of the needed solutions. Since the parent's problem was thought to be responsible for actual damage somewhere in the anatomy or neurology of the child, there has been too little effort toward searching out the methods that might prevent the "disability." A very recent announcement in an educational journal states that one of the Ivy League schools had just received "a grant of $4 million from the National Institute of Child Health and Human Development ... to conduct a five-year study of anatomical and genetic patterns associated with dyslexia." It is sincerely hoped that these researchers will realize that parents who themselves perform with difficulty are not effective teachers for their children in that same area of learning. Years and years of research and hundreds of reports all show that the most important factor in the learning-to-read process is having parents who like to read and do a lot of it with, and for, their children. Is it possible the Oscar winner's daughter is having reading problems because her mother could neither read to her nor demonstrate the pleasures of reading?

To avoid any criticism of arousing false hopes, and to anticipate the comment that there is inadequate proof of help for these children who carry this label, it is important to emphasize that there is a full awareness of the magnitude of the problem so widely demonstrated. The point being taken is that all responsible adults must make much more incisive investigations of the background out of which learning problems can arise, and make much more careful investigations of the processes which do provide the academically successful child with those skills intimately related to academic progress. If as much as $4 million were being spent on studying the successful child and his methods of developing and achieving learning skills, we could certainly arrive at some excellent conclusions. The inept and troubled individuals could then be seen as having problems for which there are some solutions instead of accepting *disabilities* that are assumed to be crippling and hopeless.

Where Might Some of the Solutions Lie?

In this effort to present a more positive view of the problems of the child who is "smart in everything ... except school," our primary attention must be directed to the sequences and processes that bring the child to a state of readiness for the classroom impacts. There are several significant statements that can provide background to this exploration of the developmental sequence, characteristically present in every human being. The first of these should be imprinted on every classroom wall and on every household bulletin board. Every adult having any responsibility for the educational continuum of any child should have to repeat it before emerging from the house every morning. A statement was made in the early 1940s by an educator who was one of the first to look more carefully and developmentally at the academic programs for teaching reading. William S. Gray, Ph.D., in his book *On Their Own Reading*, stated: "In all of our word recognition training, we must remember the child gets no meaning from the printed word—he only brings his own meanings to the printed word."[7] As one analyzes what Gray said, it is apparent that if a child is to bring meaning to words, there must be a background of experience and frames of reference into which the words fit. This also implies that the child must be able to match the printed or spoken word to his experiences without confusion and without misinterpretations. Thus, every child must collect the backgrounds that will always be available when any book, or other printed material, is approached.

Experience Is, and Always Has Been, the Best Teacher.

There can be NO doubt—experience is the *only* teacher. However, our culture is now depriving children of more primary experiences than it is providing for them, and we are expecting all children to receive their basic frames of reference from the experience of others— from parents, from siblings, from peers, from teachers, from authors—and computers. It is time we take a very careful look at the experiences every child must have if there is to be an adequate background for all of the vicarious experiences provided by the classroom, and from which we expect the child to get all of the knowledge needed to cope with the demands of the abstract symbolic tasks that must be mastered.

As we probe the dynamics of human development, we get some pertinent and crucial insights to the organization which permits one to profit from primary experiences. There are factors and components with which we must be fully cognizant if we are to so arrange the developmental opportunities within the environment of each learner. First of all, we must contemplate that *experience* and *exposure* are two very different situations. Experience demands there be personal involvement and participation and that the individual gain new knowledge as a direct result. Exposure is just exposure. Information may be presented to the individual but because there is no, or very little, participation and utilization of the information, the individual gains no usable knowledge from the exposure. As a further result, the learner gains nothing that can be called up when, at a later time, similar information is presented in which comparisons must be made.

Since we are insisting that experience occurs only with involvement and participation, we are also assuming there will be use and application of the knowledge through actions of the individual. Hundreds of publications are devoted to the discussion of perception. These generally hold that the information that comes to the individual through the inspections and discriminations of similarities and differences bring about the actions which then bring the neural organizations for internalization of the information.

Behavioral psychologists K. U. Smith and W. M. Smith, in their salient book *Perception and Motion*, hold that perception and relevant motion are two sides of the same coin, and there must be an integration of these two if there are to be any behavioral gains by the individual. They say, "It is our belief that motion and perception are inseparably related. The development of perception in the child *is* the development of motion patterns, and the only valid understanding of perception at any level is in terms of the movements that define it."[8] There will be further discussion of this later in the book, but Smith and Smith continue for more than 300 pages to establish the position that primary experience and actions of participation are the critical factors in learning. They also provide broad evidence that all of this can be positively influenced through training and practice when the visual and auditory systems are brought in to control and mediate the participation of the individual.

In a series of lectures delivered to a group of developmental optometrists at the University of Wisconsin some years ago, Professor Karl U. Smith, Ph.D., stated: "The entire human system has evolved as a result of its self-governed and self-determined selectivities of motor activity. The total development of the individual depends on the degree of supervision that vision exercises over the activities that bring about the neural integration within all information processing systems and their resulting performance."

The second sentence in Smith's statement about the evolution of the human needs much more consideration here and not just because of its great interest to an optometrically-based author! If there is to be a full grasp upon "the total development of the individual," there must be a recognition of what Smith was implying when he talked about "... the degree of supervision that vision exercises ..." Developmental and behavioral optometrists have long agreed with Gesell, who stated: "Vision is the dominant process in human behavior."[9] This statement has been frequently misinterpreted because of that confusion existing over the two words *sight* and *vision*. Thus, there has to be one more effort to delineate the two levels of function and ability in the sight and vision systems of the human. There have been so many attempts to eliminate this muddle it seems somewhat futile to try again, but " ... the total development of the individual ..." about which Smith speaks cannot be fully grasped so long as this confusion exists.

The persistent idea that the ability to identify a line of letters 8 millimeters high at a distance of 20 feet is all there is to consider in the visual process is completely untenable. It is amazing to realize that more parents and teachers understand this problem better than do some of the clinicians of various health care professions who supposedly make clinical appraisals of this aspect of human performance. *Sight* includes the inherent actions of the human eyes as they react to light and contrasts in light patterns. All of these actions occur in healthy eyes as an automatic response to light, the environmental energy for which they were designed to respond. There will be alignment of both eyes upon the area of greatest or least brightness. In the great majority of healthy individuals there will be a synchrony of alignment so both eyes point directly at the area of brightness or the object of regard. There will be pupil size changes appropriate to the variations of light brightnesses. All of these responses of the eyes take place to some extent, even in the individual who has been severely damaged by some sort of trauma. These basic physiological reactions to light are inherent functions of the eyes and operate to set these responding organs into readiness for the more elaborate internal lens action that brings the best possible light distribution across the sensitive retinae in the back of the eyes.

When these mechanical actions have occurred, the visual system is now set to receive the information the brain will draw from the light patterns. However, this visual information cannot be useful and valuable to the individual unless there is a match, or mismatch, with information which comes from at least one other information system.

This added information usually comes from posture, audition, or manual taction, or all three. When this match or mismatch of information occurs, there is a closure that assures that the information is perceived. All this brings a visual result which is much more than can be accounted for by the inherent responses of the ocular end organs (the eyes) to brightnesses or brightness contrasts. It is this closure on the accumulated information, and its interpretation for some following action, that is known to the behavioral optometrist as *vision*—a result that is greatly more than the mere light response of sight.

The confusions of these two terms—sight and vision—has been extended over the years by the standardized wall charts of various sized letters or forms. The too frequently reported performance of a patient who can read the bottom lines of this chart is, "There is nothing wrong with this individual's eyes; he has perfect 20/20 vision." This statement only means that this person can identify the next to the bottom line of letters from a distance of 20 feet. This device to categorize sight clarity was designed in the early 1800s by a physicist (not a clinician) by the name of Snellen and has been considered the determinant of "perfect vision" ever since. This degree of clarity has no relevance to the magnitude of information an individual can obtain through vision as it functions in the total integrative fashion with other information systems.

Further, there is no real determinant of "perfect vision." The misuse of this phrase can be compared to someone saying: "This pianist has nothing wrong with his hands; he has perfect pitch." Vision is the system which brings the ultimate understanding of the information which comes in through the sight system and is then enhanced or moderated by relevant information from all other information systems. "Perfectness" can be measured neither in the eyes nor by a simple identification of some sort of brightness contrast pattern. The magnitude of this ability can only be appraised in the performance of the entire visual system and its affiliates, just as the pianist's ability is appraised in the performance influenced by auditory skills related to pitch and harmony, the movement skills related to the use of both hands in combination and counterpoint, by the sense of rhythm and tempo, and the appreciation for the melody being played. Certainly, if the pianist has some fingers missing or some that are completely inflexible, the performance will be greatly influenced. If there is substantial damage or lack of ability in the *sight* organs, performance will be influenced, but it is never safe to make a final judgment of the skills of a system by making limited observations or measurements of the extremity or end organ itself. There are some one-legged skiers who are more skillful on the slopes than many two-legged athletes. It is not unusual to find a one-eyed individual with visual skills quite advanced beyond those achieved by some persons with the normal complement of two eyes.

What all this means to us now is that whether it be vision, audition, manual skills, or any other of the skills essential to performance in the present culture, the clinician must look beyond the simple and so completely inadequate (and, many times, inappropriate) tests of basic mechanical operation of an end organ. What must be fully ascertained is how well the individual has learned to use and direct each of the inherent information systems to gain the information it was designed to gain. Sight is no more than the mechanical responses of the eyes to light, while vision is the interpretation of the information obtained in conjunction with all the other information systems *when there is a need to receive and understand* signals.

This appreciation for the significant differences between *sight* and *vision* provides the reasons why the behavioral optometrist so heartily agrees with Smith and Smith.[8] The appraisal of the integrations within all the information processing systems and the performance that results comprise the area of clinical investigation that will provide the clues, and some of the answers, to the learning problems of so many children.

If there is to be a fuller appreciation of the dynamics of the total developmental sequence and its intimate relevance to the learning process, there is a need to give attention to Smith's comment: "The entire human system has evolved as a result of its *self-governed* and *self-determined* selectivities of motor activity." The reasons why I have emphasized the phrases *self-governed* and *self-determined* will soon become evident. There has been a comfortable habit acquired by many clinicians and researchers giving rise to such descriptions as "the total child" or "the total action system;" yet there has also been the continuing tendency to isolate abilities in educational and clinical programs now offered. The old mind-body dichotomy still exists, and learning is still considered a function of the mind without much consideration of the contribution the body makes in every learning act. Smith attempts to scotch this dichotomy, and another writer, long since anonymous, said it best: "Thoughts that never fully possess the muscles never fully possess the mind." The major point is this: If we are to seriously investigate how the human learns, there must be definite clarifications of the dynamics of the developmental sequences, especially those that are referred to as "self-governed and self-determined selectivities of motor activity." How these are so closely related to intellectual development is of prime importance in providing the assistance needed by so many children now having academic problems.

This need to look beyond the *psychology* of learning into the *physiology* of learning will take us directly into the dynamics of the entire developmental sequence characteristic of the human. This exploration will emphasize, first of all, that our present culture is providing too few opportunities for the child to govern and determine what his "motor activity" will be. Our culture is putting either wheels or restraints on children so much of the time that too many children are deprived of the opportunity to explore their movement possibilities, or to appraise the consequences of their movements and the tremendous importance of these movements to the entire human system. Another favorite cartoon strip shows the small child in a highchair. In the next panel the child is shown in the infant seat. Next, the child is shown facing Mother as she pushes the shopping cart. Finally, the child is pictured in the safety seat in the car and says, "I can go all day without ever touching the ground." All of these constraints, as important as they are to a child's safety, deprive the child of the self-motivated and self-directed exploratory experiences so critically important to learning what is necessary for the mastery of the environment.

As has been stated by the behavioral optometrist for the past 30 years, the child does not move merely to get tired and hungry—the child moves to explore the world, to find a place in it, and to glean all possible information from it. It all comes down to the simple fact that the child moves to learn, and all learning demands movement, the movements to act upon the information being received through the information systems. *All* learning demands the movements of doing, and it is this process of doing to learn that sets the first stages for the development of the intellect. Any omission of the relationships detailed by Smith will certainly have undesirable influences upon all development.

Then comes the question: "Why did this child not learn even though he went through the actions required of him?" Although all learning demands active participation, not all movement produces learning.

Unfortunately, just as with all learning, if the activity of the moment has no purpose for the child, the action produces little or none of the movement patterns that should be available for later activity. Muscle movements must possess the mind at the same time they are possessing the muscles if there is to be the retention and applications we identify as learning. Even we adults have been involved in activities where there was little, if any, carry-over to later actions. It is the same old story—as with learning Russian, if the individual has neither need nor interest in the practice, there will be very little learning. Smith's phrases "self-governed" and "self-determined" strongly imply *need* and that interest known as *motivation*. Thus, not all movement will produce learning, but the learning process can only reach the ultimate levels when the learner puts information received into testing and validating activities. Experience *is* the teacher and it is experience that will provide the dynamics of development.

When we humans wish to explain and communicate ideas to each other, we usually resort to a diagram or a model, which we hope will help another person to visualize and comprehend our ideas. There have been several very significant models offered to illustrate the learning process. Some of these were offered as early as 50 years ago but, like the works of Wheeler and Perkins[1] and Gray,[7] have been lost in the dust of the drive to improve test scores whether or not any learning took place, or whether or not learning processes were improved. One of these, which had great long-term impact, was the contribution of Grace Fernald[10] back in the mid-1940s. If one can find a copy of her book, *Remedial Techniques in Basic School Subjects,* one will find much that is still useful in sound, viable educational procedures. Interestingly, although Fernald identified and emphasized the most basic of the learning processes, she did not really present these in a now recognized developmental sequence. However, her philosophy became known as "The VAKT Techniques." These initials represented Visual, Auditory, Kinesthetic and Tactual procedures.

The Models

Two models will be presented here. These have come out of cooperative studies by behavioral optometrists and developmental psychologists, and it is hoped they will bring a more complete frame of reference as background for the dynamics of the human development and the progression of the learning process. The first of these models (Figure 1) should be viewed as a multidimensional lattice through which two spirals are interwoven to represent the relationships of the processes involved, and the ebb and flow of the developmental sequence through time, growth, experience, and the individuality which results from the ultimate totalities of childhood and early adulthood. This first model (Figure 1) includes a vertical spiral representing the developmental flow from conception to the ultimates in intelligent behavior. This spiral starts with conception and the genetic coding that holds the genesis for two of the dynamic characteristics of the human: the structures *for* movement and the components, or elements, that *influence* movement. These characteristics provide the human with movement patterns and sophistications (called skills) that are completely unavailable to any other being. Although other beings may demonstrate movements that are not available to man, none of these movements can extend to the expertise found in the manual, visual, and verbal abilities of man. It is these movement dexterities and skills that allow man to be the master of his environment instead of having to be satisfied with mere adaptation to it. The second model (Figure 3 in Chapter II) should also be viewed as a multidimensional lattice that represents the stellar elements of the learning process by means of which the individual utilizes his total development in the ultimate acquisition of intelligence. (This second model will be extensively discussed later.)

Figure 1, entitled "The Dynamics of the Developmental Sequence," is an effort to illustrate the environmental influences that impinge upon the person and the responses and participations of the individual in progressing through the entire sequence of self-development. Starting in the lower left corner of the diagram, one observes how this entire process is instigated by the environmental energies such as light, heat, pressure, etc. which provide the inputs to which the human receptor modes will respond. Each of these receptor modes is governed by inherent mechanisms selectively designed to respond in a particular fashion so the environmental energies can be translated and transformed into neural energies that the organism (the human) can use as the signals for action responses appropriate to the signals. Wherever the signal is received, be it by sight, hearing, touch, smell, taste, or any other receptor mode, the first response is movement as the primary effort to explore the signal. All of this developmental flow originates with the genetic coding for the performance unique to humans, and it must be fully understood that this really does begin at the moment of conception. During pregnancy this flow is primarily concerned with the innate reflex movements of the fetus essential to

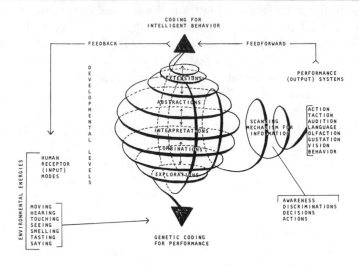

Figure 1. The Dynamics of the Developmental Sequence. Reprinted with permission from The Pathway School

the proliferation of the central and peripheral nervous systems. There is ample evidence that this neurological proliferation will not occur unless there are movements of the fetus. This is the first of the lifelong situations in which function brings structure while, at the same time, structure brings function. This is a point that will be significant to much of the discussion later in this book. As pregnancy advances, there will be an innate relationship between all this early movement of the fetus and the primitive systems of touch and hearing, but the full influence of all this interweaving can only be estimated by observations of the newborn, who demonstrates responses needing some sort of explanation. These responses will be more completely discussed later when there is a need to think about the probable relevance between this early movement of the fetus and the further development of touch and hearing abilities. At this point, the main interest is in the movements of the fetus in utero which strongly suggest the importance of neurological and physiological completions that can be appraised with tests of the newborn's "reflex" responses immediately following delivery. Interestingly, all of these immediate observations of the innate reflex responses to applied stimuli are appraisals of the infant's readiness to move or the primitive inhibition of movements, and these suggest the innate interweavings of the tactual, the visual, and the auditory systems at the most primitive level. The tremendous significance of all this lies in the simple fact that the human is specially designed for movement. The entire architecture of the human—the skeleton, the tendons, the muscles, and the involuntary nervous system which is already interwoven with at least three of the receptor modes—predicts the importance of movement to the future of the individual.

The Explorations Phase (Clinically identified as the Proprioceptual Phase)

Out of all this comes the first of the observable phases of the developmental processes. This is identified on the model as the *explorations* level, and represents that stage in the total sequence when the infant is learning how to manage and modify the movements available to him. Here, the infant spends most of the waking hours exploring the movements time and growth will allow, and finding out just what the results and consequences might be. This is the full-time occupation of the infant through the first 6 to 9 months after arrival. There is now a bright, noisy, solid environment to be explored, and these explorations bring a multitude of events to which the infant reacts in the organization of the body transport movements that will extend the explorations. These are the first opportunities for the infant to realize there are numerous receptor modes, i.e., the input systems now available that will bring light patterns, noises, and surrounding solidities where the first interweavings of the learning system are experienced. Now all these movements and the responses to the signals received bring internal as well as external messages. The previous model, as published by The Pathway School in Jefferson-ville, Pennsylvania in 1968, referred to these as the *proprioceptual responses* to identify those signals arising from the movements of the muscles, tendons, and joints involved in the actions of the moment. Previous models that I have used called this phase of the total developmental flow the *proprioception* level for the same identifications. This is the portion of the action that provides the learner with the knowledge of what muscles, tendons, and joints will do, and at the same time will provide feedback signals to the original receptor modes for modifications and revisions, which will then allow them to provide better signals for continued actions. We have spoken quite frequently here about this interweaving of signals and systems, and Birch,[4] the pediatrician quoted earlier, further states: " ... the evolution of (human) behavior can be conceptualized as the process of the development of (this) intersensory patterning." Sir Charles Sherrington,[11] another authority in the field of human development, has pointed out, "The essential strategy in the evolution of the central nervous system has not been the elaboration of new avenues of sense, but rather the development of increased liaisons among the existent major systems." It is the continuing and growing "liaisons among the existent systems" that make this exploratory phase so extremely important to the learner.

The understanding of the exploratory actions that bring interweavings and "intersensory patterns" leads us to what the performance results may be for the learner. Undoubtedly, the most valuable lesson for the infant comes from the opportunity to find out where the world is and where he is in it. This evolution of orientation arising from self-initiated movements, visually and auditorily steered and monitored "by me," and the self-determined goals, visually and auditorily chosen and sought "by me," lay the foundations upon which the learner builds self-image and position in the surrounding world plus the knowledge of the locations of all that the surrounding world contains. In this process of exploring "me," the learner finds the first masteries of the environment.

The curiosity that seems to be innate in all infants, and the advancing abilities to transport oneself through the immediate surroundings, brings a result of great importance to all later abilities. This is the organization of the two architectural halves of one's entire being. The Almighty Architect, in His great wisdom, apparently designed the human in two halves so there could be the performances so unique to man. The very business of rolling over, then the creeping, crawling, toddling, and finally walking, all bring about much more than the mere ability to move out as an upright, energy-conserving biped. This sequence brings both a unity of the architectural halves and the dynamic alternation of these halves, which, in turn, bring abilities no other being achieves. In the long, tedious process of learning all of the movements and movement patterns required for poise and grace in body transport actions, there also comes the opportunity to find out what sequences and directions of movements mean. It is these very basic experiences that will become so extremely useful when the time comes for the visual mastery of symbols. It is now fully evident that the child who does not achieve the internalizations of sequences and directions during these early experiential times will usually be the same child having extreme difficulties the educator identifies as "sequencing problems" and "reversals" in writing, spelling, and arithmetic. Interestingly, when children so identified are given the opportunity to establish more basic abilities in the movement skills, more experience and mastery of sequences and directions in movement patterns, the writing, spelling, and arithmetic problems are reduced. These are very often the same youngsters who were too frequently identified as those who could not learn well because they were "clumsy." These, too, lose much of their "clumsiness" when they master those factors of orientation now recognized as sequencing and directionality.

One more aspect of this exploratory phase must be discussed here. This is the roles that both the visual system and the auditory system play in the overall organization of the individual's orientations *with and to* the environment. There is a degree of innateness to all of the movement patterns that have led many earlier investigators to think all these would develop by themselves if given enough time. Too frequently this assumption led both parents and clinicians to ignore some of the subtle details of this organization. These must not be overlooked. A child who was unusually clumsy and who bumped into obvious objects, or who stumbled often, was frequently ignored with the comment, "Oh, give him time and he will learn better." Now more accurate observation methods are available and the informed clinician will be alert to the possibility that either the visual system or the auditory system needs evaluation. The obvious role that the basic sight system plays in guiding movements needs little emphasis here. However, there are several aspects of visual development that must be identified and evaluated as early in infancy as possible. If the basic input from the light receptors (the eyes) to the brain is deficient or out of phase with these early movement attempts, there will be the possibility of omissions in the overall learning process that will make for some severe learning difficulties later. Although the auditory system is not as prominent in its contributions, if noises that come from sources out of the field of view and their locations are not recognized, the child can be in great danger. The interweaving of these two input modes is of grave importance to the evolution of orientations and must not be passed off as insignificant to the values of this exploration phase in the developmental progression. There is no greater deterrent to the overall learning process than the absence of the visual and/or auditory contributions to the mastery and management of all transport movements.

A youngster who has been carefully observed over a period of 12 years, from birth until the present, illustrates the developmental problems that arise when one of the basic input systems is congenitally incomplete. This boy was eventually diagnosed as having "visual motor apraxia," meaning he did not have control of all the eye movements fully expected in the human. At first there had been a diagnosis of blindness by a pediatrician, who noted, "Joe will not look at me when I hold him. Therefore, he is undoubtedly blind and his parents should anticipate institutionalization as early as possible." Optometric observations of Joe's responses to his mother when she was at least four to six feet away from him, and when she appeared at distances of 30 feet or more, proved beyond any doubt that Joe's sight was completely usual in all respects. More complete optometric clinical observations brought the conclusions that since Joe could not control his eye movements and could not converge his eye alignments when looking at nearby objects, he undoubtedly was seeing double when attempting to inspect objects and faces within his manual reach. As a result, he quickly learned to avoid those activities that would create the confusion arising from seeing double when his hands told him there was only one object of regard. The relevance, however, to the discussion of the moment comes out of his increasing reluctance to move out into the exploration of his immediate surroundings as is so typical of most infants. Almost as a direct result, Joe became less and less visually alert and more and more dependent on others for guidance in all general activities.

Joe's significance here is two-fold: First, he so vividly demonstrates how inadequacies in a primary receptor mode (sight) can account for incomplete signals *feeding forward t*o this basic phase of development—explorations. As a result, there are inadequacies of the signals the exploration phase (proprioception) should be *feeding forward* to all of the succeeding phases in the total developmental sequence. And, secondly, the limited exploratory actions of this child cannot*feed back* fully adequate signals for the physiological improvements and refinements of the basic sight mode. Since the *feedforward* signals are limited, the *feedback* signals are also limited, and Joe's "clumsiness" was much more than a mere "muscle problem," needing adaptive education procedures and physical therapy treatments. He was also in critical need of sight-vision development care so all systems might have the enhancements they would not receive if only growth, time, and maturity were his lot.

Here is an example of how a problem in one of the most important input modes has had an extensive influence on all of Joe's development, and these ripple-up ("ripple-up" because Joe is still growing) effects are more and more obvious in almost every area of his development. Joe's progress through the past 12 years could provide illustrations for every detail and aspect of the developmental sequence because of the reverberating impacts of the inadequacies of his sight-vision system, the system that should have become the dominant force in Joe's total development.

References have already been made to the signals which arise from the action itself that feed back to the original input receptors—the receptor modes. Please note the diagram has double-headed arrows to indicate there are signals returning to the receptors from the basic exploratory actions as well as signals going forward to the action systems for explorations. This is to emphasize there are signals feeding backward to the most primitive receptor modes, which will then modify their actions so added signals will feed back more details crucial to the entire action system's confidence and skill. These feedback signals are every bit as critical to the entire process as are the feedforward signals that instigated the original actions of exploration. These feedback signals will bring new physiological and neurological development to the receptors, development beyond the abilities that were innately coded into them. These further developments bring more adequate responses to the environmental energies with an increase in the information that the receptor modes can then provide to the entire developmental sequence.

Most of the movements of the wakeful infant are the result of conscious efforts, and the movements that can be credited to innateness—those reflex actions noted earlier—really do not contribute much to the infant's explorations of self and environment. It is the feedback signals from the conscious efforts of the infant that bring awarenesses and recognitions to the actions just explored. Such recognitions then provide the feedforward signals, particularly in this earliest developmental phase, which lay the foundation for the relationships with later developmental levels. These feedforward signals are more likely contributors to the mind, while the innate reflex responses are more likely just the automatic firings of the primitive brain and central nervous system. As these consciousnesses expand, and as the mind develops, any degree of movement skill achieved will begin to bring primitive planning for more movements, especially those assuring more effective results if an action is repeated. This planning, which comes as a preliminary to anticipations for the next movements, is now recognized as the feedforward creating the performance over which all adults become excited as evidence that the infant is "learning something new." These are the components Gesell[5] originally suggested in his diagrammatic spirals, and which are now included on the spirals of this model. All of this is to indicate there are signals that feed back to the original input modes, and concurrently there are signals that feed forward to the more advanced developmental levels to ready them for the role they will eventually play in this entire sequence of developmental events. This is the process in which can be seen both the basic and the advanced responses that are preparing the individual to do something better the second time than it was done the first time, eventually reaching that level in which the self-directed and self-determined actions will bring the individual to the ultimate levels of efficiency and effectivity with movement patterns now performing at the subconscious levels of automation where the "right action comes without thinking."

This description of very early development illustrates the trap that can occur in the language used to describe it. There was pointed criticism earlier about the segmentations, isolations, and too specific attentions given to certain abilities even while references were being made about the "total child." A reader might think this model offers components of action and phases of development as if these were distinctly separate plateaus through which the individual should go, one at a time, until finally all were completed. This certainly is not intended. There have been frequent references to the receptor modes (the input modes) of touch, sight, and hearing as significant components of the immediate tests of the newborn. Perhaps it is because the hands, the eyes, and the ears are so obviously different in structure and placement that we fall into the trap of thinking about them as separate and unrelated "organs," each operating in its own way and for its own purposes. When one takes the time to look carefully at the performances of each of these input modes and finds how dependent each is on the others for the most primary performances, one must surely begin to see beyond their structural characteristics and recognize their operational interdependencies. Further, the just-presented discussion of the feedback and feedforward signals should bring attention to the influences that these early movements have on all of the more advanced phases shown in the model, and that the more advanced phases are, at the same time, having degrees of influence upon this first phase. The major interests and actions of the infant in this first phase are with movement, but there must also be a "planting of all the seeds" for the development of the skills that teachers hope to find in their classroom occupants. Thus, even though most of this discussion of the moment revolves around the early organization of movement and the establishment of effective movement patterns, none of these could develop without some degree of support and interweaving of all the other phases. The difficulty here lies in the need to semantically separate these phases for discussion when, in actuality, they are all interwoven and function in varying degrees of intimately related influences.

Transport Movements Lead to Manipulative Movements.

All of this becomes clearer when the more advanced movement abilities develop. The transport movement abilities usually begin to reach a skill level when the infant has had about 18 months of self-directed practice, which allows most infants to become quite effective upright bipeds. By 16 to 20 months of age, there are the abilities to walk without falling, to begin to run, and to jump with some degree of bilateral organization. These transport abilities (the more general movement patterns) are now the modus operandi permitting the child to move about in space as desired. Now the infant begins to more diligently explore and practice the manipulative movements (the more specialized movement patterns) of hands for the more selective exploration of the details of the environment. These actions, which are now so easily observed (and so frequently disturbing to parents), did not suddenly and spontaneously happen. These were all preceded by the mouthing experiences that have given the infant his first very real impressions of the "outside world" and its contents. The infant arrives with the mouth readiest to manipulate and explore the world— for obvious survival reasons. Although the first sucking actions of the newborn are innate, even these improve with use and practice, another instance of the development of movement patterns by doing something important to the individual.

It is interesting to watch the infant explore and manipulate everything he can get into the mouth. This mouthing is the first experience with solidity or softness, flavors and aromas, textures, temperatures, shapes, and weights, and all of this is preparation for the time when objects are so big they have to be explored with hands instead of mouth. Perhaps this is another of the instances in which the exploration by one action mode is preparation for exploration by another action mode. Here mouth practices the manipulations so hands will be readier to carry on the manipulations expected of them, and for which they have been so exquisitely designed. The hands then feed back signals that advance the development of the mouth, while feeding forward to offer some signals to other input modes for their explorations and inspections of those same details and qualities they will explore in their investigation of the environment. This mouth-hand relationship will become a very important organization of the movement patterns that will play an emphatic role in the readiness for the school tasks coming along much later.

There is good reason that so much time and attention has been given here to this first phase of the developmental sequence. Since movement, its development and organization from the more general transport movements to the more specialized manipulative patterns, is so critically important to all progress in learning, it has intentionally been given particular emphasis. One more aspect of all this requires some discussion. There is another of those linguistic traps involved here. One frequently hears about *gross motor* activities and *fine motor* activities as if these were two distinctly different activity areas. The words *gross motor* are usually used to describe running, jumping, skipping and even walking actions, while the words *fine motor* usually refer to coloring, cutting, pasting, and writing. The trap here leads too many adults to program gross motor *or* fine motor activities. Is the ballet dancer involved in gross motor *or* fine motor performance? Is the Super Bowl quarterback involved in gross motor *or* fine motor performance? If one thinks it through, there are both the general transport movements *and* the specialized manipulative movements simultaneously, or these individuals would never have achieved the expertise they demonstrate. Once again, it is the sequence of development for interweaving the general exploration phases with the more sophisticated manipulative phases through which every human system must go to achieve the skills available to them. It is this full sequence of action, from the earliest clumsy attempts at what may appear to be haphazard, random movements, to the ultimate dexterities that demonstrate the poise and grace of fully productive and efficient movements, that express the primary purpose and goal of human development.

The Combinations Phase (Clinically identified as the Preceptual Phase)

As more and more movement patterns are achieved, and movement becomes more of a servant than an occupation, the infant gains new acquaintances with the receptor modes. Now some spectacular behaviors can be observed as the searching, probing, and exploring child finds each of these input modes to be more interesting and more useful. Actually, these modes might now be more appropriately iden- tified as acquisition modes rather than receptor modes because they do not "just sit around" waiting for environmental energy to come along and stimulate them. Now the increasing mastery of movements allows the infant to spend time more carefully exploring events and details of the broader and deeper environment becoming available to him. In so doing, the infant finds that each of these acquisition modes is unique, having its own roles and purposes. Now the infant spends more and more time finding out what each of these modes will do for him, and what can be done with each of them. In the original diagram of this model, this level of development was identified as the *pre* ceptual phase—meaning it was a pre-perceptual facet and also be- cause the dictionary defines a *precept* as a rule of conduct, a rule of behavior. Thus, since each of these input modes has its own purpose and its own design for its conduct, the word preceptual was chosen. Careful appraisal of the performance and behavior of the adult provides immediate insights into the purposes assigned to each of these modes by the Almighty Architect. It is appropriate here and now to direct attention to some of the special characteristics of each mode.

To better understand these characteristics there should be a bit of history. A few years ago, if a person seemed to be having trouble making intellectual discriminations and identifications, he was simply identified as having a "perceptual problem," and little attention was given to why this conclusion might have been drawn. Such clinical appraisals as were done showed all "sensory systems" to be intact, "normal," and "healthy," so it was "just a perceptual problem." Scant consideration was given to *why* there might be a "perceptual problem" until several very carefully planned summer camps were conducted for the youngsters so identified. These camps, staffed by behavioral optometrists, educators, and psychologists, and under my direction, thoughtfully observed a group of youngsters who came to this pro- gram with every possible diagnostic label. The daily activities were opportunities to seek reasons for the problems each camper had acquired, as well as to guide and assist toward performance gains. Again and again, it became apparent that the campers had not learned to use and appreciate their receptor modes. The problem did not lie in an inability to understand an activity (if it was well enough designed for the individual). The problem was a lack of adequate inputs from the receptor modes. It was as if the receptor modes had not learned what they were supposed to do, how they were supposed to acquire the signals available to them. This discovery was not terribly spectacular since many clinicians, especially the behavioral optometrists, had been providing clinical opportunities for the greater adequacy of the input modes in their patients. The insightful language therapist also knew that the problem was more than the "normalcy" of the speech system, just as the optometrist knew a "perfect eyeball" did not guarantee adequacy of the visual system. What really came out of the summer camps' research was the realization that these youngsters had not learned how to combine and interrelate the input modes so there would be an interweaving of their unique abilities for more information than any one mode could provide by itself. It had always been known there are close "partnerships" that exist between some of the modes; for example, smell and taste are closely related; speech and hearing are dependent on each other; and sight and touch are a special team. For some strange reason, it was never really discovered that although these modes were designed to have special intimacies, they needed opportunities to extend and enhance their partnerships through use and practice. Even more importantly, it was too frequently assumed these "partnerships" would come about automatically, and the advanced levels where vision and audition (somewhat less obvious intimacies) would interweave should also happen automatically, and without any special attention from either educational or clinical mentors. If a student were identified as a "visual learner"—the one who succeeded by reading the text but never attending the lectures—no attention was paid to the possibility that he had not *learned* to interweave vision and audition. Likewise, the "auditory learner"—the one who succeeded by attending *every* lecture but never cracking a textbook—was given no thought that he had not learned to interweave audition with vision. The bottom line in all of this was the fact that there had to be combinations among the input modes that extended much beyond the adequacy of each individual mode.

This *combinations phase* is so critical to the developmental sequence, and to an understanding of the role that development plays in the learning process, a bit more time here will be profitable.

It is quite obvious to most students of human behavior that the seeing mode is designed and assigned to steer and monitor the individual's movements into and through the contents and complexities of the lighted world. The environmental energies provide the brightness contrasts as the clues that instigate the seeing mode to send the signals needed to guide and judge one's relationships with the environment. The best proof of this role is the extreme immobility suffered by the sightless person who is so utterly dependent on a sighted person, a trained dog, or an electronic device, which may then allow limited mobility. It also becomes quite apparent that all of the beauty and symbolic challenges of the culture are just frosting on the cake. It is still sight's primary and basic role in an individual's mobility that sets the stage for all of the following development. Fortunately, this role is usually found and practiced *because of* the inherent design of the receptor mode.

When the same attention is given to the hearing mode, it certainly appears that its primary role is to attend to those environmental energies that can be translated as noises serving as keys to the most primitive localizations as judged by the individual. This hearing mode is designed (two ears widely spaced) to provide clues to those noises that originate from sources outside the usual field of sighted view. Again, this role is usually found and practiced because of the inherent design of this receptor mode, but the basic purpose of the mode is primarily the clues it provides for the individual's mobility into and through the contents and complexities of a noisy unseen world. One's appreciations of noise qualities—tone, intensity, and all of the dis-criminations needed for the evolution of speech—are the cake frosting in this mode. First must come the skill of locating the source of the noises heard in the organization of one's orientation in surrounding space.

Too frequently, children's problems in localizations and orientations are blamed on one or the other of these two modes, and the interweav-ing of each with the other is overlooked. Joe comes to mind again. He was demonstrating problems in locating noises around the age of 4, and little concern was aroused because he was "clumsy" enough and cautious enough to protect himself; all concluded he just needed more time and practice. However, his speech was not developing as everyone thought it should, so thorough evaluations of both hearing and speech patterns were made by several capable language specialists. To everyone's surprise, he demonstrated hearing abilities quite beyond those usually found in children his age. Two realizations suddenly came. Joe was missing many noise *source locations* because the visual-motor apraxia prevented his acquiring the supporting clues through his seeing mode. His eyes moved so slowly that the noise was gone before he could look for it. Next came the realization that because of Joe's inability to get reliable clues through the seeing mode, he was missing many of these reinforcements to the speech he was hearing from others. Since there was a rather extreme problem in one mode (the eyes), the interweaving that should have occurred between seeing and hearing modes was just not happening, and what seemed to be hearing problems were actually more problems of seeing. In Joe, both sight and hearing were "normal in every respect," better than the usual acuities in both modes. Because of the deficiency in the seeing mode, both modes failed to develop the combinations and partnerships this phase of development should have brought.

Next, there is the intermodal intimacy most commonly recognized as the "eye-hand coordinations" that were so fully practiced in earlier kindergarten programs. This relationship, and the seeing- hearing relationships, will be given an entire chapter as the stellar elements of the learning process are explored. The touching and seeing mode "coordinations" are only mentioned here so the reader does not assume they are being overlooked. The major point is the importance of the amount of time and effort the infant puts into the discovery and exploration of each mode and the subtle but extremely significant interdependencies between the modes and what all of this does for the infant in the moves toward mastery of the environment. The infant finds (as does the youth and the adult in the *new* situation) that these combinations and partnerships bring explorations of the environment and investigation of the details discovered there that will form the scaffold upon which all following developmental achievements can be organized. In this process, the individual finds these intermodal relationships bring much more extensive awarenesses, and one can begin to *feel* what objects *look* like, and see what objects feel like. Now there is the possibility that what is seen can also be heard, and what is heard can be seen, and some critical foundations for the ability to read are laid down. As the infant, child, youth or adult finds how these integrations and combinations answer his curiosities and needs, there is also the recognition of values, and what should be retained for future help and use when similar environmental events or situations occur. That which meets one's own needs will be put into the "memory bank" for future reference in the progression into and through the next levels of the developmental sequence. In a later chapter the reader will meet several sixth grade students who evidently did not discover these essential intermodal partnerships long before they arrived in sixth grade.

The Interpretations Phase (Clinically identified as the Perceptual Phase)

As this interweaving and surrogating continues, providing the infant with greater appreciations of the manner in which one mode will enhance another, there comes the extensions of the critical discriminations needed in each mode. This is the process of searching for JNDs (the "Just Noticeablc Differences"), the details that bring attention to judgments of *this* chair in comparing it to *that* chair. This is probably the point in the developmental sequence when the learner finds that little differences "teach" more than do general similarities. This brings practice in the primary interpretation abilities. In this third level of the developmental sequence—Interpretations on the diagram (Figure 1)—the learner finds how to get the most information from the fewest clues. This is the process of finding how "I" fit into and interpret "my" world. In the original diagram, this phase was identified as the *per* ceptual phase since this is the major activity now. The searchings for JNDs and all of the discriminations required bring experience in making judgments of comparisons, contrasts, and relevancies that may exist in all of the details available. This is the developmental level at which the infant, child or adult (depending on the novelty of the situation faced) learns to *think*—that process that may either be very simple or very complex—in deciding on which of the interpretations one should depend for the decisions to follow. It becomes increasingly interesting to note in appraisals of an individual's performance that thinking skills can be directly clinically judged by evaluation of the efficacy of the individual's visual, auditory, and tactual discrimination skills. If these discriminations are vague, incomplete, and/or "sloppy," the thinking abilities will be vague, incomplete, and/or "sloppy." Such results will undoubtedly label a student as having "perceptual problems'" or will identify the adult who is described as "not being perceptive" in everyday situations.

Redundantly, and without any apology, the reader's attention is again drawn to the feedback and feedforward vertical arrows in the diagram (Figure 1). The more confidently one makes interpretations at this level, the more confidence one has in the information the input modes are acquiring, and the more skillful one becomes in all of the movements involved in the activity. Likewise, these interpretations and the perceptions arising from the discriminations and judgments bring opportunities for the individual to begin exploring abstractions. The most observable of these is in the development of the language one uses—that process of finding and using the words and phrases that will best express one's interpretations in establishing the adequacy of the communications one has with others. As all of this evolves and expands, the individual finds the organizations and applications of his concepts—the "packages" into which one puts the knowledge and ideas thus far achieved. These "packages" will now serve as feedforwards to the next phases in the developmental sequence.

Perhaps it is somewhat important to spend a moment here in clarifying the words *perception* (the noun) and *perceptual* (the adjective). Too frequently the parents who are told their child has a "problem with perception" are not adequately told what this label is supposed to denote. As a result, the inference is drawn that there is some mental deficiency or lack of intellectual abilities. In a very diverse sort of way, these assumptions are *partially* correct, but the misunderstandings denigrate the child, and his academic problems are then thought to be unreachable. The fact that those problems so labeled can be greatly modified with properly programmed visual, auditory, and tactual training, in which attention is given to practice in discriminations and interpretations of JNDs ("Just Noticeable Differences") must be strongly emphasized. Perceptual abilities—the ability to get the most information out of the fewest clues—are like all other abilities found in the human and will improve if given the right opportunities to improve. Such improvement is much more possible if the guidance is carefully programmed to fit into these early levels of the developmental sequence.

The Early Interpretations Dilemma

There must also be a pause at this point in the discussion of developmental dynamics to reconsider the deleterious stresses our culture is putting on children. There are more and more reports from concerned pediatricians on the number of young children who are showing up with *ulcers*. To the very best medical knowledge, ulcers are not the result of infections or viruses; ulcers are the direct evidence of stresses and frustrations severe enough to upset body chemistry. Such maladies among the adults who spend every waking moment (and some sleeping moments) trying to meet the competitions and traumas of the culture are almost an expected risk. Such maladies showing up in 3-to-7-year-olds is unforgivable, and preclusions must be found. Other responses to culture-related stressors not as spectacular but every bit as traumatic—are being demonstrated by too many children.

One of the most serious of these is the accrual of frustration and disappointment to the point where children never again find any joy and accomplishment in the learning process.

An evaluation of many of the "children's universities" and "little academies" will divulge some rather startling facts about the curricula being offered to children as young as 2 and 3, and to almost all of those children who are being exposed to "reading readiness" programs. What is most visible is the quantity of abstract and symbolic materials the children are expected to complete each day on the assumption that these children have all successfully progressed through the first three developmental levels, having already achieved the many skills each of these phases should provide. Much too frequently the programs in which the children must succeed to meet the pressures of misinformed parents and misdirected teachers include workbooks and xeroxed imitations of "ditto" sheets of the past, pages demanding visual inspections and discriminations, auditory attentions and discriminations, and manual dexterities most children of these ages have not yet achieved. The frequent result is daily tasks that become more of a frustration than an opportunity to discover and explore the abilities that should be the learning-to-learn foundations.

When one goes into some of those classrooms now set apart for special education students, these inappropriate programs are even more obvious. These youngsters, who have been assigned to this supposedly specialized and individualized educational program (the IEP), have spent even more years *not* achieving the foundation skills, and spend even more time going through the motions of completing the abstract and quite meaningless pages with little, if any, acquisition of knowledge they can apply to everyday living. Too many of these children are coming to the "special" tasks with too little of the underlying abilities and skills which must be present if the students are to "bring meaning to the word," as emphasized by William S. Gray so many years ago.

The Abstractions Phase (Clinically identified as the Conceptual Phase)

The fourth level in this developmental model becomes much more significant to the entire process of achieving the thinking skills so critically needed in today's culture. The original diagram identified this phase as the conceptual phase. The updated diagram shows it as the *Abstractions* phase—the level, already briefly introduced, as the time when the learner "packages" his interpretations for the primary purpose of building communications with others. This communication must now be recognized as much more than the imitations of one's mother tongue for the speech demands of the immediate milieu.

Probably one of the most significant of all the skills the human can acquire is the skill of drawing and writing. This ability to congeal one's knowledge, ideas, and personal philosophy so these can be passed on to others not within hearing range of one's voice is a stupendous developmental advancement. The previous phase sets the challenge and the practice area. This phase sets the patterns of intellectual development. As editorialist William Raspberry so succinctly states in one of his excellent columns on the education of children in *The Washington Post*, "It simply is not possible to listen to people who use the language well and believe them to be stupid or hear them use language poorly and believe that they are bright. More than that, people who learn to use the language well become more confident, more test competent, more teachable—and brighter. And yet we spend too little time making our children competent in written and spoken English. It may be the best thing we could do for them." Here Raspberry is summarizing quite clearly what these developmental levels are all about. He is especially touching the fourth level in this model in which the ability to put thoughts and ideas into representative symbols determines and demonstrates the intellectual progress of the individual. Here the individual gains the skills of applying and extending all of the experiences, skills, and concepts of the previous organization into the personal philosophy for intelligent productive activity. Now a single word, a phrase, or a drawing will contain the components of all the experience the individual brings to it. Here the superiority of the human is clearly demonstrated. Further, it is here we can observe the efficiency of the innate design for energy conservation that comes through the use of a word as a replacement for all of the overt actions required to demonstrate a meaning. Now the four letters j - u - m - p take the place of all the effort and energy needed to lift oneself off the floor with a sudden muscular thrust of the legs to overcome one's weight and the influence of gravity. Now the learner will bring meaning to the word that is not inherent in the four letters. Because of the thoughts that accompany the combination of those four letters, the meaning will "occupy the muscles as they also occupy the mind." The meaning is complete, and the printed word *jump* will bring a tingle to the leg muscles, still another example of the feedback mechanism.

The Extensions Phase (Clinically identified as the Cognitive Phase)

The spirals drawn into the model continue to represent all the influences that feedback and feedforward bring to the developmental sequence. The vertical arrows in the middle of the diagram (Figure 1) illustrate how each level communicates with earlier levels, and, at the same time, passes some information on to the higher level so it is being prepared for its organization. As this occurs, the fifth level in the diagram—*the Extensions phase*—that was previously identified as the *cognitive phase*—brings the learner into performance and behavior also completely unique to man.

As all of the previous levels are fully and diligently explored and organized, the individual finds he can move on into creativity as a product of the prediction, imagination, and the anticipations on which one can depend in all areas of behavior. The individual is now able to move into the abilities and skills that allow the design, completion, and utilization of the symbolic abstractions on which civilization depends. Here the individual finds how symbols can be used as time-binders, how the printed word, or artistic rendering, can encapsulate thoughts and ideas for others across time and space.

The Second Spiral in the Model

The second spiral seen in the upper right corner of the model represents the search and review of the larger spiral for the information the individual needs when faced with an entirely new situation or problem. This second spiral is labeled the "Scanning Mechanism for Information." Please note that where the first spiral started at the bottom of the diagram—at "Genetic Coding for Performance"—this spiral starts at the top—at "Coding for Intelligent Behavior." This is to indicate that when an individual faces a new problem, there will be an instantaneous search throughout the upper levels of knowledge for previously acquired information pertinent to the new problem. If there are inadequacies in that pool of knowledge, the search will continue down through all the levels of developmental experience until the most relevant information now needed for comprehension and decisions is found. There could be instances in which this search might have to return to the first level where the earliest movement patterns would provide the clue needed for the solution of the new problem. Amazingly, this entire search or scanning for essential information is an instantaneous process and should all happen within one-fifth of a second, or the search is of no help. In fact, if this scanning of all the previously acquired knowledge takes longer than one-fifth of a second the result is confusion and distraction from the original problem that set off the search. If, on the other hand, this scanning catches the needed information out of the developmental sequence of personal experiences (illustrated by the larger spiral), there is an instant phenomenon known as the "ah-ha!" phenomenon, which brings the answers and the understanding needed for the new problem.

The "Ah-Ha!" Phenomenon

This phenomenon is worth a bit of discussion here because it is such an important part of the observations to be made of the developing individual. This "ah-ha!" is the sudden flash of conclusions reached by the person when all the pieces of the puzzle fall into place and comprehension is reached. The verbal expression for the name given this event is: "Ah-ha, now I see!" or "Now I understand!" This is illustrated by the cartoonist as a light bulb flashing on over the character's head. It is easily observed in the facial expressions, which show the actual brightening and pleasure the individual achieves when this level of comprehension is reached. This is such an important point in this scanning process that every learner should be carefully watched so there can be reasonable confidence the learner has achieved this closure and hence the answer appropriate to the problem at hand.

The Scanning Sequence

Once again, recognizing the dangers of oversimplification and the traps that lie in the words sought to describe this thinking sequence, four observable characteristics of this scanning mechanism can be identified. These are detailed here because of the role each plays in the total development of the thinking and learning process in the human.

Step 1. The *Awareness* Facet

This is the sudden realization by the learner that he does not instantly have all the information needed to solve a new problem. This is the recognition that the background of experience and knowledge must be scanned to find the clues and details that can then be applied to this new problem. It is the instant when the learner recognizes there must be a review—a scanning—of all previously acquired information that can be brought to bear on the new problem. Thus it is not only an awareness that key bits of critical information are not immediately at hand, but is also the awareness that this search must occur. This complex process includes the awareness that there is probably some relevant information tucked away somewhere in one or more of the developmental phases the individual has experienced and organized. Of course, this latter awareness will be present *if* the development phases have produced all the abilities, skills and extensions they were intended to produce. Here is the first instance in which the learner's confidence in his own developmental sequence will emerge. Here is where the learner knows he can face the risk of a search that may not provide the clues needed for immediate solutions. The extent of this awareness will give the learner the confidence needed to find and accept errors or absences of information. The courage to say, "I do not know"—the admission that will then allow the learner to continue the search—is an even more important aspect of this facet.

Perhaps this is an appropriate place to comment that a primary side effect of some of the drugs given to children with learning/behavioral problems is the dampening of this awareness so important to the entire learning process. As previously mentioned, this scanning process must take place in one-fifth of a second. Several of the drugs being used may reduce muscular activities, but there are too many instances in which the resulting dullness slows down the scanning and thinking process the classroom demands, thus producing "noise on the line" and neurological "static" that will override and/or distort the messages which should be coming through. There certainly must be a better way to help the overactive child than the drug way.

The alert clinician and/or teacher learns to observe the facial expressions demonstrated by the pupil who suddenly realizes there is a need to search his background of experience for the information needed. And these observations are important to the manner in which the involved adult will assist the learning into the scanning process. The facial expression is usually one of surprise or sudden concern over the idea that something is lacking. The learner's eyebrows usually go up and eyes widen as if trying to look more carefully into one's memory. In contrast, if the learner is *not* aware that he needs added information, the facial expression is usually one of being content with the limited information present, and there is little if any curiosity about the answers that have been reached. Although these observations are difficult to describe, the adult who is sensitive to a child's ability to learn will consistently identify the facial expressions accompanying the stresses of the learning process. The importance of these observations lies in what the clinician and/or the teacher does to guide the student. In the first instance, the adult should encourage the child to "keep thinking," to "take a good guess," and to again review the related experiences. This can be done by suggesting possibilities relevant to the problem of the moment, and this will be the encouragement that assists the learner to keep searching and thinking. If the second situation exists, and the learner is so confused that little or no search can be started, the adult *must* find a way to rephrase or reconstruct the question so that the learner can come to grips with it at some level of understanding. The actions the adult takes in either instance can well determine the success or failure of the student with results that will either support and lead, or frustrate and destroy. This awareness facet is such an important take-off point for every learner that it must be fully appreciated at all times.

Step 2. The *Discrimination* Facet

In this facet, the learner marshals thoughts to make the search and review as productive as possible in the split second allowed. This marshaling must include the first discrimination of what information is missing or what information is needed to attack the problem. This demands an appraisal of the familiarity he has with the new problem and an immediate recognition of the particular developmental area that most likely holds the pertinent details. What are the most relevant previous experiences? Will they provide the needed information? How appropriate to the new problem are the previous experiences and the bits of information they contain? If the first chosen developmental level does not help, which other developmental levels should be probed? And all of these questions must also flash through the learner's mind in that same one-fifth of a second.

It is now apparent to the learner that the sufficiency of developmental organizations, especially those in the level of *Interpretations* in the original spiral, will come to his rescue *if* that phase of development was fully explored and established. Here, as in earlier practice, the relevant JNDs must be examined to find the specific details needed.

The alert adult—clinician or teacher—will quickly recognize the facial expressions that indicate the help the learner needs. The student who has had some background of experiences with which to attack the problem of the moment will frown, scowl, and demonstrate the search for the needed details. Here, the adult need only make the simplest suggestions, and the student usually brightens and completes the move to the needed answer. In contrast, the student who is "lost" in the process will show expressions of confusion and frustration, and if not adequately assisted, will turn away and make no effort to solve the problem. In the latter situation, the adult *must* guide the student through the details of the relevant discriminations and may need to help the student retrace most of the early developmental levels to find the discriminations he can make for solution of the problem.

This *discrimination* phase is such a critical part of the development of the entire thinking process and is so fundamental to the next phase in this series, it must be given extra attention in the preschool years. This practice in the thinking skills every child must achieve was the purpose and goal of Frable's methods when he "invented" kindergarten for children not yet of school age. It was also the foundation of all that Montessori brought into her program of early assistance for the children being discarded as "retarded." Both of these pioneers arranged conditions so young children could gain the facilities of making the best possible discriminations for the speed and facility involved in thinking how to solve problems. There is a tremendous need today to go back to the programs that fully recognize there is *no* magic in any of the so-called readiness programs until the learner has found the magic within himself.

Step 3. The *Decision* Facet

The learner must also be able to make decisions about the worth of the information coming out of the discriminations just made. There must be instant decisions such as: "Now that I know what information I have, how can I make use of it?" "Has my previous experience with this information given me everything I need to be confident this will be useful now?" "Is it really worth my doing something about it now that this added information suggests the end result will not be useful?"

Although all of these decisions may seem to be quite similar to the discriminations made in the previous phase of this sequence, there is a major difference. Now the learner must go beyond knowing what the noise, the object, or the event is and must decide how to use this information for his own purposes after the problem is solved. It is here that all the information scanning produces must be sorted out for the most effective and appropriate performance that lies ahead. The individual who gets caught short at this point is often described thusly: "Oh, he seems to know what to do but he just can't make up his mind."

This is the phase in the thinking process so frequently bypassed by a question in which the answer is embedded or suggested. The learner needs to make no decisions because the question, or the questioner, has already made it for him. "This is a felt-tipped pen for heavy black lines, isn't it?" includes the discriminations and the decisions, and all the learner has to decide is whether to agree or disagree. This decision is not a learning decision on felt-tipped pens. It is only one of compliance with what the other person says and contributes to the adult's too frequent supposition that this sort of question teaches something. There can be NO dispute—no learning takes place *unless* the learner makes the critical decision about the value and usefulness of the information. If this decision is not made by the learner, there will not be the desired progression to the next development in the thinking sequence with any degree of self-confidence and self-reliance. The learner must be his own authority, and will be, IF there can be the confidence that pertinent decisions are based on alert discriminations with decisions that will reliably serve the learner's personal needs.

Step 4. The *Action* Facet

There are frequent references to "splinter skills," those unusual abilities some individuals develop that seem to be completely isolated from other similar abilities—for example; the All- American athlete who is a symphony of movement, poise, and grace during a sports event and a complete "klutz" on the sidewalk or the dance floor. This individual seems to make excellent decisions as long as they specifically relate to the game in which the unusual ability is visible but demonstrates a definite inability to think clearly in other situations where he should be expected to also perform well. How can such behavior be explained?

It would seem reasonable that if an individual practiced repeatedly and diligently in the exact patterns the instructor required, without any need to make discriminations and decisions about his own needs and goals, then a splinter skill could quite easily evolve out of the desire to please and satisfy the instructor. Thus, this athlete can operate at top form as long as the game goes exactly as the scouts have predicted it would go. If, on the other hand, the opposing team or the opposing player changes the play patterns beyond the "splinter skills" of the carefully trained "conditioned reflexes," the athlete becomes an instant disappointment to other team members, the instructor, and the alumni. "He just can't seem to make up his mind!" and this becomes much more observable under the stresses of close and intensive competition be it a sports event or a Friday morning test in the classroom. Rote memorization of arithmetic facts can be a "splinter skill" *unless* there are also those decisions on how and when to use these facts.

All of this emphasizes the tremendous importance of the learner's ability to put decisions into suitably productive actions. Such actions provide the learner with the proof that the decisions were correct and appropriate to the problem of the moment. These can be either overt actions, observable to others, or covert and subtle actions best described as "thinking it out." If for any reason the learner needs to verify a decision, he may review the actual movements suited to the problem. In such an instance, the learner scanned his experiences, and finding there are still some details missing or some difficulty in making the discriminations needed or a lack of confidence in the decision that must be made, the learner goes back to those developmental phases where he can re-explore the actual movements that are relevant. In some instances there may be the need to carry the review through all of the phases of the developmental sequence in the search for the clues needed to attack the new problem. There may be the need to act out the most basic transport movements for the exploration of the decisions to be made; there may be a request from the learner for repetitions of the noise, or the learner may use his voice to repeat the noise heard; there may be a need to visually reinspect the object or the symbol more extensively for the discriminations on which the decisions can be made. Any of these actions will slow the learning process and may seem to be causing further confusion but they may actually be a confirmatory process—a trying on, or trying out, so there will be more success the next time such a situation might arise. The desirable performance at this level in the scanning procedure, however, is very much less of this slow and detailed review of so many phases in the developmental sequence and much more of the covert thinking it through "as if" the original organization was being repeated.

Granted, "splinter skills" are better than no skills at all. However, any limitations that occur in the discrimination facet will bring limitations to the decision facet, which will then in turn bring limitations in the next facet—the *action* facet—and these final limitations can be quite the opposite of "splinter skills." At the very moment this chapter is being given another editing, there has been an example of what catastrophic results can happen when limitations occur in the discrimination facet. A young naval officer made an inaccurate and limited discrimination of a list of aircraft known to be flying in a specific area. As an immediate result, he and several other officers made decisions that brought about crew actions resulting in a missile strike on a passenger jet mistaken for a fighter jet. Almost 300 people lost their lives because of an inaccurate discrimination. And, equally tragic, several naval officers and highly trained radar specialists will never recover from the trauma of this stressful moment.

All this brings another point that is more immediately relevant to the occupants of our classrooms. There is an aspect of this sequence that is too often taken completely for granted. We adults know from our own learning patterns that since these covert actions are not visible to others, the assumption is made that the new learner knows what he would be required to do correctly in response to the information being received. We too frequently assume that the new learner has already so well established a learning pattern and has sublimated it to the habit level, he has no need to act out a solution for his own verification. This can be misleading to us and unfair to the learner. It can be the reason for an adult's mistaken supposition that the learner does know all that will be needed at another time at another place where a similar situation will demand appropriate behavior. If we are really concerned about guiding the new learner in the development of thinking skills, we will find it to the benefit of all to occasionally ask the learner to demonstrate what actions would be chosen as a result of the discriminations and decisions made. The primary classroom "Show and Tell" time needs more use and expansion than it is usually given.

The early learner will provide the alert observer with clues to the degree of ability and confidence he has achieved. The facial expressions here are most apparent; the child will have an expression of confidence that appears immediately following a very brief pause for thinking. There will usually be an upward gaze as if searching for and contemplating his own mental impressions. In contrast, the learner having difficulty will again show expressions of perplexity and uncertainty and the confusion that will delay or prevent the needed action.

This brings us to the computer programs thrust upon children in the primary grades "because they will need to know about them later." It is disturbing to observe these youngsters being entranced by what the computer does in place of the practice of making discriminations, decisions, and appropriate actions. The artificial intelligence now put into a microchip will never—and *must never*—be the replacement for the thinking practice just discussed. The billion-dollar Aegis computers involved in the naval accident were accurate. It was the breakdown in thinking abilities that accounted for the tragedy. Dare we assume that the artificial intelligence of the computer will do it all at the push of a button?

A recent visit to a primary classroom provides an example of the computer lessons some children are receiving. The child seated before the computer is told that the letter "S" stands for *square*, and if this letter on the keyboard is pressed, the computer screen will display a square. After the child "produces" a few squares, he is told the letter "L" stands for *larger*, and if a bigger square is desired, the "L" key is all that needs to be pressed. Sure enough, the "L" key is pushed, and the computer screen shows bigger squares. The child does not discover that the letter "S" might also stand for *smaller*, or that the letter "L" might stand for *littler*. Finally, if the child wishes to take "a picture" home to show parents what he "drew," the printout key is pushed and the "picture" rolls out for display on the front of the refrigerator at home.

The major fallacy in all this should be obvious to every adult, especially to computer specialists on the school staff. The child learned absolutely nothing here but how to poke a computer key with a forefinger. There were absolutely none of the directions of hand movement needed to *draw* a square; there were none of the stop-turn-go experiences of turning corners at the proper time and place to make a square, let alone any experiences of making the square larger or smaller. As a direct result, none of the muscle senses and movement patterns combined with visual patterns were experienced that would provide the learning so critically essential if the child is to really know everything that will allow the comprehension of what the letters "s q u a r e" really mean so that thoughts can fully possess the muscles and then more fully possess the mind. How can these children who never explore and experience the movement differences between a square, a rectangle, and a triangle ever be ready to progress through the developmental sequence and the thinking processes the usual classroom tasks demand? What practice was there in complex directions of the special movement patterns needed for writing (or drawing) the differences between "b" and "d" so there will be none of the "reversal" problems haunting so many children? It is now becoming more and more apparent that the hours the primary child spends in the computer labs (now considered such an important part of the child's preparation for the future) will do very little more than extend the splinter skills of poking with a forefinger.

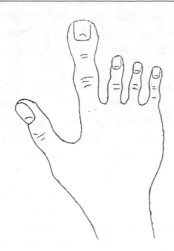

Figure 2. The Hand of the Future. This diagram is offered to illustrate two important developmental points: 1. Function determines structure more than structure determines function, and 2. "Use it or lose it." Illustrated here is the forefinger, which is developing as the primary poking and acting finger, while the thumb merely gets large enough to manage Velcro. All the rest of the fingers fade away because of disuse.

Since human evolution has repeatedly shown us that the part we use the most grows the biggest (witness millions of pear-shaped youngsters whose "most used" part has grown the biggest) and the part we use the least degenerates and may even disappear, what does the future hold for the most marvelous of all tools—the hand? Figure 2 suggests this possibility. Even more alarming is the possibility that the child of the future will not achieve the concepts of shapes and sizes required for any and all symbolic performance.

Undoubtedly, and beyond all argument, there certainly are more effective computer programs than the one just described. I will be among the strongest proponents of the computer as a means of extending the values of the abilities and skills achieved by the human. The point is, however, that the computer must never be allowed to replace the manual skills and the concomitant thinking skills that must be acquired before the computer will become the servant it should become. If any computer program even begins to substitute for basic skills, it must be promptly discarded or put aside until the child is developmentally ready to be its master.

The Ultimate Purpose of the Scanning Mechanism

The diagram of the model used in Figure 1 shows arrows from the scanning spiral which point to the "Performance (Output) Systems" now considered to be the primary determinant of human behavior in contemporary culture. Actually, these output systems are the ultimate reason and purpose of the entire developmental sequence and the scanning mechanisms described here. Further, these output systems come about as the direct product of all the feedback and feedforward signals so influentially present throughout the entire living and learning experiences of the individual. The input modes feed forward into the developmental sequences; the developmental sequences feed forward into these performance systems. Eventually, to complete the organization of the individual, the performance systems feed forward to the behavioral coding, which then feeds back to the input modes— and the entire process starts all over again—but now in the amazing 200 milliseconds, one-fifth of a second.

At the ultimate level, each of these aforementioned performance systems develops its own special characteristics that will eventually add up to skills far exceeding the primitive abilities of the original input modes with which each of the output systems was architecturally linked. For example, the seeing mode (at the input level) acquires brightness contrasts and patterns to which it was designed to respond. These signals instigate mental explorations and combinations of the signals from the related input modes. Then come interpretations of these combinations, abstractions, and finally those extensions and elaborations relevant to the original light patterns. And all of these evolving organizations are scanned and given the further attentions of the information analysis process. Now, the visual system is capable of interpretations and abstractions the seeing mode could not possibly achieve. Now, because of this very elaborate and complex series of events, the visual system can interpret sizes, weights, solidities, textures, and temperatures that only the touching mode could originally offer. Or, the visual system can now reach translations of musical notes printed on a page of music as if they were actually being received by the hearing mode. Or, the visual system can now inspect a carefully photographed table full of food (as in *Better Homes and Gardens* magazine) and bring appreciations of the aroma and the taste of the food as if it were being eaten. In similar manner, the visual system can translate music being heard into a mental picture (a visualization) of the printed page of the musical score being read by the singer or the instrumentalist. Likewise, the visual system can translate the characteristics of objects being manually explored into mental pictures (a visualization) to achieve still further a visualization of the printed symbols which would properly describe the objects. All this explains the tremendous differences between *sight,* which takes place in the seeing mode (the eyes), and *vision,* which comes as a result of the entire developmental sequence illustrated in this model.

It is this constant exchange and integration of information that make all of these output systems so unique and important to the development of intelligence. It is the constant flow of feedback and feedforward signals and the speed and accuracy of the scanning mechanism that bring these output systems to their ultimate levels of performance in the act of thinking. And it is because of these specially advanced abilities—abilities not possible at any previous level of action—that these performance systems are considered as *output* systems producing results previously impossible. It is not surprising that thoughtful clinicians and researchers now think of these performance systems and intelligence as part and parcel of each other. Neither is it surprising that these same thoughtful clinicians and researchers have now found ways to enhance and extend these systems—and the intelligence that is the product—through the properly guided practice by the individual. After all, isn't this the purpose and goal of our entire educational system?

Postscript:

This postscript must be added to this chapter because the research into the intimate relationships between eye movements and body balance and audition brings new information faster than this book can be written. Researchers at the University of California at San Francisco have reported that they have found that certain brain cells learn to be repeatedly tuning and organizing their connections until they get a new skill built.[12] The particularly interesting aspect of this recent research is the evidence it provides that the motor skills of the vestibular and ocular systems must be learned, or relearned, as a child grows, a person ages or has changes in vision, or if an accident or illness impairs sensory or muscle performance. Since eye movements are so closely related to visual efficiency, and since body balance is so closely related to the vestibular system, and very relevantly to audition, the behavioral optometrist becomes very interested in this research. These new discoveries about brain-learning circuitry come from studies of eye movement skills found in all mammals, including humans, and the researchers are confident their studies involving monkeys may pave the way for more studies to help humans. This confidence is built upon the evidence that learned eye movement patterns provide a model system for all learning in the mammal.

Stephen Lisberger, head of the UC research team notes: "Complex motor patterns such as playing a Beethoven piano sonata, or the fielding and throwing of a baseball are not executed correctly on the first attempt. Rather, initial efforts are corrected, refined and finally (sometimes) perfected by motor learning." These researchers have identified three neural pathways in the brain responsible for the integration and organization of the ocular movement and body balance (vestibular) actions. The first pathway is not influenced by learning. "Its job is just to give the system a kick in the right direction at the earliest possible time." The other two pathways are "accuracy" and "error" signals and are definitely involved in motor learning. "The job of the error pathway (which receives feedback from the eyes and inner ear) is to calibrate the accuracy pathway. As the system gets tuned, the contribution of the error pathway goes down and the contribution of the accuracy pathway gets better," Lisberger says. After repeated adjustments and organizations based on sensory input, the neurons gradually settle into new, more accurate firing patterns in what researchers say amounts to motor learning.

The primary reason that this new research is of such high interest to behavioral optometrists is its relevance to the vision therapy the optometrist provides, and its explanation of the positive results demonstrated by so many patients who have had the benefit of this clinical care. It brings further substantiation to the contention that vision is the result of motor activities of the human and is learned just as all other inspection and interpretation skills are learned.

Chapter II—The Stellar Elements of the Learning Process from a Developmental Perspective

A s has already been suggested in a number of ways, the developmental sequence in the human is a complex and involved series of events and accomplishments taking place over a comparatively long period of time—a lifetime. Further, much of this *covert* sequence can only be observed and described according to the *overt* behavior of the individual. This is the behavior that serves to illustrate the phases and interweavings occurring *within* the individual. And then, as has been noted, the interpretations of the observed behavior will depend almost entirely on the biases the observer brings to the proceedings, and the conclusions reached will heavily depend on the clinical interests of the observer.

Fortunately, there are aspects of the human's learning process that are much more visible than are the developmental sequences discussed in Chapter I. Where the individual's development is really only evaluable as time passes, and as growth and abilities appear, one's learning can be judged almost the instant it is happening. Some of these observations have also been discussed in Chapter I. Although the learning process includes all of the receptor (input) modes and all of the performance (output) systems shown in the first model diagram, there are three stellar elements of the learning process that can be observed and appraised in the flashes of their happening *if* one is alert to the evaluations and interpretations that can be made. The three elements to be discussed here are those having the greatest relevance to the tasks presented in the contemporary classroom. These are: manual skills, visual skills, and verbal skills—the three ability areas all adults depend on in their judgments of a child's intellectual process. These judgments come because the evolution of each element, their interrelationships, and the manner in which each is used to solve problems make them more visible than the other elements in the learning process.

The Learning Process
The model presented in the next diagram (Figure 3) illustrates the

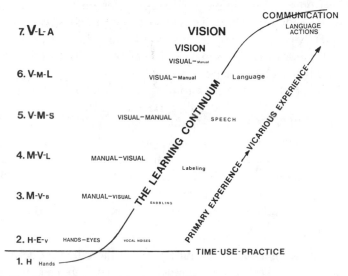

Figure 3. The Stellar Elements of the Learning Process

interweavings and the interrelationships existing here. What the diagram is intended to illustrate, above all else, is the basic fact that if these interweavings and interrelationships are not achieved, the entire learning continuum will not complete and expand to the ultimate levels the human can achieve. I contend that this diagram, added to the developmental sequence previously discussed in Chapter I, illustrates the evolution to the genius level. If all phases of this evolution are fully explored and organized by an individual, the ultimate potentiality of the individual will be the result. If the reader thinks this contention is too optimistic, a step-by-step review of the diagram is essential.

The horizontal line across the bottom of the chart represents the time of birth, and the fact that time, use, and practice are the most essential aspects of all the elements in the learning process. Each level, from 1 through 7, is identified with letters and words of various sizes; sizes are used to suggest the prominence of the element represented by each of these letters. The smaller the letter or word, the less prominent the element is in the total learning continuum that extends from the moment of conception to the moment of expiration. The time span illustrated here is from the last trimester of pregnancy through the time in which the most learning takes place, the years from birth to maturity, and is labeled here "The Learning Continuum." This continuum is also described as the period of time when most individuals move from primary movement experiences on to the abilities that allow the individual to utilize vicarious experiences *as if* these were completely personal experiences. As the individual moves up through all of these levels, exploring and organizing himself, the letters and words on the chart change in size proportionally to represent the decrease or increase in the prominence of each element. The larger the letter or word, the more dominant and influential that particular element will be at that time in the total process. The ultimate level of accomplishment on this chart is shown as "Communication"—the level of performance when the individual achieves the greatest possible communication with the world and its contents, and with all of those other individuals with whom, and from whom, he can benefit through personal participation, observations and/or reading.

Level 1. The Smallest H

This is that prenatal level during which the touch mode is finding itself when hand comes into contact with the mouth. Here the smallest H indicates that the major experiences of the fetus may well be the hand-to-mouth actions and the earliest sucking practice of mouth on thumb or fist. This is the fetal action that begins to set the stage for all of the available movement patterns of thumb, fingers, and hand that will eventually lead it to the development of the unique skills it achieves as the ultimate output tool for human performance. (Parenthetically, it seems the use of the word "tool" here, and its frequent use later, is unbefitting to the action levels being described. The Japanese artisans do not refer to their action instruments as "tools"; instead they call them "dogu," which roughly means "instruments of the way"—contributors rather than accessories—something that aids and abets in the process more than merely being an object in the action. In this sense, the hand, even at this level, is already a "dogu" in the learning process.) This importance of the hand and what it is contributing to the learning process can be predicated upon the ability some infants have in finding and mouthing their hands almost immediately after delivery, behavior that certainly suggests there has already been some use and practice with these body parts.

There is something quite wonderful about the fact that the fetus finds and explores hands at this very early time. General movements of the fetus are an exciting experience for the parents, and especially for the mother who makes judgments of her daily progress through those late weeks and days of pregnancy. The refinements of the general movements into the special movements of hand to mouth are significant indicators of the organization of fetal movements even in utero. Here, there are the earliest examples of learning to direct and control movements in preparation for the many more elaborate movement patterns to come.

It is obvious that the sight-touch interweavings do not occur at this prenatal level. The dark environment provides very little stimulus to the sight mode and brings no opportunities or reasons for "looking around" to "see" what is happening. There is very scant evidence that eyes open at any time during gestation. Thus, there is no mention of eyes on the diagram at this level.

Perhaps, however, there should be some notation to represent the hearing mode at this level. The same sonographic and x-ray techniques allowing views of the fetus sucking on a thumb will allow views of the startle response of the fetus to loud noises. Many mothers report the calming of the fetus when soothing classical music is played where the fetus might "hear" it. The "scientific journals" sold at the supermarket check-out counter frequently report babies' prenatal response to noise. One of these "scientific" publications filled an entire front page with the story about the parents and the obstetrician who could hear the fetus singing Italian operatic arias. As strange as all this may sound, there is more and more thought being given to the influences of noise on the unborn baby. However scientific or unscientific it may be, there are many evidences suggesting there might very well be opportunities for the hearing-speech mode to have some prenatal practice. Carefully repeated observations of infants who were surrounded with soothing music while in utero suggest that they were more auditorily alert after birth. Since there is so much difficulty in properly researching all this, it seems better to leave this aspect of the learning process for more study. Thus the notation of prenatal hearing development has been left off this diagram.

Level 2. H and E Larger With a Very Small V

This is the early post-natal level, the neonate level, when the new infant begins to demonstrate the TNR, the tonic-neck reflex. This was given extensive attention by Gesell[9] in many of his publications. This is a movement pattern, seemingly quite reflexive, in which the infant's eyes (identified here as a small E) find the hand (the small H) when the infant lies on his back in what Gesell describes as "wakeful relaxation." One arm is fully extended off the shoulder; the infant's head is turned toward the extended arm, and the eyes are attracted to the hand as the fingers are flexed. It is as though the infant discovers a part of himself, and there are repetitions of the actions in manners that certainly seem to be more than sheer happenstance. The infant's facial expressions here are often those that also seem to express a curiosity and an interest in the event. It is quite as if the infant is finding there are related parts—one part that can be consciously moved and another part that can consciously watch it all happen.

In a room where there is uniform illumination, this pattern of movements occurs as though the infant wants to continue the explorations, and to practice them over and over. In such a room, the position of the arm and hand seems to attract the eyes, and both left and right TNRs will be explored. At this level, the behavior observed leads one to think it is the hand directing the actions with eyes following because they are attracted to movement. Undoubtedly, there is considerable information being fed into the developmental process even at this very primitive level, and there are probably signals already being sent on for the first combinations of mode imprints—in this instance, the sight-vision complex.

In rooms where there is a particular area of brightness, such as a window, the eyes are attracted to the light source. As the head turns to obtain the best possible light distributions over the retinae of both eyes, the arm extends to that side and the expected TNR pattern will follow. If the crib is rotated so the light source is now on the other side of the infant, the eyes will again be attracted to the brightness, and again the TNR pattern will follow. These two situations, one in which the hands seem to lead, and the other where the eyes seem to lead, may be the first observable evidence of mode reciprocity and the reciprocal interweaving, which will eventually be of such great importance to the learning process.

Imagination leads one down some interesting paths when one wonders what thoughts might be going through this very new sample of humanity. Does he say, "Ah, what is that out there that wiggles?" "Hey, I can make it wiggle so it is fun to watch." "Oh, there is another one off the other way." "Hey, these both belong to me, and I can make them wiggle or be still." "Are these the same things I have been putting in my mouth?" "If I keep watching them when I do put them into my mouth, will I be better able to be sure these do belong to me?" "I did this for quite awhile yesterday, and now I can do it better than I did then. Guess I am getting better with practice." "Guess I will watch this part of me out there to see what else it can do." "Hey, I feel and see it touching something that is not my mouth. Guess I had better take a good look to find out all I can about this new situation."

Of course, the pure scientist may ridicule all this imaginative account of the internalizations which might be occurring here. The observations of the neonate make it very difficult to assume that all of this growing relationship between hands and eyes is simply the result of genetically innate patterns. Many observations lead to a conclusion that here is an example of the most primitive level of the learning process—the occasions where neither hands nor eyes are the more prominent input and action mode, but where each of these finds it is related to the other, and where one or the other can instigate the explorations of this relationship. One quite definite conclusion does arise here after continued observations of these wiggle and watch, watch and wiggle activities. The hand does seem to be the leader in the early explorations that provide the most opportunities for this first combination of two input modes. Here is the earliest chance for an observer to see the genesis of the intimacy in which the hands and the eyes will eventually depend on each other for information each can use, for ways to serve each other, and even to serve as surrogates for each other. If this all seems to be too imaginative and esoteric, please give thought to the established fact that if the infant does not find and fully explore this combination, there will be very definite lacks in both the tactual and visual performance systems, which strongly suggest the TNR patterns were not present for this early exploration. The observable deficiencies in the development of hand-finger skills expected in the curious, probing and touching infant a few months later can certainly seem to be the result of an absence of the TNR experiences in the neonate. In contrast, those neonates who spend much of their waking time fully exploring both right and left TNR postures seem to start off with some of the basic bilateralities that will be so important later. Likewise, the neonate who experiences only the right *or* the left TNR seems to be predominantly *unilateral* with difficulty attaining the full organizations of bilaterality. This apparent unilaterality was interpreted by Gesell as the first indication of "handedness" that would be more definitely observed later. Nevertheless, the profit from early actions that bring information for use in later actions is the gist of the entire learning process in the human, and the tonic-neck reflex action patterns are vivid examples of this process in the earliest weeks of life.

In this same period of developmental progress, the infant discovers the ability to make noise. Of course, there usually has been a very early experience with a loud noise resulting from deep breathing actions. It does not take long for the infant to find there are some variations available, and these variations bring varying results. One sort of loud noise will bring something to the mouth that is more satisfying then a thumb or fist. Another sort of noise will bring relief from discomfort, and yet another variation on this theme will bring the attentions and comforts of being patted and stroked, lifted and held as the bonding process evolves. Then, too, there is the discovery of the small gurgling noises, apparently coming from deep inside, noises to be played with, to be explored, to be manipulated. These are so enjoyable that the infant frequently spends many waking moments "talking to himself" to *learn* the variations possible. When he finds there is a way to listen to the little noises being made, there is also the discovery of how to listen to the noises that come from other sources or from another person. The earliest phases of the communication process are evolving, and *learning* how to differentiate between internal vocal noises and similar external noises brings some of the same combinations and interpretations coming out of the hand-eye experiences.

All of this brings ample evidence to any observer that Level 2— where hands and eyes find each has a purpose, and where vocal noises bring some awarenesses of internal and external signals—is the foundation level upon which the individual will build the three stellar elements of the learning process for success in the classroom. If any one of these three elements fails for *any* reason to gain its own place or relationship with the other two, there will certainly have to be some very careful review of this introductory level for the "readinesses" expected a few years later.

A review of these basic elements certainly does not mean the preschool child should be returned to the TNRs and gurgling practice of the infant. However, there certainly must be every possible emphasis on those simple activities demanding hand and eye combinations, and the sort of talking and listening practice where each of these abilities is given challenges for discriminations and interpretations. It is essential, at this developmental level, that the activities be full of obvious likenesses and differences to assure everyone that the child *is* made aware of what hands and eyes are for, and what the simplest vocal noises include. Of greatest importance here, the adult assisting the child in these activities *must* give responses that show the child that he has elicited the response. Remember, please, there must be feedback even at this most primitive level if there are to be advancements in the learning process. When a parent hears the cry that signals hunger, or the cry that signals discomfort of loneliness, it will be the action the parent takes that serves as the feedback the infant needs for the added practice and refinement of this very early communication ability. Such feedback is every bit as critical in all other areas of the earliest organization.

Level 3. A Much Larger M, a Larger V, and a Small B

This is the level in which parents begin to talk about the personality their child is now showing. Individualities do begin to show at this level because each of these three elements begins to manifest an increase in its own abilities. This is an exciting time because the infant shows more familiarity with hands, and these hands will be used as "instruments of the way" in the manipulation and exploration of the crib and bath toys. Now the infant begins to demonstrate an alertness and awareness of the visible surroundings. There is more visual searching for those objects touched. Although Gesell[9] stated that the infant "takes hold of the world with his eyes before he does with his hands," one can very confidently state that the degree with which the infant takes hold of the world with his eyes certainly depends on how much manual contact, exploration, and experience there has been. Psychologist Samuel Renshaw, quoting M. D. Vernon, another psychologist, frequently reminded us that "vision develops under the tutelage of the active touch."[13] Level 3 represents the time when the hand (and touch) is becoming active enough to practice the reach-grasp-release sequence upon which Gesell put so much emphasis.

Interestingly, since Gesell's milestone work in the 1930s and 1940s, the behavioral optometrist has found this sequence should now read: reach-grasp-*manipulate*-release. There *must* be more than a mere reflex closing of the hand on an object touching the palm. There must be an exploratory manipulation of the object *plus* the early visual attentions and inspections defining the first interpretive combinations of this entire continuum. Now it is as if the infant were thinking, "What I am feeling is interesting—I wonder what it looks like." The infant's eyes will take a quick look at the object *after* it is touched, and one can be quite confident in assuming the hand does the leading and the eyes do the following at this Level 3. Here is an even more vivid example of the systems' combinations that are so much a part of the total design of the human. Earlier note was made of the flick of the eyes toward noise as an indicator of the hearing-seeing relationship. This flick of the eyes toward a touched object is the sign of the early touching-seeing relationship. If there is any lag, or lack, in the growing relationships of these two input modes, it can certainly be observed at this level, and the early concern it deserves can be given to it.

The seeing-hearing relationship now begins to take on more prominence. Where touch is the leader in the manual-visual combination, now vision is the leader in the seeing-hearing relationship. The vocal noises now become much more patterned, and this becomes more like a babbling related to what is touched or seen. The infant now does much more experimenting with vocal noises, and this babbling seems to have a vague resemblance to words being used by those nearby. Language specialists have difficulty decoding words out of this babble in spite of parents' insistence they hear family names. Nevertheless, there is practice in sounds, and the alert infant will return to a pattern of babble when familiar objects or situations occur. One can begin to observe a growing relationship between what the infant touches, what the infant sees, and what vocal noises the infant seems to associate with the seeing and touching actions. If the infant looks at, touches, and gurgles over a new rattle, expansions of previously laid foundations will certainly occur. This full exploration of all three elements brings the interweaving of visually guided hand actions with relevant vocalizations. This combining of the sight-vision mode with the hand-touch mode with the speech-hearing mode has repeatedly been proven to be the most significant and productive act in the entire learning continuum. The human faced with a *new* task, at any age, will return to this Level 3 review of the interrelationships of these systems to assure the successful actions for the completion of the new task. It is the dynamics of their interrelatedness that make these three elements so significant to the entire learning process.

Level 4. A Much Larger M, a Much Larger V, an L Bigger than the Previous B

The much bigger M and V now represent a much more elaborate and advanced relationship between the touch-manual complex and the sight-vision complex.

Where the M was bigger than the V in Level 3 (to show that manual actions were still leading), both M and V are equal in size in Level 4 to show that a new interpretative relationship is evolving. The manual actions may still do much of the leading but the visual inspections and discriminations now begin to bring added information to the manual actions. Now it is as if the sight-vision complex serves as a support system to the touch- manual complex, serving to verify what hand manipulations are bringing to the information search. Although hand may make the primary explorations and manipulations, the sight-vision complex now assists by adding JNDs (Just Noticeable Differences) not available to the hands. For example, two textures might "feel" the same but the sight-vision inspections are needed if each is to be fully identified. A 25-cent coin and a bus token may feel almost exactly alike inside the purse, but usually they both must be brought out for the sight-vision inspections to determine which will serve the immediate need. By this level the hands have acquired many skills and dexterities but they cannot fully perform their duties, in many instances, without vision as the final judge.

This is the level in which too many individuals miss opportunities for skill development. The "benefits" of civilization have seriously deprived at least two generations of children of opportunities to achieve the manual-visual relationships this level of development is emphasizing. There are three kinds of switches that turn on various devices. Most toys are now battery-operated, and remotely controlled by one or two switches. Now neither the switches nor their resulting actions demand any real hand dexterities. Shoestrings no longer need finger skills—Velcro does it all. Children are being "programmed" in special education classrooms (and in too many standard classrooms) so the manual-visual skills are not needed. If the essential manual-visual skills are not present, substitute activities are found, and the child will continue to miss the learning opportunities that should have occurred before any of the symbolic tasks of the classroom were ever faced.

A local newspaper ran a story indicating that manual-visual integrations are not being carefully enough considered. This story concerns a county's attempt to restudy the special education procedures. It opens: "Hundreds of ... county pupils may have been labeled as learning disabled but are not, and possibly have been isolated in classes for the handicapped, according to school officials." It continues: "Children with learning disabilities, such as motor skill dysfunctions or hearing or speech loss, make up 55% of this county's handicapped student population." (Note, please, there is no mention at all of the sight-vision complex problems being itemized here, and which might be major contributors to the learning problems of these students.

Perhaps these youngsters all demonstrated "perfect 20/20 vision" on the wall chart, so the sight-vision complex was not even considered.) Later in this news piece there was announcement about plans to "restructure" the special education program: "The plan, which must still be voted on by the Board of Education, would allow teachers to use alternative methods to help slow learners. For example, 'children who have trouble writing could use puppets to present their book reports.'" What about the "alternative method" of helping the children with writing lessons in which opportunities exist for the acquisition (instead of replacement) of the manual-visual integrations so helpful to all the students in the standard classroom? A much bigger question: How will puppets (as a substitute for writing) provide any of the developmental experiences so critically needed by these children who have been incorrectly thrust into the "learning-disabled" category?

The L in this group of letters represents a developmental advance of tremendous significance because this is the level at which the human infant discovers the ability so completely unique to humans—the ability to establish interpersonal relationships with vocal noises more specialized than the babbling that brought desired attention. This L in Level 4 is for Labeling—the refinements of the vocal noises that can now serve to establish identifications and classifications for all the hands can touch and all the eyes can view. Now the infant begins to discover that he is the labeler, and even if the labels chosen are not the same as those used by others nearby, these vocalized labels become the packages into which people, things, and places can be categorized for both past and future references. Even practice on these labels elicits responses from others which reinforce, confirm, or correct the vocal noises being made. When Father walks in and baby vocalizes "mamamamamama," the response of the father conveys the message that the vocalization should have been "dadadadadada." After some help and more practice, the baby can imitate others who insist that "bybybybyby" is the vocalization for someone's disappearance.

These labels not only bring an advancing relationship with others, they also begin to alert the baby that eyes will "see" differences, and hands will "feel" differences. There will now be instances that can be expected, and the first anticipations are experienced. If what we humans call *memory* is thoughtfully analyzed, it seems quite possible it cannot become available until this labeling ability is achieved, to some extent, by the baby. How could anything be "remembered" if it were not categorized as some sort of a special item or event? Further, how could any anticipations be experienced if there were not some experience on which these expectations could be based? And the big question now is: How could any of this development occur unless there were all the very concrete manual and visual practicings that provided "somethings" to be labeled? Thus, this Level 4 represents the actions that bring the very young human up to the possibilities of the masteries of identifications, interpretations, and abstractions that will establish a baby as an individual. Perhaps this is the time when the baby first begins to find the differences between the personal primary experiences and the vicarious experiences he will be expected to interpret as if these were primary and personal. Perhaps there is more than a chance that here in Level 4 the child will find the "readiness" needed for all the classroom expects of him. This instant of discovery that what is felt and what is seen can be translated into some sort of label is also the instant when the real concrete world can become an organized and internalized mental abstract world. If all of this is true, there are some explanations why this is the level to which every learner returns to clarify quandaries and to eliminate confusions. And maybe this is the level in this continuum during which the young child should gain more of the skills and confidences needed before being thrust into academic abstractions in "nursery school," like reading, writing, and arithmetic!!

Level 5. A Much Larger V, a Much Larger M, an S the Size of the Previous L

These letters represent the shift the child must now make when moving into a world with less and less of the personal primary experiences that have been so enjoyable and reliable in the collection of information. Now almost every learning situation is one in which the child is expected to translate another person's experience as if these were the child's own. I cannot forget the early years of optometric clinical practice when the youngster who was asked, "Why don't you like reading?" would reply, "My dog's name isn't Spot, and I do not know anyone named Dick or Jane." Here was a child trying to communicate that since his dog had a different name, and his acquaintances were not Dick and Jane, there was no match between his experiences and those he was expected to vicariously appreciate. This is not one bit different from an adult's *disinterest* in a book on some totally strange subject in which there is no possibility of experiential comparisons. As Gray[7] said it, this youngster could bring no meaning to the words in the reading text. He was begging for printed words to which he could bring meaning out of his *own* experiences—what reading is really supposed to be.

It is at this level that the sight-vision complex begins to reach the hierarchical dominance Birch[4] wrote about in the 1970s. Now the visual system takes the lead away from the manual system—the lead in the inspection, discrimination, interpretation, and comprehension process. Now this visual dominancy, which rises out of memory and anticipations, permits the summations and comprehensions that will save time and energy in making decisions. Even with all this advancing skill, there will be instances when the visual scan and interpretation process can be misled because too many things look so much alike that the manual system must come in with either confirming or contradicting details so the final decisions can be trusted. Two little containers stored on a shelf—the same size, color, shape, and label—have visible characteristics but still do not let the viewer know that one is empty and the other is full of lead BBs for an air rifle. Only when both are manually grasped and lifted does the critical difference become apparent. Now the manual system becomes the supporter for the visual system, and for the information no other system can provide *if* there is no store clerk around. If there is any question or doubt, the very skillful and adept visual system will still have to fall back on the manual system. At this level, however, the individual learns just how much the visual system can be relied on and how much dependency on the manual system still remains.

The increasingly bigger S in this series at Level 5 represents still another major step forward in the developmental sequence and the learning continuum. Where, in the previous level (Level 4) the child was finding the values of his own labels, there is now the awareness that spoken words can provide information beyond that which either the visual or the manual system can provide. Now the relationships between these three elements are expanded and greatly extended by the speech sounds both self and others provide. Many situations arise in which the output actions of the visual system and the manual system can be represented by spoken words. Now the visual system and the manual system become more and more input systems, and the speech system becomes the "instrument of the way," the "dogu," for both of them. The breadth and the depth to which this speech system can now develop will still depend heavily on both the visual and the manual experiences for the true meaning of the words to be spoken, but there is now a reciprocity and a surrogating not previously possible. Experiences vicariously instigated by the words of others become almost as real and reliable as primary experiences. The boy who disliked reading because his dog was not named Spot can now visually and manually "pretend" the dog in the story is like his dog, even with another name, and there can now be the meaning the book's author hoped there would be. Here in Level 5, vision is still the leader because it is the only input, analysis, and output system capable of meeting the symbolic task; it is the only system able to translate the printed word into the visualizations which then permit the communications between individuals.

The contemporary classroom presents some problems for vision that even speech will not help to solve. There are letters and numbers in the classroom tasks which look so much alike, and some which sound so much alike, that confusion adds frustration to the learning process—for example, the lower case letters "b" and "d," "m" and "n"; the capital letters "C" and "G," and even the capitals "B" and "D." If visual and/or auditory discriminations are slow or undependable, the manual system *must* come in to help to eliminate the confusion. If the learner is able to return to the manual system so he can "draw each of these to get the feel of each of them," the confusion disappears. The adult will say, "Let me get my hands on it so I can be sure." But in almost all daily instances, the visual system leads and the other two systems follow and serve to support and complete whatever task the visual system encounters.

Now Level 5 brings the awareness that a listening ability must develop if the child's words will have matchings with the words of others. In Level 4 the child could choose his labels, which were frequently quite adequate for the results desired. Many of these words were "cute," and parents repeat them in the appropriate situations, reinforcing the child's use of such completely personal vocalizations. One of my children came up with a private language definitely suggestive of some mysterious Oriental ancestry. He would say "wang-ho" and point to the ice cream store as we drove past. It did not take long to realize he was using his personal word for "dairy cone," and we, as young parents, thinking this was cute, perpetuated his word by asking, "Would you like to have a wang-ho, Jim?" Here, a child was using vocal sounds to replace the visual inspections of the several stores and to replace any manual efforts to point out the store having the most interest for him. Probably the most exciting aspect of all these advancing reciprocities is the evidence that Level 5 is the forerunner and the preliminary organization of these three stellar elements for all they will accomplish in Level 6.

Level 6. A V Still as Large, an M now Shrinking, and an L as Big as the V

These letter sizes depict the dominant role that the visual system is now playing while the manual system is beginning to have a less prominent part to play in the learning process. Vision now is more definitely the leader but still needs the manual system for occasional verifications and reinforcements. If the sight-vision complex finds itself a bit unsure, the touch- manual complex comes to its rescue with some double-checking. For example, if the learner is not quite visually confident about the differences in "b" and "d," the touch-manual complex rises to the occasion to draw each one to assure the sight-vision complex which is which. As a rule, however, the sight-vision complex is so much the leader and the dominant element in this level of the learning process that the touch-manual system is used as the tool of the visual system—again, the "instrument of the way"—the complete servant that will usually follow the directions without having to go back down the developmental scale to "get the feel of it." In Level 5, the sight-vision complex says, "I think it is a square," and the touch-manual complex says, "Yes, I have just checked it and it is a square." In Level 6, the sight-vision complex says, "That *is* a square," and the touch-manual complex says, "I will make one for you." Now the touch-manual system becomes the tool wielder to complete the decisions of the sight- vision system.

Please take full note that the letter L in this series is now as big as the letter V. The verbal abilities developing in the previous level are now becoming a *Language* of communication both within the child and in his relationships with others. Language now permits the child to make more complete internalizations of the situation bringing more complete organizations of these three elements so important to the learning continuum. Vocalizations (either sub-vocal or audible) move from single words to sentences, and the ability to listen takes on new importance for the matchings that must occur. Now, the child finds the "cute" baby-talk vocalizations do not satisfactorily represent the visual and manual systems as the single speech sounds previously did. Jim, repeatedly falling back on his "Oriental genes," would say, "Kee wang-hi mo." By now we had begun to analyze the strange language of this youngster and realized this particular phrase was spoken only when Jim was with his grandfather and when a scheduled passenger plane flew over. Eventually all decided Jim was saying, "See the airplane, Grandpa." Knowing these odd syllables were not going to be meaningful to others outside the family, we became wise enough to help Jim find the words all others use in such a situation.

Now, as the bigger L becomes the symbol for *Language* abilities and interweavings, it also takes on added stature as the symbol of the *Listening* abilities that must develop. As language abilities emerge more and more, there is a growing intimacy with vision, and what can be so expressed brings vision to new levels of ability and performance. Just as labeling back in Level 4 put "packages" on everything the sight-vision complex could explore and all the touch-manual complex could manipulate, now language becomes the time-binding process that allows the visual system to visualize past experiences and imagine future experiences. And all vicarious experiences can take on more and more value as significant contributors to the total learning process in the classroom.

Level 7. A Still Larger V, and a Large L with a Large A

Here in this top level of the diagram, the very large V indicates that the sight-vision complex has reached its full dominance in the learning continuum and in the hierarchy of all those systems related to performance in the classroom. The large L and the large A now represent all the *Language* abilities and the *Action* abilities available to the human. The sight-vision complex is now the ultimate input mode and can use both language and action as its ultimate output servants. Here there are the uniquely superior skills of the human for unmatched performance and behavior in an extremely demanding culture, all of which continue to progress and expand through the feedback and feedforward signals traveling from and to each of these stellar elements of the learning process. All the actions available to the individual support and reinforce the language available to the individual, and then both of these support and reinforce all of the visual skills available to him. Action does, language explains and describes, and vision puts all of these into imagination and creativity. The final and supreme result is communication with self and all others, which will then, in its turn, instigate the repetition of the entire process at a more advanced level at which geniuses develop.

A return to reality allows the recognition that handwriting is the most observable and appraisable example of the ultimate levels just described. Handwriting also provides the reasons why Levels 5 and 6 are so critically important to classroom success. The ability to write one's thoughts legibly enough to assure full communication not only illustrates these learning elements, but this ability also clearly illustrates the intellectual level the individual has achieved. The frequently expressed notion that learning to write is not important "because this is an electronic world of computers and word processors run by secretaries who will put all the necessary words on paper for us" is completely unconscionable! The electronic scanners and cash register "mathematicians" at check-out counters have become a necessity because too many high school graduates could not compute the totals, write a receipt, or make change correctly. Now, typewriters have built-in dictionaries to correct spelling for the graduate who has not mastered the basic words of the English language. Too many graduates have decided there is no need to communicate by writing letters because the telephone will "reach out and touch someone." As a general result, there is at least one generation of young adults incapable of writing numbers and words, a generation that cannot communicate with others *or* themselves. This aspect of the wave of illiteracy can be directly traced to the fact that children have not been given the opportunity to learn to write, to express themselves, to communicate, and to rise to the intellectual potentials given them by virtue of their membership in the human race.

The tremendous importance of the ability to write will be given extensive consideration in a later chapter. It is given emphasis here because of the role it plays—indeed, must play—in the learning process. The broader understanding of the sight-vision complex and its role in learning, and the broader understanding of both speech and writing as the observable illustrations of the developmental sequence that must underlie *all* classroom performance will certainly provide a framework upon which all educational guidance must be programmed *if* there is any desire that more children be smart in everything ... *including* school!

Chapter III—Understanding the Sight-Vision Complex from A Developmental Perspective

N one of the learning and/or performance modes discussed until this point has generated more confusion and misconception than has the sight-vision complex. It is difficult to understand why this confusion persists when there is so much evidence and so many explanations about the abilities found here. Undoubtedly, part of this confusion stems from the varying methods of appraisal used by psychologists, ophthalmologists, traditional optometrists, and behavioral optometrists. The frame of reference used by each of these disciplines as a base for their clinical treatment of the problems found in this system is probably the biggest reason for the misconceptions. Thus, the definitions of sight and vision used to explain the purposes and roles of each influence the concepts on which these clinical disciplines perform. Amazingly, each of these disciplines is completely convinced that its particular concept is the only correct one, and communications between them are limited. The semantics each uses to describe its particular concepts provokes the confusions that William S. Gray[7] implied—each discipline brings its own meaning to these words, ignoring the depth of the semantics others are using. The major concern in all this, however, is not the lack of communication between the disciplines; it is the damage done to the children who suffer the penalties of the disagreements between disciplines—the damage of inadequate, or even incorrect, clinical care for the problems they must endure. Lamentably, the longer these disagreements exist, the more children (and adults) will continue to fail in the increasingly complex visual tasks of our culture.

The philosophical backgrounds, the concepts, the semantics, and the current clinical procedures have all been repeatedly described for the information of all. Biases and prejudices are like habits, much easier to acquire than to cure, and another attempt to clear the confusion seems like an exercise in futility. It is worth trying again here, however, for a number of reasons:

1. The non-clinical audience will not bring the same biases and prejudices to this chapter and can thus appreciate a clearer understanding of the role the sight-vision complex really does play in the

learning continuum.

2. There is an increasing number of clinical professionals who sincerely want to end the confusion so that more children can be given the help they need and can have.

3. Those who continue to ignore the huge reservoir of indisputable evidence will just have to be bypassed so there is an end to the misconceptions passed on to parents and teachers, misconceptions that are now blocking a greater understanding of the problems and some of the solutions.

This chapter will be entirely directed to the greater understanding of the sight-vision system and its primary role in classroom tasks. Such discussion limitations to the sight-vision complex come because of my primary interests, and because I am not qualified to offer a similar discussion of the other two stellar elements of the learning process. I have had quite enough of critiques offered by individuals who do not belong to the discipline being criticized. The clarifications offered here are presented in the hope that all will gain a better appreciation of the *real* problems—the problems of children in trouble. If this can occur, the misconceptions and the miscommunications can be bypassed, and all children will profit.

Most obvious to all who are trying to assist children in the learning process is that the three stellar elements presented in Chapter II must be consistently appraised as the child progresses. The manual abilities are quite easily evaluated by the manual skills the child demonstrates. As the model so clearly illustrates, attention must be drawn to the fact that almost all children are arriving at the classroom without having achieved the manual dexterities needed for all of the feedbacks and feedforwards itemized in Chapter I. The presence or absence of manual dexterities provides the clues to the child's readiness for the primary classroom tasks.

Verbal skills are also quite easily appraised. As a child gains the mastery of his mother tongue and the communications skills this mastery should provide, adults can make immediate judgments of the child's readiness for the academic experience. In this same analysis, adults can usually judge the adequacy of the child's hearing abilities and the resulting auditory skills. It is important to note that the language process a child achieves can be well judged by the degree of verbal skills the child achieves.

In contrast, visual skills are not so easily observed. Parents cannot see how well a child "sees" in the way they can see how well the child uses his hands or hear how well the child speaks. The 150-year-old wall chart containing various sized letters can completely mislead judgments of this skill area. If there is to be a fuller appreciation of the sight-vision complex and the role it plays in the overall learning process, there must be another attempt to reach some better under-standings of it.

Demands of the Contemporary Classroom

The usual classroom is a major part of the lighted world in which children live, and since the sight-vision complex's primary purpose is the guidance and monitoring of all human activity, the classroom is really 100% visual. What the title line for this paragraph really means is that at least 80% of classroom tasks demand visual inspections, discriminations, and interpretations. This should not be misconstrued to suggest that manual skills and speech skills are not involved in many of the classroom procedures. The statement does, however, emphasize that vision plays the dominant role in the vast majority of all classroom work.

All this certainly is true of every reading activity. There is little doubt (even among the most adamant pathologists) that reading is primarily a visual task. As the judicious observer appraises the behavior of the student trying to learn to read, the role the visual system must play in this effort becomes more and more evident. One obtains a greater understanding of the statement by Smith and Smith[8] in which they speak of the "degree of supervision that vision exercises over ... neural integrations within information processing systems" when the sight-vision complex is more fully understood. One is reminded of Birch's statement[4] about the hierarchial dominance of the visual system in reading readiness. It also becomes quite obvious why Gesell[9] stated that vision is the dominant factor in human behavior. The beautiful film "The Embryology of Human Behavior,"[14] edited and narrated by Gesell, clearly illustrates the vision development of the infant and how this development prepares each infant for the reading tasks of the classroom. It is all of these evidences, from the individual's behavior and the judgments of many authorities, that lead the behavioral optometrist to make such thorough and extended appraisals of vision development before jumping to simplistic conclusions based solely on the reported clarity and recognitions of small letters on a wall chart at a distance of 20 feet.

The Sight-Vision Complex

As is true of all the input-output complexes, the sight-vision complex must have achieved all the appropriate skills. The developmentally oriented optometrist will carefully evaluate each of the functional components of this sight-vision complex to determine the capabilities and/or the inadequacies that can be identified here. Since there is no other input-output complex capable of inspecting, scanning, discriminating, and interpreting the printed page, this complex must be fully evaluated to determine the level of skill that has been achieved or the magnitude of assistance an individual will need to achieve these skills. Careful appraisals of both the successful reader and the individual with obvious delays in reading performance have brought very reliable data worthy of attention here. The following chart of the incidence of problems in the sight-vision complex as found among elementary and junior high school students, and among many groups of juvenile delinquents, reveals the critical details of the visual skills needed for success in reading. These data have been repeatedly verified by other studies of many groups across the nation, and the only questions that still arise come from the inconsistencies in the techniques for observation and appraisal. When the same observation procedures are carefully controlled, and the same critical judgments are repeated, all observers reach the same conclusions. This consistency of results verifies the importance of the sight- vision complex to the entire learning process.

This chart is self-explanatory but to be sure there are no misunderstandings, some brief comments are indicated.

Visual Discriminations

This ability is usually mislabeled *visual acuity.* The old wall chart has confused so many individuals, there must be clarifications here. The expression, "You have perfect vision. You can see 20/20 on the chart." is one of the greatest misstatements made by professionals. The chart measures acuity, not vision. Vision is the *interpretation* of what is seen. If one is very familiar with the item or object in view, it will be seen well enough to identify, and thus any "test" score will be higher than it would be on an unfamiliar item. The commonly used wall chart has been well described as being more of a test of alphabet familiarity than it is a test of sight clarity. If one knows what a street sign should look like, it will be seen and discriminated correctly and from much greater distance than will any other street sign that is totally unexpected.

Incidence of Visual Problems that Interfere with Academic Progress
Age 8 to 18 inclusive

VISUAL SKILLS	Top 1/3	Mid 1/3	Low 1/3	Spec.Ed.
VISUAL DISCRIMINATIONS This is such an individual ability, it does not readily submit to percentages of occurrence				
VISUAL SCAN AND INSPECTION	12%	32%	65%	96%
VISUAL SYNCHRONY	10%	35%	65%	95%
VISUAL ATTENTION SPAN	5%	15%	40%	88%
VISUAL-TACTUAL INTEGRATIONS	3%	12%	20%	90%
VISUAL MEMORY (COGNITIVE IMAGERY)	10%	50%	65%	85%
VISUALLY STEER AND MONITOR There is another area of visual ability not usually given adequate consideration in the appraisal of problems children have in school. This is identified as the ability to visually steer and monitor one's own movements in his environment, and is one of those abilities that should emerge from all of the other visual abilities. This needs to be included in this chart because so many children have been incorrectly labeled as "just too clumsy to learn" while actually this, too, is a visually-related learning problem				
VISUALLY DIRECTED MOVEMENTS	5%	12%	20%	78%

There is an up-side and a down-side to visual discriminations as these determine reading abilities and comprehensions. These discriminations not only have a primary dependence on familiarity of the item or object being viewed, there is also a critical dependence on what the viewer *wants* to see. The up-side is found in what educators know as "context reading"—the discriminations and recognitions of words that bring sense to the context of the sentence or paragraph. Context reading is a large part of the skill demonstrated by the speed reader with 95% comprehension. Insofar as it is clinically possible to judge, such readers are probably "seeing" all the words in considerable blurriness but go on discriminating and interpreting quite adequately because they "know" what the sentences should say. This blur situation probably exists *until* a completely strange, or very unfamiliar, word is encountered. At such an instant, the reader is brought to a halt and must shift into even better than 20/20 acuity to determine what this word is and what it might mean. Even now, the meaning the reader wants a word to have can greatly influence discriminations of it, and the reader may "see" another word the reader thinks is more appropriate to the context of the sentence. The speed and almost total accuracy of visual discriminations can be of great assistance to the "good" reader, and it is the skill level desired by both the reading teacher and the student who has many pages to read in a short period of time.

The down-side appears when what the reader *wants to see* becomes a big factor in the meaning he should obtain. There are so many words in the English language that look so much alike they can be too easily misread if the reader has decided these words should have meaning other than the actual denotation. In such a situation, the entire meaning of a sentence, a paragraph, or an entire message can be wrongly influenced by what the reader *wanted to see* there. The passenger jet tragedy in the Persian Gulf is again a vivid example of such an error. The psychologists who investigated the incident reported, " ... once crew members identified a plane ... as an F14 fighter, it became difficult for them to change their minds .... That is what they hoped it was, what they wanted to believe, and so an F14 is what they saw." The government's official report states, " ... some of the men monitoring the screens and digital displays may have distorted the information they were receiving in an unconscious effort to make available evidence fit a preconceived scenario."

A splendid example of seeing what one knows he should see is found in a picture optometrists have been using for 35 years to illustrate the difference between "sight" and "vision"—between just *seeing* something and *interpreting* what is seen. Figure 5 is an illustration of something very common and frequently seen by many people. It demands imagination and recall to decipher—to decode—it. Many readers of this book will have seen it in optometric offices, so it will not present problems of interpretation. If there is nothing but confusion, and all possible efforts have been made to "see" it without success, see Appendix B for some help. Then return to this figure and note the differences in the interpretations now possible.

Figure 5. WHAT IS IT?
This fascinating picture is not an illusion. It is an actual photograph of a familiar subject.

This picture has been used by behavioral optometrists for the past 35 years to illustrate that the human can really only "see" what the human knows—that *vision* is the ability to interpret what is being looked at no matter how clearly the picture is printed. If the reader has never seen this picture before, rotate the page 90 degrees until the WHAT IS IT LINE is at the viewer's left. Inspect this picture carefully and identify whatever is possible before turning to Appendix B for added clues.

The results of visual discriminations on which both momentary and daily decisions will be made, is much, much more than simple "visual acuity," and even the clarity of sight at the input mode level will be influenced more by the feedbacks from previous knowledge than it will by the anatomical or physiological status of the end organs (the two eyes). Certainly, the possibilities for the most effective sight-vision complex performance are greater when the end organs are most efficient in their basic operations, but the actual discriminations depend on much more than an absence of any condition that is clinically described as a "refractive error" needing "corrective lenses." Finally, the mere presence of 20/20 acuity brings no guarantee that the individual will automatically and fully interpret everything that must be visually appraised. The clinician who casually states about a child, "The problem in learning cannot possibly be a visual problem because he has 20/20 vision," is guilty of making critical judgments on much too little information. This might be compared to the clinician who does no more than count a pulse and then state there is nothing wrong with an obviously ill patient. In both of these examples, the incomplete evaluation borders on clinical incompetency and should never be accepted by anyone seeking clinical assistance. There is now such a wealth of viable knowledge and information that no clinician should be allowed to make such unacceptable diagnoses.

The reader will note that no percentages of the incidence of visual discrimination problems are shown in Figure 4. This detail is so completely dependent on the individual's personal experiences and interests that it cannot be set into statistical percentages. The variables are so numerous and broad that the clinical judgment of this visual skill will depend on the training and acumen of the observer.

Visual Scan and Inspection

The movement patterns achieved by the sight-vision complex that are most essential to classroom achievement are those directly involved in the visual survey for the recognition of the contents of printed pages, computer screens, and teachers' demonstrations. Most of these movement patterns demand the particular skills of scanning the horizontal lines of print on the textbook page, the vertical scan of columns of numbers in math classes, and the multi-directional movements needed for picture or map inspections. The basic horizontal, vertical, and diagonal eye movements are used and practiced in all wakeful moments when the infant visually explores the lighted world into which he has come. These movements are very general and extremely varied in infancy, while these same movements must become very specialized and controlled in all of the classroom tasks. Thus, the horizontal visual scanning movements required in reading are the very special manipulative movements that can only come out of the experience and practice in reading activities. Where the infant freely and randomly moves eyes in roaming visual exploration, the student is expected to have achieved the movement controls needed to keep his place on the page at all times without having to use a finger or a marker to keep visual attention on the task. These very special movement patterns and the skills that must be achieved by the reader must have the attention of anyone having an interest in visually-related learning problems or learning-related visual problems. All of this is especially pertinent to the child who has been categorized and labeled in the school records as "learning disabled." A very conclusive study done under government grant and completed by a school nurse in a primary school shows that children given the opportunity to gain these horizontal eye movement abilities made significantly greater progress in their reading classes than did the control group that had only the usual reading lessons.[15]

Unfortunately, there have been many disputes over whether or not these sight-vision movement patterns determine the ability to read, and these disputes do nothing more than cloud the issue with unnecessary controversies. Some of those who insist there is no relevancy between speed and accuracy in these sight-vision movement patterns and reading success have based their conclusions on brief and inadequate observations of a few carefully chosen individuals who had learned to read in spite of obviously unskilled movement abilities. There are many large buildings around the country full of evidence that some human performance skills have been achieved even when motoric abilities are terribly restricted for some reason. One must immediately ask, "What levels of performance might have been achieved, with less stress and frustration, if the involved individual had not been confronted with such motoric restrictions?" Desire, need, interest, determination, motivation, and personal goals are but some of the incentives that must be considered before such judgments are made by anyone! Such judgments are some of the examples of the preconceived notions which so influence clinicians that the full clinical details are not explored. These clinicians "see what they expect to see." The contention that specialized sight-vision movement pattern skills are unimportant to classroom tasks makes no more sense or logic than to imply that special finger movement pattern skills are unimportant to the concert pianist.

There have been many paragraphs now devoted to the discussion of *movement* patterns. It is just as important we realize that these skills must also include the control of no *movement*. How, when, where, and why to stop movement are just as much a part of movement skills as how, when, where, and why to start and then direct movement. In fact, this ability to stop moving is one of the most difficult for infants to develop. The momentum factor in any sort of movement is what must be controlled, and the human "braking abilities" demand a lot of practice. This is especially true in eye movements where the eye-globes are set in such moist, fatty cushions with "12 enormous muscles, 100 times stronger than they need to be,"[16] to effect the movements. Yet, the ability to stop eye movements for the visual inspection of critical details becomes a major part of the reading act. If there is any lack of skill here, and the reader overshoots or under-shoots the word needing inspection, confusion is certain. In such a situation, time and comprehension are both lost. Once again, the importance of the sight-vision complex's movement patterns must be considered in any appraisal of reading abilities.

There must be further comment about these sight-vision movement patterns and the ability to read. The presence of excellent skills here will not guarantee reading success. Reading is still an individually unique ability that must be learned, and like all else learned, it depends greatly upon the individual's need and desire to read. It must be strongly backed by experiences and developmental organizations that will fully allow the reader to bring meaning to the printed words he is expected to read. These sight-vision skills will not in and of themselves guarantee reading ability, but the absence of these skills can certainly guarantee more difficulty than the student should experience in every aspect of the reading assignments. The skills of mobility for the speed and accuracy of visual scan, and the skills of controlled immobility for stopping to inspect, cannot be ignored. The acquisition of these skills will make the entire learning process much easier for both the student and the teacher. The absence of these skills can make every reading task fatiguing and frustrating for both student and teacher.

The reader will have already noted the usual categorizations of student abilities on the chart (Figure 4). The frequency of problems in visual scan and inspection are most alarming in all groups because this is a direct indication that too many students have not achieved the skills here that could be a support to their academic efforts. The evidence that 96% of the youngsters in special education have such problems should be a flashing red light to every educator and clinician. Unfortunately, it is here that so much "controversy" exists between those who insist these students should at least be given the opportunity to gain these skills, and those who insist these skills have nothing to do with academic progress. The nay-sayers insist there is no "scientific evidence" such attention will assist these students in spite of the thousands of clinical reports of definite improvements in classroom performance. Such evidence is fully available to whomever will read it.[17] One is reminded of the old Chinese proverb "No book contains any information until it is opened and read." Finally, one must ask the nay-sayers how they would design "scientific studies" that would allow one group of children to practice something directly related to their classroom efforts and prevent a control group from such practice? When it comes to practice in the performance of anything involving participation where learning could occur, there are few placebo possibilities. One group cannot swallow a pill that has "skill vitamins" in it while another group swallows an exact duplicate but with the "skill vitamins" left out. To top it all off, how can the group so desperately needing help be deprived of any opportunity of benefit with absolutely no possibility of harm? If one-third to two-thirds of the usual classroom population demonstrates a problem in a sight-vision complex that obviously relates to 80% of their classroom time and effort, how can it be ignored? Is it possible such controversy is a product of prejudices rather than a legitimate and sincere question about abilities undeniably related to academic achievement?

Visual Synchrony

The reader will have noticed that the chart (Figure 4) shows too many students demonstrating problems in this aspect of visual performance.

Because of its importance to the brain's ability to interpret all of the signals it is receiving, this phrase needs a bit of exploration.

The usual clinical term for the adequacy of the ocular performance representing this synchrony is binocularity, and this term is usually used to describe simply how well the two eyes are apparently teaming—i.e., doing the same thing at the same time. The classical explanation of this teaming is based on the notion that the brain needs fusion, or complete overlapping, of the "images" that are supposedly "focused" on the retina by the optical elements—the internal lenses in each eye. One hard fact must always be remembered. The eyes, like any and all parts of the human, will only do what the brain tells them to do. Thus, the "fusion" of light reaching each retina actually takes place in the brain. This matching of the information being sent into the visual centers of the brain will be accomplished by the brain so it can obtain the most useful and appropriate information it needs for the elaborate integrations with all the other informations arriving from all of the systems related to the visual task of the moment. The magnitude of visual synchrony is much more than simple alignment and teaming of the two eyes. It is the total matching of all signals pertinent to the interpretations the brain is seeking. As a result, what may seem to be a problem of "ocular misalignment" that is commonly called a "binocular problem" may actually be a system timing disparity, or a disparity of system signals that interfere with the integrations the brain needs to obtain the most information. The 1981 Nobel Prize winners D. H. Hubel and T. N. Wiesel have made great contributions to the understandings of brain development directly traceable to the magnitude of the influence of the early organization of this synchrony of the two eyes, and the following synchrony in the signals to the visual cortex. This is "must" reading for the student of the sight-vision complex organization.[18]

By genetic design, a design that occurs only in the human visual system, the two eyes should be physiologically matched with each other so there is the best possible chance that the signals they send to the brain are of equal quality, equal intensity, and with simultaneity in transmission. When this happens, there is the best chance the brain can, and will, integrate these signals with all those other bits of information arriving from systems related to visual information. If, for any reason, this simultaneity is disturbed or disrupted, the result will be less than ultimate. Thus, there is reason to hope that each of the signal input systems—each eye and its neurophysiological components—is most efficiently available. If, for any reason, there is a reduction of the signals that should be generated by the end organs or their muscles, there is reason to consider the proven methods of improving the operational abilities of these. If this is properly accomplished through carefully programmed and guided clinical practices, the signals the system is expected to carry to the brain will be more adequate for the brain's use in the total integrative process. There is no difference in the principles of enhancement of the visual system than there would be in the enhancement of the manual system for the concert pianist. This is what the behavioral optometrist presents as visual training or vision therapy.

There is another facet to this visual synchrony that is of extreme importance to each individual. Since this design is expected to give the brain the light signals that arise from the entire visual spatial field, the visual periphery takes on added significance. This visual field is the 180+ degrees of the total field of view "out front" of the two-eyed person. Careful evaluations of the awareness of the signals from the visual periphery provide clues to some of the problems the youngster with learning problems demonstrates. Quite frequently these students are labeled hyperactive and excessively distractible. The evaluations of how these individuals respond to stimuli coming from this visual periphery can reliably indicate how much difficulty the brain is having in achieving the desired synchrony. In addition, these individuals have rather severe orientational difficulties and are not as fully aware of peripheral environmental clues as they should be for confidence and comfort in busy surroundings. In such situations, this wide field can contribute disturbances the brain cannot integrate, and confusion results. When carefully designed vision therapy[19] was made available to some students so identified, their spatial orientations improved, and their hyperactivity and distractibility were greatly reduced. Many of these students were no longer in need of the drugs so frequently prescribed for these problems.

This visual synchrony is seriously influenced when the brain does not align one eye with the other eye. This condition of serious misalignment, known as "strabismus" among clinicians, is *very* rarely a cause of any learning problems. The individual unfortunate enough to have one eye turned toward the nose, or turned out to one side, has usually compensated visually and emotionally for the situation so well that this is mostly a cosmetic problem. As in any compensation, the individual would undoubtedly perform better if the strabismus were not present, but studies repeatedly show little if any interference in academic progress because of it.

As serious as strabismus is to the ego strengths of an individual, even more serious from the academic standpoint is the situation in which both eyes *appear* to be aligned but visual synchrony is not present. This is one of the visual situations so easily overlooked or misidentified by incomplete clinical evaluations and diagnoses. If visual synchrony is not fully developed, the child may actually have double sight when fatigue sets in. Since diplopia (the clinical term for double sight) usually cannot be observed by parents or teachers, and since the child has no way of knowing others do not also have similar distortions, this loss of synchrony is almost always completely missed by the casual observer. When the alert clinician finds such a situation and asks a child if he ever sees double, the answer is usually in the affirmative. Then, when the child is asked why he never complained about it, the usual reply is, "Doesn't everybody see like this?" Manual clumsiness and verbal problems are easily recognized by teachers and parents, but visual clumsinesses are not nearly so easily identified. Every child demonstrating unusual fatigue or frustration on extended near-distance visual tasks should be asked about this possibility, and if there is *any* doubt, complete clinical attention *must* be sought. Diplopia, or even the *tendency* for doubling, can have much more deleterious influences on the learning process than an actual strabismus. The first learning component to be lost is comprehension, and this then demands rereading and rereading until frustration drives the learner away from the assignment. These inconsistencies, which may occur in the sight-vision complex, can eventually influence the entire developmental sequence and be a major deterrent to intellectual development and the literacy so many students are seeking.

Distractibility and hyperactivity, touched upon briefly two paragraphs back, need expansion here. Equally subtle and difficult to observe is the lack of visual peripheral awareness that almost always accompanies these undesirable behaviors. Observations should include how a child behaves and performs in situations that require an alert awareness of his immediate surroundings. How often the child bumps into objects in passing or how easily the child "gets lost" even in familiar places or how unaware a child might be of what is happening in the immediate surroundings are the behaviors to appraise.

In spite of the recently issued reports that children are not so affected, most children become so entranced by the television show they enjoy that they do not hear others speaking to them or trying to get their attention. However, if any child demonstrates an extreme centrality of visual attention that provokes statements such as "Are you blind? Didn't you see that chair? Why don't you look where you are going?" the situation warrants further investigation. This is often the same child who unintentionally wipes every school desk clean as he passes and accidentally plants a foot in the wastebasket on the way to the pencil sharpener. This child may be the "klutz" on the playground who is constantly bumped around by other children. He may demonstrate a definite preference for having his face buried in a book and may be the best reader in the class, with all promise of becoming extremely nearsighted in the process of constant adjustment and adaptation to a very limited visual spatial world. Or the total opposite may be true, and this child with so little visual confidence in his visual periphery can be the most outstanding example of an attention span so short that little of the assignment is completed because of the distractions.

Whichever of these behaviors may be noted, thorough clinical help *must* be sought as early as possible. The dangers of incomplete or misinterpreted testing will be discussed in a later chapter. Here and now, the important point is: *Do not delay evaluations* since so much of the developmental foundations and learning processes depend so heavily on basic sight-vision competencies.

The positive side of all this is the availability of the clinical care directly pertinent to such problems. The clinician who is fully alert to the overall significance of visual synchrony will spend at least an hour or an hour and a half and may need more than one appointment to fully evaluate the problems and the mediations available. Much of the clinical time will be spent observing the youngster's performance on tasks similar to, or representative of, the classroom desk tasks. If such near- distance task performance is not investigated, neither the patient nor the parents can be assured this visual synchrony has been properly investigated. The time needed to find the problem and the time needed for its elimination is much less than the time it takes to repeat a grade in the effort to become a more successful learner.

Visual Attention Span

This ability has also been touched upon in previous comments. The number of children who demonstrate this sort of problem, as shown in Figure 4, demands additional discussion here, and there will be even further comments later. The point that now needs to be made is that this is a very complex sort of problem, and it cannot be too haphazardly observed. The part that peripheral visual awareness plays in the ability to "pay attention" has been noted, but it is important there be full recognition of the part that auditory skills also play. Since audition is such a prominent receptor mode for signals arising **outside** the field of view, what may often appear as a deficiency in visual attention span may actually be too great a sensitivity to auditory signals. This may definitely be the situation if there is any difficulty in the area of visual scan and visual inspection. If there is so much lag or delay in sight-vision movement abilities, if the individual is unable to shift visual attention quickly *without head movements*, and if head must be turned to find the noise, then this can completely disrupt the visual attention to the task at hand. What may appear to be a super-sensitivity of audition (to the point where noise is too distracting) may be a lack of visual scanning skills. If the student can take a quick glance to be sure the noise is of no consequence, the head is not turned and the visual attention is not disrupted. Thus any attack upon the problems that appear to be attention span problems must consider the underlying and relevant situations that may arise from both of these input modes.

This ability—visual attention span—is much more than the manner in which a student can keep concentrating on visual materials. It also includes the ability to visually encompass more than a single number or word at a glance. One of the most positive results of carefully conducted tachistoscopic (short flash exposures of letters, words, or numbers) practice is the increased breadth of visual span of recognition. When this sort of practice is properly provided by a well-trained clinical assistant, there is almost an automatic increase in how much the individual can visually grasp in extremely short periods of time. This breadth of visual grasp is closely related to the speed and accuracy of the visual discriminations in reading. Further, there is an interesting gain in reading comprehension when this practice is properly offered and skills are accomplished by the student. Thus, it is not just the ability to stay on a reading task without being distracted, it is also the ability to gather more signals at the input mode level. The more that is gathered the more there is to discriminate and interpret, and learning increases with less stress and fatigue.

This span of visual attention is greatly influenced by still another component of the input mode. The ultimate efficacy of the entire sight-vision complex depends very heavily on its ability to seek and hold symbol clarity for inspections and discriminations of critical details. This has been referred to in the discussion on visual synchrony. Like all other input modes, any demand that keeps the system on a restrictive task (like reading) for extended periods of time (like homework) without relief brings a satiety that can either distort or even eliminate the validity of the signals the system is designed to send into the total developmental sequence. Eighty percent of the classroom tasks include these situations where an input system is expected to provide consistent and continuous information in spite of the stresses entailed. The demand that the sight-vision complex must operate at desk distances over long periods of time will in and of itself bring both constrictions and restrictions to the movement patterns involved. To these stresses are added those being fed back from the mind when there is a special demand for comprehension. When any of these stresses bring any degree of fatigue or any mismatchings anywhere along the spirals of the developmental sequence, attention span will immediately deteriorate. Under such circumstances there are only two solutions the individual can reach: either there will be a concession to the stress, and the entire system will distort in some manner in its attempt to relieve the stress, or the individual will turn to some other less stressful activity. These are known as the "fight or flight" responses, and the sight- vision complex provides an example of this in its "fight" to overcome the stress by becoming "nearsighted" or by choosing "flight" and avoiding reading because of its discomforts and frustrations.

I am fully cognizant that most of these pages will be interpreted as though everything here relates only to infants and children. On only a few occasions have there been references to adults, and these were in such general terms that they might not have been noticed. The fact remains, beyond any doubt or dispute, that as long as one is alive, regardless of age, development and learning are still a part of every waking moment. Neither of these is as evident in adulthood as they are in early life because the adult has so well established physical stature, size, and behavioral habits, and because there usually is less and less challenge to learn new skills. There is one aspect of life that remains as fully in force as it ever was at any time since birth—this is the "fight or flight" response just discussed. If the impact of stress is persistent enough and lasts long enough, the individual will make the choice to either solve the stress or escape the stress. There is no part of any of the daily responses to the stresses of this contemporary culture where this is as evident as it is in this aspect of visual performance now being discussed. The sight-vision complex is now faced with the need to adapt ("fight") or escape ("flight") because of at least two major cultural impacts: daily traffic congestion and the computer screen.

The daily hours millions of adults spend at the steering wheel of their automobile impose extreme demands for visual peripheral attentions and skills that exist in no other area of activity. The need to literally "drive" an amazing number of cars other than the one occupied is a tremendously stressful visual task. It requires a constant visual alertness and a constantly shifting apprehension of all the forces every other car presents, as well as the vagaries of the drivers of the other cars. "Depth perception," the ability to judge distance and placement of everything that surrounds one and one's place in the total visual field, must not fade for even an instant during the miles on the freeways at 60 miles per hour, or at 20 miles per hour when an impatient driver insists on changing lanes without warning to anyone. Although clarity of sight assists in this activity, it is much less important than visual attention span and its reliability. If every accident occurring on the nation's highways were fully evaluated, more than 90% of them could be directly attributed to some failure or critical deficiency in the visual performance of the individuals involved. Somehow, somewhere, at some instant in the time preceding the accident, visual discriminations and decisions upon which visual attention is based, would have been insufficient to some degree. The number of individuals whose "fight" in these stresses brings undesirable adaptations is inestimable, and the loss of life under these circumstances proves that these stresses are impacting on more than the individual at the steering wheel. Reading all the traffic clues is every bit as demanding as reading all the office communications.

The other cultural stress now impacting on millions of adults is the computer screen. This comes closer to being a return to the stresses of the classroom than any other situation now faced by adults. The computer affords all of the stresses the child had while learning to read and reading to learn. The major difference comes in the pressures and demands of the modern office or plant to maintain a high rate of individual production, lest the boss find someone who can.

There have been a flood of media attempts to bring solutions to the problems the computer has imposed on the millions now using video display terminals (VDTs). Research and surveys of the problems coming from the "fight" response of all those who want to keep their jobs has brought forth a myriad of furniture designs, all promoted to eliminate the fatigues and body contortions now created at the computer. Research continues on whether the computer causes baldness or miscarriages. There are hundreds of workman's compensation cases in which wrist or arm damage is blamed on the computer. What continues to get the least attention are the many changes in visual comfort, visual performance, and, eventually, visual abilities. The sight-vision complex is so adaptable to the forces impacting upon it that the discomforts and distortions in its performance are seemingly taken for granted so long as "corrective glasses" can be obtained that recover the loss of sight clarity for the drive home on the freeway at the end of the day. The amazing number of office workers who have had to obtain new glasses after a few months of intensive computer use provides alarming evidence of the results of the "fight" response made by the sight-vision complex. The tremendous number of individuals who have sought another occupation because the "flight" response is open to them should also draw more attention to this particular impact of an electronic culture.

Why is all this time spent describing stress situations and the maladaptations being accepted? Because the mediation of these problems is the best kept secret of the modern day! This entire book is directed at the developmental sequence and the learning processes that are characteristic of the human. The underlying contention of this book is that since all of these characteristics are extended and enhanced through use and practice, there certainly are positive and constructive procedures available to the human to reduce or eliminate the destructive and negative adaptations made by the sight-vision complex. Must these adaptations *always* be concessions and sacrifices to the advancements of civilization? Isn't there some way to direct these adaptations so the advancements of civilization become opportunities for the advancement of the individual as well?

There are very definitely *some* viable and reliable solutions to *some* of these stress problems that are so deleterious to the sight-vision complex and its performance capabilities. The first attack must be directed at the stresses that arise in the near- centered tasks of the classroom and the computer station of the office. This attack demands the sort of evaluations of visual performance that brings more attention to how effective and durable this performance is at near distances in contrast to the simplistic evaluation of the symbols on a wall chart 20 feet away. How clearly and how efficiently a person sees at the distances needed for driving on the freeways is almost a direct product of how durably and efficiently one performs on the near tasks. The millions of adults who have become "nearsighted" as a result of long, intensive hours at the VDT are examples of this, as they also are examples of how children become "nearsighted" as a direct result of long and intensive hours in the textbooks. There is now ample evidence that the deterioration of visual peripheral awareness and skills needed for freeway safety can be traced to these same nearpoint stresses of computer and textbook.

The proper evaluations of these areas of visual performance—visual scan and visual inspection, visual synchrony, visual span, and all of its components—must be completed while the receptor modes (the eyes) are neither directly nor indirectly traumatized by any sort of drugs, either those ingested by the patient or those introduced by a clinician. The clinical evaluations can only be reliable when the receptor modes are operating as fully and as efficiently as they can at the moment. Any drug put into the eyes that is touted as a "relaxant" is usually a paralytic and will almost totally eliminate any possibility of obtaining the clinical data needed for either diagnosis or solution to the problem. If such a drug is deemed necessary for a more complete examination of the internal status of the eyes, it must be introduced at a time when it will have no subsequent influence upon the performance capabilities of the receptor modes. This detail is still the choice of the patient, and many clinicians are fully capable of making the sort of evaluation needed without the use of deleterious drugs.

The signs and symptoms are most evident to the individual himself and not easily recognized by the lay observer unless that observer has been alerted to what the signs will be. The deterioration of visual attention will be noted first in the increase in fatigue while on any sort of "reading" task—in the classroom, at homework, on the computer. This will become apparent when the visual attention time span is reduced or when there is noticeable blurring, or "smearing," of the print. One who personally experiences this will have no doubts about it, and the frequently recommended "solution" for the computer operator is to blink more frequently or to take breaks every 15 minutes in spite of the fact that both of these "solutions" can also seriously decrease productivity.

The student may not complain about such signs of visual difficulty since he may not know this is an unusual situation and may be assuming that all other students have the same blurriness as "part of the job." Since it is impossible to see or hear another individual having these problems in the same way that one can observe stumbling or clumsiness or hear speech problems, such signs may be present for a long time before being identified as an unnecessary interference with visual performance. Under such circumstances, a student may have already been classified as "lazy" or "lacking motivation" or "the class clown" or "a discipline problem"—all as a result of the "flight" solutions chosen by the student.

The clinical literature of the eye-care professionals (the ophthalmologist) and the vision-care professionals (the behavioral optometrist) is full of the diagnostic clues and mediations for this problem. Unfortunately, the clinician who prescribes glasses solely for sight clarity on the distant wall chart will overlook this problem. In high contrast, the clinician who gives careful attention to the abilities of the entire sight- vision complex for all the near-distance visual tasks our culture includes will use the most pertinent clinical methods for the elimination or modification of such problems. The usually successful solution is provided by judiciously prescribed glasses, specifically chosen to relieve the stresses described in the previous paragraphs. The informed clinician will give full instructions and recommendations on when such glasses are to be worn and will probably give specific instructions on how they can support and enhance visual performance on constrictive and restrictive tasks such as reading, studying, detailed handwork, typing, and computer tasks. These glasses will *not* be prescribed for clarity of sight on the wall chart! They *will* be prescribed for efficiency and efficacy on near-distance tasks.

Such glasses are sometimes incorrectly appraised by the uninformed clinician who prescribes only for sight clarity on the wall chart. This clinician will most likely criticize such a prescription and discourage its use. Both patient and parents must remember such near-wear glasses are identified as "stress- reducing glasses" by the clinician who is more fully aware of the impact of the complicated visual tasks our culture is presenting. The clinical literature is now filled with research and clinical data[20] on the values and validities of such clinical procedures, and the bulk of it is so great it can no longer be ethically disputed.

Visual Tactual Integrations

This aspect of the entire sight-vision complex will have detailed exploration and discussion very soon. However, the reader's attention must be called to the fact that the usual three standard classroom groups (manual, visual, verbal) have the lowest incidence of problems here. This can be very reasonably explained by the developmental importance of the intimate relationships existing between the visual mode and the manual mode. This intimacy is notably absent among those students in special education, and this certainly should hold some quite obvious messages for educators. It has great significance to the developmentally oriented optometrist who long ago found that learning opportunities enhancing this intimacy had almost spectacular results in the overall progress of students thrust into special education without proper evaluations.

Visual Memory (Cognitive Imagery)

This item on the incidence chart (Figure 4) will be more fully discussed when some of the educational tests are discussed in the next chapter. There must be some comment here for two reasons: (1) there are so many students who demonstrate problems in this facet of the role the sight-vision complex plays in the classroom tasks; and (2) because the ability to achieve visualizations—cognitive images in the mind—is so critically essential to basic reading comprehension and spelling abilities. Interestingly, many authorities now contend that the skill levels achieved in this visual ability can be directly correlated with intellectual skill levels. One fact stands out—skill in what the behavioral optometrist calls *visual memory* is certainly very relevant to productive imagination and creativity. Although this is another of those abilities difficult to observe as it is happening, its products are easily recognized. Every test used by educators to investigate "perception" and "perceptual abilities" includes probes of "visual recall." Visual memory, visualization, mental imagery or visual recall—whatever it may be called—is undoubtedly the ultimate level of skill in the entire developmental sequence *and* in the total learning process.

One of the educational test batteries to be examined in the next chapter describes visual recall by stating: "This involves the ability to recall dominant features of one stimulus item or to remember the sequence of several items." This may be interpreted as a simplified description of this particular ability so unique to humans. Experimental psychologists and behavioral optometrists know how extensively this ability influences *all* human behavior in all degrees and levels of the interpretations and comprehensions of every aspect of all things visible, and, in many instances, what has been previously seen but then becomes invisible. Further, these clinicians are vitally interested in the contribution of the visual-tactual organizations that have undoubtedly laid solid foundations for the organization of visual memory.

There must be consideration of the much broader aspects of this ability if its significance to the learning process is to be understood. Carefully controlled observations by highly qualified researchers in the field of infant behavior[21] definitely suggest there is *memory* behavior as early as 3 months of age if there have been visual experiences and manual manipulations of objects used to elicit what certainly appears to be viable evidence of *recognition—re* cognition; *re* call. By the time many infants are 6 or 7 months old, there is repeated behavior strongly suggesting that visual memory (visualization) permits the baby to hold a degree of contact with Mother when she walks into another room out of the infant's sight. In such a situation, there is also the significance of auditory signals the baby receives when the mother talks to the infant from the other room. In addition, infants show more curiosity and give more attention to a new toy put in the crib. This new response to a new toy strongly suggests the infant can visualize the old one well enough to put the old one aside so attention can be given to explorations of the new one. These observations, with variables controlled and carefully repeated, give credence to the conclusions that visualization abilities are developing much earlier in life than many investigators had thought. There is added credence to the contention that these skills are learned, are not totally innate, and are certainly much more than a mere ability to "recall dominant features of one stimulus item or to remember the sequence of several items."

Besides the tremendous role visualization plays in reading comprehension, its role in spelling ability is also significant. Certainly there are a number of words in the English language so phonetically valid that "sounding them out" elicits the correct spelling. However, our very difficult language has too many words that do not spell as they sound, or sound as they spell. In every one of these exceptions to the phonetic consistencies, the speller must be able to visualize the words if correct spelling is to be achieved. Visual memory will also have a great influence on the magnitude of the meaning one can bring to the printed word. Again, we must remember Mr. Gray's comment about "not getting meaning *from* a word, but bringing meaning *to* a word." The meaning one can bring to a word, whether printed or spoken, will be greatly determined by the breadth and depth of the visualization the word generates. Likewise, a picture, which is supposed to be "worth a thousand words," will be only as valuable as the number of words that will be visually influenced. Rube Goldberg, the famous cartoonist, said: "We humans communicate not just with words but almost entirely through visualization."[22] His drawings of complicated mechanical devices that created a series of actions and events could not be appreciated unless the viewer could visualize all of the action factors suggested in the cartoons. Goldberg's cartoons brought great emphasis to the fact that if a picture were poorly drawn or a story poorly told, the viewer or the listener could not create appropriate and matching visualizations. If visualizations were poor or incomplete, the picture or story was discarded and not remembered. And no communications would have been established.

Visually Directed Movements

This final item on the incidence chart is included only to reveal a part of the reason why so many of the individuals receiving our attention can be "smart in everything ... except school." The percentages here emphasize that actually doing something brings success of performance not as available when movement is not part of the problem-solving process.

"Refractive Errors"

The conditions generally known as "refractive errors" need some clarification in this discussion of visual problems. These are not listed as problems that influence academic performance because the proper clinical evaluation of these refractive problems brings the prescriptions that usually compensate for the ocular conditions which exist. There are three of these conditions usually mediated with what are frequently labeled as "corrective" glasses. It is essential the reader know that glasses so prescribed do not "correct" the problem in any manner. Such glasses only compensate for the distortions in the sight-vision complex arising as a direct result of adaptations to undue stresses on the biophysiological system.

The problem now becoming most prevalent among children is "nearsightedness" (myopia), the condition in which the individual sees more clearly at near distances than at long distances. Next in frequency of occurrence is astigmatism, the condition in which clarity of sight is reduced at all distances. The third is "farsightedness (hyperopia), the condition in which sight clarity is usually quite adequate at all distances, but the individual performs visually at long distances with less stress than at short distances. Many books have been written on each of these conditions, the possible etiology of each, and the most effective clinical care procedures. It is now evident that the care provided can bring either positive or negative results. These issues are best discussed in full detail with the clinician of choice, and the individual seeking vision care should be very sure that all questions regarding expected influences of "corrective glasses" and long-term prognosis are thoroughly answered. It is essential here to note there are aspects of each of these conditions that can be worsened rather than ameliorated if "corrective" glasses are the only prescription offered. Much more detailed information can be obtained by contacting the Optometric Extension Program Foundation, 2912 South Daimler Street, Santa Ana, California 92705. The College of Optometrists in Vision Development, P.O. Box 285, Chula Vista, California 92012 is another source of valuable information. Both of these sources can also provide names and addresses of many clinicians who have prepared themselves to provide the special care these conditions require.

After literally hundreds of research reports, clinical explanations, and many interdisciplinary discussions, it is clear that confusions and "controversies" remain. The greatest disappointment is the totally unnecessary and unjustified impact on the children who continue to suffer problems as the arguments rage on. Added to the muddle are the misconceptions propagated by the continuing articles published by inadequately informed educators. If there is to be an increase in the understanding of the sight-vision complex and its dominant role in the learning process, some undeniable facts must be included here.

First, if the proper glasses are prescribed and properly worn, these three refractive conditions should create no interference in a student's learning process. In fact, the proper glasses can provide definite and impressive reductions of the stresses of the near-centered academic assignments with less fatigue and improved comprehension as a result. A large number of researchers and authorities from optometry, education, and ophthalmology have agreed on this point.

In 1953, Helen Robinson, Ed.D., then director of the University of Chicago Reading Clinic, published an important monograph on reading problems following research conducted by educators and optometrists.[23] This is a broad report of extensive investigations of vision, visual performance, and visual conditions as these relate to reading skills. In this monograph, Arnold Gesell wrote: "Refractive errors which yield to optical correction are not in themselves likely to cause reading difficulties. The use of cycloplegics (drops) in refractive examinations interferes with testing of visual functions at near distances. But, nearpoint is the area where reading anomalies become manifest. Accordingly, it is desirable in suspected cases to apply a battery of far and near orthoptic tests and visual skill tests. Such tests serve to reveal abnormalities of fusion (visual synchrony), fixation and projection (visual inspection), faulty visual flexibility (visual scan), maladjustments and spasms of accommodation (visual discriminations and interpretations), and special errors of refraction. Inconsistent conditions are more handicapping for reading efficiency than are fixed ones. It is the alternate phorias (errors in spatial judgments), the intermittent squints (intermittent misalignments of the eyes), and the periodic central suppressions (suppressions of the input signals from one or both eyes) which contribute most to reading difficulties."

Second, all studies of the influence of such visual conditions emphasize that evaluations must fully and carefully consider much more than the refractive status of the eyes and include carefully designed appraisals of the entire sight-vision complex as it has been described in the previous two chapters.

Third, because the vast majority of the classroom activity demands extended periods of visual attention to near-centered, desk-distance tasks, all evaluations must give much more consideration to the efficiency and durability of the sight- vision complex at these distances of task demand. This means, as Gesell stated, that much more than distance sight clarity and the usual wall chart tests must be made to determine just what sight-vision difficulties might be present.

Fourth, the clinical evidence now overwhelmingly proves that glasses that might be completely appropriate for distance visual tasks can be completely inappropriate for academic tasks like reading and all desk-distance assignments. For specific example, the glasses that quite adequately provide the nearsighted person with distance clarity may so increase the stresses of the near visual tasks that there are extensive interferences with comprehension in reading and similar symbolic tasks. Further, these "distance" lenses frequently create added nearpoint stresses that lead to an increase in the nearsightedness if they are also worn for all near tasks. The informed clinician in both disciplines usually prescribes lenses that are appropriate for both far and near tasks, usually in bifocal form, because clinical experience has reportedly shown both an increase in the ocular problems and a decrease in academic performance when such lenses are not prescribed.

Regrettably, the confusions and controversies still remaining can be traced to the age-old differences in the basic clinical philosophies of the disputants. Since all humans have great difficulty with any philosophy that does not agree with the one first learned and sincerely believed, the urge to defend a philosophy frequently takes on added biases and prejudices. Such an undesirable and unnecessary situation has arisen that continues to perplex and disturb parents and teachers, especially those trying to reach some of the solutions to the problems being demonstrated by children in academic difficulties.

A Policy Statement

In 1972, a small committee of clinicians issued a statement for the American Academy of Ophthalmology, the American Association for Pediatric Ophthalmology, and the American Academy of Pediatrics. Typically, and understandably, the biases and prejudices of these clinicians determined their judgments, and this was reflected in the policy statement they issued. This policy statement has been reissued and widely circulated in a dozen or more "clarifications" in the intervening years, and the most recent one comes from the American Academy of Ophthalmology with the latest "clarifications." Sadly, these statements have added nothing but confusion to what the sight-vision complex really is and to the role it plays in the learning process. This situation has been too often seen as "controversy" between these medical groups and two or three non-medical groups who have been prominent in the search for understandings and solutions. There have frequently been indications that this "controversy" has been promoted as a distraction to cover the clinical ignorances and research paucities of the groups issuing such statements. On the positive side of all this is the latest edition of this policy statement, which very strongly suggests that the Academy of Ophthalmology is catching up with the research and clinical developments coming from those several non-medical disciplines that have been making significant contributions during the past 30 years. This latest edition holds interesting promises for the cooperation and communication which may now evolve.

This most recent policy statement deserves investigation with the greatest possible objectivity and with children given higher priorities than any given to the clinical disciplines that have been in such deep conflict. There are so many gains evident in it that the "controversy" should now begin to fade and become much less of an interference to the desired progress.

This statement opens with two summarizing recommendations for care:

1. "Early medical, educational and/or psychological evaluation and diagnosis."

2. "Remediation with educational procedures of proven value, demonstrated by valid research."

Neither of these statements can be denied, but both of them need extension to assure the inclusion of the evaluation, diagnosis, and remediation that is actually required. Certainly, there can be no dispute about the need for *early* intervention, or the importance of *"educational procedures of proven value, demonstrated by valid research."* It is extremely important that these recommendations go far enough to adequately and properly include the "proven" and "valid" contributions in "diagnosis" and "remediation" from several clinical groups not mentioned here. Apparently, the medical groups are the only ones not yet aware of the help available from groups who do not consider themselves to be "medical, educational or psychological" disciplines. Since communication seems to be opening, some of this confusion may be clearing.

This latest policy statement offers a paragraph as "Background," and most of this statement is beyond any question. The final sentence, however, again suggests some limitations in the understanding of the phrase "visual perception." This sentence states: "Research shows that simple deficient *visual perception* of letters or words accounts for inability to read in only a small minority of children; the majority suffer from a variety of linguistic defects." Does this statement really imply that visual perception is not a part of linguistic skills development? Is it possible that the usual medical model of vision and visual perception is still limiting these abilities to sight clarity and the simple physiological functions of the eyes? Do these clinicians still think of visual perception as a completely separate entity in this total ability to read? Hopefully, Chapter II may give these clinicians some added insights to the dynamics of the learning process for reading and all other academic tasks.

This policy statement then goes on into "Evaluations and Conclusions" about "learning disabilities, including the dyslexias." The entire gist of this first statement is completely correct except there is again the limiting identifications of the clinical disciplines that can make important contributions. The emphasis here is on assessment as "early as possible to identify individuals at risk for learning disabilities." There can be no argument with the insistence that early assessment is of greatest importance.

The second paragraph brings another suggestion of the limits of the clinical model that lies behind these statements. "Eye care should never be instituted in isolation when a person does have dyslexia or a related learning disability." One cannot avoid the feeling that this is a pretty naive sort of statement for any group or person to make. It does reveal the tremendous differences in the basic philosophies that exist among clinical groups who provide eye care and those who provide vision care. It appears that the medically oriented groups are still holding to the philosophy that the end organs (eyes) are all that need attention; if these are "normally aligned" and "have 20/20 acuity," no further consideration need be given. This philosophy holds that if the eyes are "normal with no refractive errors," there can be no "eye" reasons for learning problems. Does this philosophy also hold that these "normalcies" then shift the problem to the educator and/or the psychologist, and this referral avoids the "isolation" mentioned?

An opposite view, held by hundreds of behavioral optometrists, was best stated by Arnold Gesell in 1949: "The development of vision in the individual child is complex because it took countless ages of evolution in the race to bring vision to its present advanced state. Human visual perception ranks with speech in complexity and passes through comparable developmental phases. Moreover, seeing is not a separate isolable function; it is profoundly integrated with the total action system of the child—his posture, his manual skills and coordination, his intelligence, and even his personality make-up. Indeed, vision is so intimately identified with the whole child that we cannot understand its economy and its hygiene without investigating the whole child."[9] This second paragraph of the newest medical policy statement does extend beyond previous editions by saying, "Children identified as having such problems ('dyslexia or a related learning disability') should be evaluated for general medical, neurologic, psychologic, visual and hearing defects." Isn't this what Dr. Gesell was saying 40 years ago? Parenthetically, it is most interesting to find this policy statement now including vision as a probable seat of a "defect." However, one wonders if the "vision defects" included here are those that the medical profession find only in the eyes themselves.

This second paragraph ends with another of those comments that no one can deny. "If problems of this nature are found, corrective and/or remedial steps should be applied as soon as possible." It is splendid to read this point on the urgency of early care so that further, unnecessary deterioration of learning abilities does not occur.

The third paragraph contains several ambiguous statements that may not really dispel much of the lamented confusions. "Since the decoding of written language involves transmission of visual signals from the eyes to the brain, it has, unfortunately, become common practice to attribute reading difficulties to subtle ocular abnormalities, presumed to cause faulty perception." It is extremely difficult to believe such a statement still appears in print from any source. There is so much research coming out of the past 30-plus years that the reading process is so complex, and so widely influenced by so many factors, that any tendency to attribute reading problems to ocular abnormalities as a "common practice" suggests another limited view of both the reading process and the role of the eyes as the original processors of the light inputs they receive. This statement would be much more realistic if it were rephrased to read: "Since the decoding of written language (and, hopefully, *printed* language) involves transmission of visual signals from the eye to the brain, there must be a recognition that some ocular problems can have a negative influence upon the reading process with the possibility of detriment to perception." This point has been discussed earlier in this chapter and should need no further comment now.

The next sentence in the paragraph is another that has been repeatedly clarified in optometric and psychological literature. "Although eyes are necessary for vision, *'visual perception' depends on the interpretation of visual symbols by the brain.*" The underlined part of this sentence appears in italics in the policy statement perhaps to emphasize the medical profession's new understanding of "visual perception." If the goal of this statement is clarification, it might be much more helpful to restate it as follows: "Although eyes are necessary for sight, visual perception is the brain's interpretation of all the signals that arrive in the visual cortex and may be quite extensive even when sight is absent."

The final sentence in this paragraph brings added questions. "Remediation directed to the eyes alone cannot be expected to alter the brain's processing of visual stimuli." If there is any comprehension of the complexity of the visual system, as noted by Gesell, it is almost totally impossible to direct remediation to the eyes alone. Even if it were possible, this would very definitely alter the brain's processing of the stimuli it would be receiving from the entire sight-vision complex. The only philosophy that isolates the eyes from all the other information input systems undoubtedly holds that "eyes can be treated in isolation" and this notion was discarded many years ago by most of the disciplines concerned with human development and the learning process in humans.

There is still another paragraph in this third conclusion that may suggest the limits of the clinical philosophy behind the entire policy statement: "Indeed, children with dyslexia or related learning disability have the same incidence of ocular abnormalities, e.g., refractive errors and muscle imbalances (including nearpoint convergence and binocular fusion deficiencies) as children without." Many questions are immediately spawned by such a flat and all-inclusive statement. What tests were used? Were there in-depth probes of ocular and visual consistency, durability and efficiency or were only wall chart distance acuities investigated? Were all tests done without the drops that create a temporary paralysis that has extensive impact on the entire sight-vision complex? What tests of stress impacts on the entire visual system were conducted? What observations of the magnitude of the integrations between the manual system, the verbal, and the visual system were completed? Assuming that the flat statement of "same incidences" could be accurate, were the same number of farsighted, nearsighted, and astigmatic youngsters found in the two groups? If this was actually the result of the study that brought this conclusion, the group sizes must have been very small, and the individual differences which exist in every other human performance area would have been such a unique situation that this research should have had wide publication.

A closely related question must be asked: Has the committee composing this policy statement completely overlooked the world-wide attention that has been given the research and publications of the famous Canadian scientist, Hans Selye, M.D., Ph.D.?[24] This man's investigations and conclusions on the impacts of stress on the human show beyond any doubt that no two individuals react to stress in exactly the same way. Further, extended stress can have severe impact on all the physiological systems in body functions. Selye's major thesis has been that excessive amounts of stress over prolonged periods of time lead to frustration and failure and to extreme adaptations and/or distortions of the physiological mechanisms. This work has swept every clinical discipline, and the ophthalmologist cannot possibly ignore the impact of such stress on the internal pressures of the eyeball with glaucoma being a too common result. How can there possibly be a neglect of the impact of stress on all other ocular functions and eventually all visual perceptual results?

The contemporary optometrist has been reporting the results of stress on the visual system for many years. In summary, the most common clinical observations show that most valedictorians and other highly motivated students are most likely to be nearsighted before they complete high school. In contrast, the youngsters in the special education classes, where there is a distinct difference in the intensity of motivations and academic task pressure as well as much less time devoted to study, are very seldom nearsighted. The old question of whether the nearsightedness makes the valedictorian or the valedictory drive makes the myope is of no real consequence. The major point is the great clinical evidence that the magnitude of stress can bring physiological changes that would bring distinct differences between the two groups of children addressed in this sentence. This statement will have to be supported by extensive valid research before it can be accepted as a viable conclusion, and the reader is again referred to the chart on incidences of visual problems presented earlier in this chapter (Figure 4).

Still another question must be raised. Even if it could be proven that the same incidence of ocular abnormalities exist between children with dyslexia and learning disabilities and all other children, shouldn't there be careful thought given to the fact that such "abnormalities" would have a much greater impact on learning-disabled children than they would on usual students? If there is any possibility that youngsters with learning problems are victims of poor integrations of several of the learning modes or confusion in the process of scanning and interweaving the stimuli from related information processing systems, could these youngsters cope with "ocular abnormalities" as well as the usual student? Would the mixed and/or incomplete signals from the "ocular abnormalities" cause more confusion in the interpretive processes the academic tasks demand of the youngsters with learning problems? Isn't it quite possible that the totality of the entire process would be more severely influenced in the youngster who has not developed the coping methods the "easier" learner would have achieved? Somehow the established and well proven philosophies of human development have to be brought into the consideration of this policy conclusion.

The fourth conclusion states, "Correctable ocular defects should be treated appropriately. However, no known scientific evidence supports claims for improving academic abilities of dyslexic or learning-disabled children with treatment based on: (a) visual training, including muscle exercises, ocular pursuits, or tracking exercises or glasses (with or without bifocals or prisms); (b) neurological organizational training (laterality training, balance board, perceptual training." There is much more to this paragraph, but this opening statement must be examined without delay. Here are statements that have created more confusion and distress than any other sentences in the entire set of conclusions, and these suffer from rather extreme ambiguities.

Certainly, "ocular defects should be treated appropriately"! There are wide differences in opinion on what the appropriate clinical treatments are, but with the exception of myopia (nearsightedness), the inappropriate glasses do not usually create a severe problem. This is probably true because the farsighted and astigmatic patients will discard "inappropriate" prescriptions because of the increased discomfort that may often occur. The nearsighted person is trapped by what seems to be such a spectacular improvement in long distance clarity that these prescriptions are usually worn in spite of some discomfort at reading.

The statement about "no known scientific evidence" raises some serious questions. First this statement reminds one of the popular library poster that states, "He who does not read is no better informed than he who cannot read," and this seems very appropriate here. The evidence is so great and so widely available it is difficult to understand how it has been missed by the composers of this policy statement. One single report presents 218 references in support of visual training as one clinical approach to some of the solutions of learning-related problems.

Some specific clarifications must be offered. What do these medical experts mean by the phrase "muscle exercises"? There are numerous members of both the medical and non-medical specialities who have known for more than 30 years that visual training is much, much more than simplistic "muscle exercises." Medical researchers determined in the late 1800s that the ocular muscles are 100 times stronger than they need be to move a moist, well cushioned eye in its orbit. There is certainly no need of any sort of muscle gymnastics to strengthen muscles already many times stronger than need be. Instead the behavioral optometrists, some occupational therapists, school nurses, classroom teachers, and educational psychologists long ago shifted attentions and interest to practice procedures that assure the individual of speed, accuracy, and durability of the visual scan and visual inspection abilities essential to so many classroom tasks.[25,26] The skills of visual inspection, visual scan, and visual discrimination are all dependent on so much more than muscle strength that the phrase "muscle exercise" is neither applicable nor relevant.

In 1970, two years before the first policy statement was jointly issued, Sir Stewart Duke-Elder, the absolute ophthalmological authority, published the fifth volume of his series of textbooks for the ophthalmologist.[27] In this particular text he wrote, "It should be remembered that biologically the eyes were adapted for relatively simple purposes ... to look for enemies and food; and although, from long custom, we accept the conditions in which we live today as normal, it by no means follows that the eyes have evolved sufficiently to fulfill the exorbitant demands of unremitting close work imposed upon them by a highly complex and artificial civilization. The more is this understandable when we remember the functional minutiae required for the attainment of accurate vision with the high degree of coordination necessary between movements of the two eyes as they fulfill the requirements of binocular vision. It is understandable that this complex of the visual apparatus tends to make it less capable of withstanding the long-continued strain than a cruder and less highly specialized mechanism." Later in the same textbook, Sir Duke-Elder discusses "visual exercises" and writes: "The facilitation of the processes of seeing is exemplified in comparison between the efforts of a child who fixes each letter in his early attempts at reading with the practiced reader who can interpret print with a glance which does not require fixation even on each word; it is the difference between the facile ease of the practiced golfer or skater and the strained efforts of the tiro....Repetitive exercises, by facilitation of the perceptual processes and the provision of an accumulated fund of memories and associations to aid interpretations, are an immense aid in the art of seeing." Here, in a few sentences, Duke-Elder answers almost every point of the conclusions drawn in medicine's statement #3, and gives import to the extensive work of Hans Selye. In so doing, he quite fully describes what the behavioral optometrists, the informed occupational therapists, school nurses, classroom teachers, and some educational psychologists have been offering in their efforts to assist children to better skills for use and application to the learning processes.

There is exciting and much more recent research now being reported that is very pertinent to this discussion.

A recent account, titled "Plasticity in Brain Development,"[28] provides many new insights to the plasticity that exists in the brain, and how visual experiences can influence this plasticity. The scientists reporting this research wrote: "Even though the basic organization of the brain does not change after birth, details of its structure and function remain plastic for some time, particularly in the cerebral cortex....Experience—sights, smells, tastes, sounds, touch and posture—activates and, with time, reinforces specific neural pathways while others fall into disuse. A childhood imbalance in the use of the two eyes, for example, will cause permanent deficits in the visual perception through the underused eye." This is exactly why the behavioral optometrist insists on proper and complete evaluation before the "deficits" can occur. This most recent report concludes: "We are only beginning to understand how molecular events influence the structure of neurons and how these structural changes are translated into changes in brain functions. As we try to answer such questions, we hope to get closer to understanding how the external world comes to be mirrored in the microscopic structure of the brain. Ultimately, the answer will lead to a profound appreciation of how each individual person, in spite of being formed by inexorable genetic processes, is also the unique product of experience."[28] The behavioral optometrist has been contending for the past 35 years that if carefully programmed visual experiences could be available to individuals, there would be changes in the behaviors that are representations of changes in brain function. There has been insufficient "pure scientific" explanation for the changes specifically achieved by optometric visual training, but the indisputable changes in classroom and occupational performance cannot be ignored.

One cannot help but wonder which clinicians and/or specialists are being indirectly identified in the fourth conclusion. This author knows of no optometric colleagues who would even think of claiming their clinical procedures are "cures" for dyslexia and/or learning disabilities. Disclaimers to this effect have been published frequently in the past 15 to 20 years. The contemporary optometrist who is providing well validated and carefully designed vision care does insist that if the visual system is more integratively present and more adept in all of its behavior and performance, the individual certainly will be more available to the teacher who has the responsibility of making the direct attacks upon the learning problem. In this manner the optometrist serves as a resource or support clinician to assist the educator to have more positive effects in the academic program for which the educator is responsible.

Tucked into this same criticism of visual training is "... glasses (with or without bifocals or prisms)." It certainly should not be necessary to rehash this detail. As has been clearly stated, the purposes of "glasses—bifocals or prisms "—are clinical questions about which there is too much argument to pursue it any further here. The committee would be of greater service if its efforts were directed at better understandings of what the judiciously prescribed lenses can do for the improved performance of the sight-vision complex.

The same sentence, part (b), discredits "neurologic organization training (laterality training, balance board, perceptual training)." The phrase "neurological organization" also calls attention to the work of the 1981 Nobel Prize winners D. H. Hubel and T. N. Wiesel.[18] These two Americans were awarded this prestigious prize for their work on the organization of cellular information processing in the visual cortex of the brain. Theirs is one of the most significant of all studies of neurological organization that is so casually discredited here. In addition, the parentheses contain several incomplete and flat implications needing scrutiny. Is helping a child to know the "right" and "left" sides of his body, that our culture reads and writes from left to right, that laterality and directionality are intimately related concepts, "laterality training"? Is the primary teacher's efforts to help a child understand numbers and what they represent "perceptual training"? Is the effort to assist a student in how to make discriminations and decisions, on which conclusions are to be drawn, "perceptual training"?

This paragraph then continues: "Furthermore, such training may result in a false sense of security, which may delay or prevent proper instruction or remediation. The expense of such procedures is unwarranted. They cannot be substituted for appropriate remediational educational measures." What is being said here? Almost every single "treatment" mentioned is part and parcel of every educational program in some manner or degree. Do these create a "false sense of security"? In whom? Which of these is too expensive? This entire paragraph contains many incomplete and confusing suggestions that will only add further bewilderment to parents, teachers, and patients. What is the committee's intent with all of these blurred comments? And, to add even more confusion, the final sentence says: "Improvement claimed for visual training or neurologic organizational training typically results when those are combined with remedial educational techniques." Most of this paragraph condemns "visual training or neurologic organization" and ends up admitting these can bring improvements when combined with educational techniques. First these procedures are condemned and then they are recommended. Which is it to be?

The fifth conclusion in this entire publication is positive and to a point on which no one will disagree. It states that the teaching of dyslexic and learning-disabled children and adults is a problem for educational science. (This paragraph should have also commented that these problems cannot be ignored by *any* clinical discipline having any ability to contribute to some of the solutions to these problems.) It continues to emphasize the need for proper testing, proper identifications of the type of problems that exist, the importance of early care, and the numerous reasons that may exist for the problems. It makes a special point that no single educational approach is applicable to all children, an apparent recognition of the individualities of children. It concludes with a most interesting comment—one this policy statement has never before included. "A change in any variable may result in improved performance and reduced frustration (including placebo benefits)." Here, after more than 25 years of an opposite position, this committee has come to the conclusion that any one of the many variables can be positively influenced and that such can result in improved performance. Does this finally mean that even those training procedures that can improve visual functioning (one of the most prominent variables in the learning process) may bring improvements? Does the credit now being given to "placebo benefits" express an admission that procedures the committee cannot fully explain may also contribute to the progress of the individual?

When one stands off and reviews this policy statement as disconnectedly as possible, some intriguing thoughts come to mind. Here is the official statement of the beliefs and conclusions reached by three prestigious clinical groups. Careful analysis of this most recent publication by this triad reveals that it still contains more negatives than positives. There are redundant "evaluations and conclusions" on what must *not* be done, on procedures these groups consider to be improper or which will prevent help and cause unwarranted expense, with several implied warnings of danger and possible detriment to children. One must ask: Are all these negatives based on experience with "procedures of proven value, demonstrated by valid research" or are all of these nothing more than "the evaluations and conclusions" coming out of the understandably biased opinions of these three disciplines without scientific data to substantiate them? The numerous contradictions to the growing wealth of information coming from well-qualified investigators in many disciplines cannot be overlooked. Reading and rereading this policy statement uncovers only three specifically positive points: (1) the importance of early diagnosis, (2) early remediation, and (3) the need for a multidisciplinary approach to the entire problem. The rest of the entire document merely restates well-known and indisputable aspects of the problem and offers only those suggestions that any ethical clinical profession is expected to offer because of their special training and their inherent codes, rules and standards of professional conduct.

The closing paragraph of this policy statement is a repetition of the opening policy proclamation, but it certainly does bring a question about why it is presented at the final point in the document. It states: "The American Academy of Ophthalmology, The American Association for Pediatric Ophthalmology and Strabismus, and The American Academy of Pediatrics strongly support the early diagnosis and appropriate treatment of persons with dyslexia and related learning disabilities." Is "strong support" all these three groups are offering? What is the difference between the support now being offered by these medical groups and the strong support being offered by parent groups, educator groups, and other professional groups? Does the adjective "strong" suggest something more than that being expressed and contributed by others? Should the reader infer that "strong support" includes extensive research that only these groups can provide out of their clinical expertise? Or is the "strong support" they offer nothing more than repeated issuance of this policy statement which expresses their "evaluations and conclusions" about the problem? Is this final sentence about "strong support" being added to smother any thoughts that members of these three groups have *not* been supporting such programs up until now—but will from now on? Is this only an expression of the maximum help they are capable of offering to the thousands of individuals needing much more than "early diagnosis and treatment" of their learning problems *after* they have occurred? Although there is an extreme paucity of medical research now being conducted on the critical relationships between many chronic pathologies and learning problems, each of these clinical groups could bring spectacular assistance to the search for better understandings of learning difficulties in the human, especially in the *prevention* of these problems! It is not enough to simply talk about "a problem for educational science" and then to step back and offer only "strong support."

Here are three professions very closely related to the physical and mental welfare of every individual who must perform in the academic environment. The pediatricians could especially be a source of extensive help in expanding a much greater parent- teacher awareness of all aspects of childhood development and child health. They could bring desperately needed clarification of the effects of drugs on learning, even such drugs as aspirin and particularly the too frequently used Ritalin. The physicians who are the eye, ear, nose and throat specialists could bring numerous insights and significant guidance on the performance problems that do arise out of the pathologies that undoubtedly do influence language development. The ophthalmologists could bring added information and insights on why amenable disorders of the sight organs *do not* contribute to learning problems and how these disorders should best be cared for so they will not progress to become interferences in the academic progress of students. Such information could eliminate many of the misconceptions about the sight-vision complex now existing.

Instead of making all these very real contributions that are needed so desperately, this triad of medical specialists seemingly has assumed the judicial position in which they assume the prerogatives for determining what the final word is on some of the problems, what the solutions should be, and who should or should not be qualified to make contributions to the search for needed answers. If there can be a sincere effort on the parts of all the clinical disciplines involved that will bring communications and cooperations for the benefit of all children, the guidance that parents and teachers need so badly will result. This can only occur, however, when each of the disciplines opens itself to the contributions each can make and to the recognitions of the limitations each suffers. Such openness will not come about tomorrow, but it must come soon if the loss of another generation of school children is to be avoided. Fortunately, there are more and more speech and language specialists being added to school staffs. The physical education teachers who have been dismissed from primary schools because of budget problems will have to be brought back to help children gain the motoric skills they need. Both the speech and language teachers and the physical education teachers can be supported and reinforced by the extended employment of elementary music teachers. Eventually, there will have to be consideration given to the addition of the professionals who can provide the guidance all teachers need in the development of all the visual abilities the symbolic culture is demanding. If there is a real concern for the future of thousands of children now lacking readinesses for the classroom impacts, these additions cannot be delayed much longer.

One more aspect of this "controversy" is being kept alive by statements such as those just considered, i.e., the frequent criticism of the efforts of the clinical disciplines who are seeking some answers to the many problems now epidemic, the criticism that these efforts are "unscientific" because the positive results being reported are based on "anecdotal evidence." One could ask the very silly question about why 53% of doctors chose Bayer aspirin "to have it in their backpacks when they climb mountains." Was this 53% determined by scientific research in which there were three carefully chosen groups of mountain climbers, one group that carried Bayer, a second group that carried aspirin, and a third group that carried sugar pills (the placebo)? Was their mountain climbing ability then judged on the basis of which group reached the summit of the mountain first or on the basis of the "anecdotal" reports of the climbers about what influence the Bayer aspirin had on their climbing ability?

I have worked my way through at least 50 cardiologists at one level or another since the original big strike in 1965. In this 20-plus years of varying episodes, ranging from simple angina to three heart pacers to triple bypass surgery, there have been exposures to every conceivable scientific instrument and equipment to measure and appraise the existing physical conditions. Unfailingly, after every possible test has been run—from dozens upon dozens of electrocardiograms to CAT scans, sonograms and arteriograms—there has been the personal conference with one or more cardiologists. Without exception the questions are asked: "How are you feeling now?" And: "Are you having any difficulties or discomforts?" Several times, my reply has been: "You now have all of the data from your elaborate tests. What is your judgment of how I am doing?" Their reply, without exception, has been: "All your tests show that you are making excellent progress *but* how are you feeling, and are you experiencing any problems?" Twice, to cardiologists with whom a professional friendship had evolved, I said, "You should be able to answer those questions because of your splendid tests on all of your splendid scientific equipment." Their reply each time: "Our elaborate testing can only tell us that the machinery seems to be working well. It can never tell us what the patient is actually experiencing, or how well the patient judges his progress to be. When it comes down to the final analysis, we must depend upon the *anecdotal* evidence we can gather from the individual patient." One of these cardiologists, a professional who had earned my complete respect and confidence, then commented: "Any clinician worth his salt knows that what the patient tells him and what medications seem to be working best within the particular situation are what count. It is the (anecdotal) reports the patient gives us that determine what medications we will use regardless of any research data given us to read."

As one contemplates all of this a bit further, it becomes quite apparent we will want teachers who are child oriented instead of curriculum oriented to use the procedures and materials that will bring the desired results regardless of any research data offered by any publisher. It is the anecdotal reports from one teacher to another teacher that finally determine what will happen in the classroom. And this is exactly as it should be if the children's individualities are fully considered! Why is it that the highly touted "scientific research" that is carefully designed to control all of the variables of children's individualities (supposing such is possible!) so frequently comes out to be completely irrelevant to what the children need for progress in the academic environment? Somehow, there will have to be the realization that "scientific research" and "clinical research" are most often not compatible and probably will neither support nor contradict each other even though they may be directed at efforts to reach understandings of the same problem. What is now being identified as scientific research usually strives to find and identify the single most indisputable cause of the problem, while clinical research seeks to find the most appropriate solutions to the problem when all relative factors are considered. This critical design, bringing these eliminations, may discard the element that holds the significant secret to the individual's needs. Further, this may be the variable that can *only* be identified by anecdotal evidence that releases the detail needed to determine the program that will allow a return to the basics which must be sought and identified.

Without any question both scientific and clinical research must be done, but there can be no expectancy that either one will ever substitute for the other. Both must be done for the information each will provide, but each must be kept in realistic perspective as we search for the information we must have to find the reliable solutions to the problems now evident. There can never be any expectation that anatomical, physiological, or neurological structures will ever completely explain the behavior that arises from one or all of them.

If and when there is criticism of clinical methods "unscientifically based on anecdotal reports," it becomes important to look behind the criticism to determine why such a charge is being made. Is it being made to camouflage the lack of understanding of the critic, or is it being made to distract the listener from added investigations of the help that might be available for children in academic difficulties? One must always ask such critics about their dependence on "anecdotal evidence" before their criticisms are accepted. As this most apparent smoke screen is cleared, progress toward some solutions can be expected.

I am aware that many readers may think too much time and too many words have been accorded the sight-vision complex and the clinical observations, appraisals, and discussions thereof. This has not occurred just because of my optometric training and developmental interests! It comes because there is so much evidence that the sight-vision complex plays such a dominant role in all human behavior, *especially that behavior and performance expected in the classroom.* Gesell wrote very clearly on this point. "The pre-eminence of vision in the sensory-motor construction of the human action system is reflected in the input and output arrangements of the retina and brain. The retina, with its multibillion sensitive points and polarities, is receptive to an enormous range of impressions. Retina and brain are sensitive enough to detect the light of one candle 14 miles distant. Speaking as a neurophysiologist, Warren McCulloch, Ph.D. (late of

M.I.T.) points out that each eye alone has more than 100,000,000 photoreceptors, each of which is either signaling or not signaling at a given moment. This means the eye can exist in 2 to the hundredth power states, each of which corresponds to a unique distribution of stimulation. Each eye transmits as much information to the brain as does all of the rest of the body. It can send in a million impulses per millisecond. For the whole organism, including eyes, the input (to the brain) has a maximum of three million signals per millisecond."[9] Thus, the entire learning process is so wholly reliant upon the the sight-vision complex that if it is not fully understood, the learning process cannot be fully understood, especially in the classroom where 75% to 85% of the learning tasks are visually centered. Further, there must be the full recognition that any force, either internal or external, that brings any changes in the patterns of light across the retina will have an impact upon the functioning of the brain which will then impact upon the learning process.

Hopefully, this chapter will have brought some added appreciations of the sight-vision complex and the appraisals and mediations needed to assure that this major contributor to all aspects of human development will fulfill its role and purpose to the benefit of the individual. This chapter has had another purpose. This reach for greater understanding of the sight-vision complex will hopefully bring a readiness to strive for a greater understanding of the words and phrases being used to identify both abilities and problems in the learning process.

Chapter IV—Identification of Difficulties in the Learning Process from a Developmental Perspective

A ll adults striving to understand the children who are "smart in everything ... except school" are searching for explanations of the learning deficiencies demonstrated by these children. Since diagnosis alone is worthless, there is also search for training regimens that will modify or eliminate these learning deficiencies. In spite of the devotion and sincerity of these searchers, their efforts may have brought more confusions than solutions. Perhaps some of the difficulties have arisen because there is too much effort spent in trying to find single causes and panaceas. Perhaps the inter-system deficiencies and the interdependencies of the system have not been given enough attention. (Some of these significancies have already been addressed here.) Or perhaps the lack of familiarity with the developmental sequences and the role of each of these elements in the learning process has allowed the searchers to spend too much time on what the child is expected to do, with too little time spent on the child's developmental readiness to meet the expectations. Whatever the reasons for our too frequent difficulties in really helping these youngsters, there certainly is no doubt about the confusions and misinterpretations now existing in this whole situation. The more often one analyzes the tests designed to identify learning problems, the more often it seems these probes all approach the child's problems at too high a developmental level. These probes characteristically assume the individual with academic difficulties has successfully passed through all of the foundational levels and can perform at the levels required for the advanced symbolic tasks of the classroom. Consequently, the test results are interpreted to prove what the child *cannot* do instead of proving what the child *can* do and where his successes could be. Added to this confusion is that which arises from the misuse and misunderstandings of the words and phrases used as labels   both for the problems and for the youngsters having the problems. The definitions that come from Public Law 94-142 have certainly been no help, since they have added to the widespread mislabeling and the misassigning of thousands of children into classrooms in which academic progress is not expected.

Identifying the Problem

An unknown Chinese philosopher is credited with saying, "If one wishes to deal accurately with something, first one must always call it by its right name." A much more contemporary semanticist, S. I. Hayakawa, Ed.D., comments, "Whatever language one happens to inherit, it is at once a tool and a trap. But like other instruments, languages select, and in selecting what they do select, they leave out what they do not select."[29] One might well add to Hayakawa's comment: " ...and in being so selective, what is left out may well be the detail that could have guided us out of such traps." All this particularly applies to our need to reach for and achieve a better understanding of the labels being used. While these labels can be a "tool," they are also too much of a "trap" because of the incomplete or inaccurate meaning given to them. As traps, there are too many negative and deleterious impacts on the youngsters we are striving to help.

THE LABELS

It is important we all realize that almost all of the labels being used to identify the child or the problem are *symptomatic* words instead of *causal* terms.

Learning Disability

Right off the top is the much too commonly used phrase *learning disability*. This label alone has probably brought the greatest single trauma to literally thousands of children *and* adults! As traumatic as this label can be, even greater trauma results when the abilities that are present and available to this individual are overlooked so he is actually prevented from developing and enhancing those abilities that *are* present.

In the usual events surrounding the much too common use of this phrase comes the horrible mistake that the label describing the symptoms becomes the label for the cause. Thus we hear such comments as: "No wonder he cannot learn, he has learning disability." Or, "He is learning-disabled so he will not be able to do the more advanced classroom tasks." It certainly seems it would be much more positive and appropriate to discuss these difficulties as "academic learning problems" since academia is where these are most evident, and since problems have solutions if only we are diligent and smart enough to find them. Remember the little maestro who insisted that even the rocks, trees, and flowers have music in them if we can just learn how to "get it out."

This is not just idle talk in defense of the concepts emphasized in this book. The clinical evidence coming from the developmental/behavioral optometrist, the developmentally oriented speech and language specialist, the developmentally oriented adaptive physical education teacher, and the developmentally oriented psychologist very strongly validates significant progress in both academic and general cultural areas when a more fitting appraisal brings greater understandings and help. Such clinical evidence can, and must, clear away negative labels that bring negative attitudes in children as well as adults. We must also realize these labels and attitudes are most often relative only to the classroom performance—if they have any validity at all.

About 40 years ago, there was an opportunity to observe and evaluate a tall, handsome 16-year-old youth placed in a famous reading clinic in the Philadelphia area. He was a classic example of a student with severe difficulties in all of the symbolic programs of the usual classroom. He was placed in a group of youngsters 8 to 10 years old who were "reading at the second grade level." To soften the trauma of having to go to classes with "all those little kids," this attractive young man was made the editor of the second grade newspaper, following the staff conclusion that this activity would bring vital experience with words more interesting than those in graded textbooks.

As every reader will guess, the records on this young man were extensive. Every possible educational and psychological test then available had been administered in innumerable schools during the previous 10 years. Every academic regimen and every commercially produced educational program had been utilized with only limited gains. Deeply buried in this pile was a report from a primary counselor who had added some random notes about this young man's interests and his hobby. Here were details about his extensive activities as a ham radio operator. He was active and prominent in ham radio emergency groups in Central Pennsylvania and was considered by experts in that group as one of the most capable Morse code operators. Further, he had completely assembled all of his own radio equipment. Either this report was completely fallacious or this young man had skills of symbol translation all of the teachers and tests had overlooked.

After some added staff discussion, he was moved from editor of the second grade newspaper to author of a series of articles on why and how he got into ham radio operation, and how another person could do the same. With the enthusiastic help of the faculty in this special clinic and the motivations stimulated by outside interest in the articles, he progressed from second grade reading level to sixth grade level in less than three months' time. He continued to delight the faculty with his further progress. The magic in all of this was this young man's interest in radio and his desire to pass his expertise on to others. The change in faculty attitudes supported his enthusiasm and provided the guidance he needed. The emphasis on his needs in the underlying developmental levels instead of on his academic failures gave him the means by which to gain the reading abilities for which there was every potential. Granted, this is only an anecdotal report on one person, but similar progress has been made by so many others since this experience that the methods of attack and the results obtained cannot be ignored. The "experience reader" composed by this student has since been developed and used by many teachers, but there are still too many children not receiving such help. The real point here is this: the labels do not correctly or appropriately lead to the underlying reasons for the problem and too frequently generate attitudes and opinions that guarantee failure.

An opportunity for a most meaningful and confirming conversation came just a few months ago. It took place at the Charles County, Maryland, Special Olympics where Bill Demby was the honored guest of the day. Demby is the Vietnam veteran who lost most of both lower legs to a missile, and who has been seen by millions as he plays basketball on a Dupont Company television commercial. We were talking about the negative words that are so unthinkingly used to describe the youngsters who were participating in this event. Bill said, "None of the labels are any good, and you certainly cannot tell anything about a person just by looking at him. Neither can you depend on the books which tell all that is wrong, and what these individuals cannot do. One just has to throw the book away, give the individual the right opportunities, and then stand back and watch him go." Thank you, Bill. Having been there, you know exactly what it is all about!

Dyslexia

The second most damaging label now being used is *dyslexia*. Here, again, the label for the symptom has become the label for the cause of the problem. We too frequently hear, "Oh, he cannot learn to read; he has dyslexia," as if it were some sort of pathological illness that was "caught" from another family member. Those who continue to insist upon pathological explanations insist there is a hereditary reason for this problem because too many parents cannot read as expected so their children have been "infected." One has only to carefully observe these family situations to be reminded that one who has not achieved a skill has great difficulty in teaching that skill. It most often is more likely a matter of deprivation than an issue of contagion. Actually, when this word is used to describe the difficulty an individual is having, the speaker who says, "He cannot read because he has dyslexia" is merely stating, "He cannot read because he cannot read."

As with so many of the other similar situations being discussed here, the problem is often part and parcel of related learning problems usually seen in the classroom. Certainly, as the informed educator says, "This student has difficulty in decoding and interpreting the printed symbols of our very difficult language." This same individual may very well be the successful power plant supervisor or the Olympic gold medal winner—like those who so frequently appear on television to promote commercial reading training programs. It is always interesting to find these individuals capable of decoding all sorts of environmental signs; it is just the *printed* words on which they fail.

There needs to be a much broader interpretation of the words *read* and *reading*. The infant *reads* the mother's tone of voice and her facial expressions very early. All of us *read* the body language of others. Even the individual with "severe reading problems" learns to *read* many of the stimuli which do come to him. The Oscar winner who had no difficulty learning lines if they were spoken to her certainly had an auditory *reading* process available to her.

Two general reader categories were set up many years ago as alert educators sought the individual differences they knew were important to their students. There were "visual learners" and "auditory learners," those who were more skillful in gathering information through one of the learning systems than through the other. The visual learner frequently found it quite unnecessary to listen to the teacher; there was only the need to carefully read the textbook. The auditory learner, on the other hand, found it unnecessary to read the textbook; it was only necessary to attend every class and listen carefully to what the instructor said. Both of these individuals had learning problems, but neither of them were "dyslexic" in the sense this label is so often misused. The critical issue is that either one or the other of the individual's input-output modes is not able to make the discriminations and interpretations needed for the contributions the mode should be making.

The label *dyslexia* is certainly incorrect and inadequate if there is to be an attempt to assist the learner in overcoming any sort of problem with the mastery of the symbols of our culture. Using this word as the cause or reason for the problem is totally unacceptable. The only acceptable approach is the evaluation of the developmental sequences, and the available learning processes, to find where and how to assist the individual in acquiring the discrimination and interpretation skills each of these two systems need. Then the auditory learner can also be a visual learner, and the visual learner can also be an auditory learner.

Dysphonetica

This is another of those Latinish sounding words now being included in some of the reports parents receive. This word supposedly means *dysfunctions* in *phonetic* abilities which then can be heard in a youngster's mispronunciations and/or confusions of several speech sounds. This label is not frequently encountered unless a clinician or an educator is especially attracted to the phonics approach to reading instruction. There is now an active national organization insisting that all reading problems can be solved with full attention given to phonics (the sounds letters make) and the phonetic approach for word attack. Too often these enthusiasts become so involved in the auditory aspects of phonics that the other contributors to the reading process are overlooked. Again there needs to be the reminder that audition and vision are so closely and intimately related that neither the visual approach (sight word recognition) nor the phonics approach (the sounds letters make) will succeed in isolation. Arnold Gesell expressed it very well in a personal conversation with me in the mid-1940s. "One cannot begin the study of any part of the child without immediately discovering there is a lot more child attached for equal consideration." This comment especially applies when one inspects the phonetic inconsistencies that exist in the English language, inconsistencies which demand that visual inspections and discriminations are more revealing than auditory attentions and discriminations. There can be no disputing that phonetics can provide a number of clues to word attack, and there are many excellent rules for guidance here. In high contrast, there are too many words for which the rules do not apply, and the learner must then fall back on other clues. The ending *ough*, for example: if the *"b"* in the word *bough* is changed to an *"r,"* the *ough* portion requires a completely different pronunciation. If this same word *rough* is preceded by a *th*, the *ough* again takes on a completely different sound. These are but a few of the examples of how the changes in *ough* are signaled by the visual discriminations of one or two very important letters. Even this is not the entire story. In the word *slough* one must somehow gather the concept expressed in the sentence to know which pronunciation is proper. *Slough*, as in "sloo" means a stagnant swamp. *Slough* as in "sluf" means to cast off or shed outer skin. *Slough* as in "slou" is a city southeast of London. The sight-vision input is the same in each instance. The hearing-audition signal is different in each instance. The meanings are specific and cannot be interchanged. The only clue, and the final one, must come from the entire sentence and the context of the paragraph in which the sentence appears if the reader is to know which pronunciation is proper and which meaning is valid.

To identify a reading problem by labeling it dysphonetica is like labeling it dyslexia. These simplistic words serve little purpose; they simply engender confusion and misunderstanding of the developmental problems that probably may be the real issue needing identification and guidance. Too frequently these Latinish sounding words are used to make reports seem more scientific, and none of them have yet been supported by any kind of controlled scientific research showing them to be anything other than labels for the symptoms exhibited. Mispronunciations are not the causes—they are only the symptoms.

Dyscalculia

This word is usually found only in "scientific" reports in special clinical journals and rarely used in reports to parents. It has been used to label the situation in which there supposedly is *dysfunction* in *calculations*—the use of numbers. It needs but brief comment here since it is now hoped the reader will recognize that these words are inappropriate and used to disguise the user's lack of familiarity with the developmental problems that really do underlie the student's inability to use numbers in contemporary classroom tasks.

However, the deep concern with the epidemic lack of math skills, as it is now reported in so many news reports, is not new. I had the privilege of presenting courses in child development and vision development at Texas Women's University Department of Special Education in 1964. One of the teacher groups was a class in mathematics concepts and programs for the elementary grades. After a couple of discussion classes, the group was assigned the task of identifying the foundational concepts required for success in math. The teachers were asked to itemize the concepts and the vocabulary the student must have that would be relevant to the concepts. This group of master's degree candidates unanimously agreed on the following:

Concepts Necessary for Success in Math Courses

First Concept: Size
Relevant vocabulary: big, little, small, large, long, short, tall, high, low, wide, fat, narrow, thin, deep, broad, great, light, heavy, thick

Second Concept: Amount
Relevant vocabulary: few, more, less, least, much, often, fast, slow, all, enough, none, some, many, several, any

Third Concept: Placement (Direction)
Relevant Vocabulary: up, down, around, across, to, from, toward, away, through, top, bottom, close, far, here, there, left, right, up, down, inside, outside, under, over, below, beneath, beside, between, behind, past, above, on, off, upon, before, after, in front, forward, backward

Fourth Concept: Sequence (Distance)
Relevant Vocabulary: near, far, close, here, there, where, top, bottom, first, last, second, third, fourth, fifth, sixth, seventh, eighth, ninth, tenth, next, beginning, end, now, soon, later, day, night, when, morning, afternoon, evening, fast, slow

Few readers will likely have given much thought to the concepts that were itemized by this group of elementary teachers, particularly in the light of these being basic to math courses. One need only review that nouns are the language of objects, places, and people; verbs are the language of actions; and many of the adjectives we use have direct language relevancies with numbers. The concepts these adjectives express are the same concepts we use numbers to express. The part that the language skills play in the understanding of numbers is another aspect of the diagram of the stellar elements of the learning process as diagrammed in Figure 3 in the previous chapter.

Interestingly, every one of the adjectives the educators chose is also related to the manual-visual and visual-spatial organization of the individual. There must be an extensive experiential background in visually directed and monitored movements if these words, or their numerical translations, are to have full meaning. There should be some obvious clues here for both parent and teacher regarding the developmental opportunities which exist that will eliminate or prevent such a label as *dyscalculia*.

Dysgraphia

This word is being used more often now as computer enthusiasts insist the VDT (video display terminal) will be the answer to "writing problems" or dysgraphia. We are now hearing, "He should not be expected to write out his assignments. He has dysgraphia." Translated, this merely means, "He cannot write because he cannot write," and again the symptoms have become the "causes" of the problem. The "disability" mentality previously discussed takes over, and instead of being given the opportunity to achieve manual dexterities and the letter and word shape skills needed, the computer (the typewriter, or a puppet) is recommended as the circumvention for the problem identified as dysgraphia.

It takes few observations to discover that the individual so labeled has not acquired the manual dexterities needed for the complexities of the writing act. If one goes back to review this individual's preschool developmental history, one frequently finds there was not the use and explorations of hands and the hand skills that should have occurred. This lack of manual development is why Legos and all the similar playthings are so important to the child. Here also is the tremendous value of the original Montessori programs in which hand activities and hand dexterities were so fully emphasized. It is this preschool period of experience in manual abilities that lays the foundations for the perceptual skills discussed in Chapter I.

If these manual abilities do not advance to writing abilities, there will also be the critical difficulties in thinking abilities as discussed in Chapter II. The bottom line is that dysgraphia—or whatever it does mean—should never occur in any individual. If there is a problem that can be so described, it should never be allowed to continue. This point is so important to the entire thesis of this book, it must have further discussion.

The ability to put one's thoughts into legible symbols for communication is undoubtedly the step in the entire sequence of human development that really sets genus homo apart as being superior to all other living creatures. This is that ultimate level where the visual system guides and monitors the most complex of all refined manipulative systems speech for vocal expression and manual dexterities for graphic expression. These manual dexterities must progress through a developmental sequence just as do all other movement patterns the humans must acquire.

This brings us face to face with a long-standing argument over what kind of handwriting should be practiced by the learner: *manuscript* printing (as is now commonly used in the usual primary classroom), or *cursive* writing to which the young student is expected to shift in third and fourth grades. Manuscript printing was introduced as the "proper" way to learn to write, using the reasoning that these hand printed letters would look more like the printed letters in the textbooks. This would then make it easier to achieve reading skills. It is difficult to rationalize this explanation when the mechanical and physiological operations are so much more difficult in the completion of "printed" letters and words.

All physiologists have long known that big movements are more easily learned, and that these then can be refined into the more specific manipulative movement patterns. Observe a small child learning to feed himself, and you will see the progression from full arm movements to the more refined arm and hand movements. This very same progression is observed as the learner moves from the whole arm actions of using a crayon for coloring to the refined arm and hand movements for writing. Further, the *line and ball* patterns emphasized in manuscript printing do not provide the differences in the direction of movements inherent in cursive letters. Take a moment to print the *"b"* and *"d"* in large sizes. Then write the cursive *"b"* and *"d"* in similarly large sizes. The differences in the directions and fluidity in the directions of movement, and the contributions they make to the internalizations of the movement patterns will be most obvious.

Before leaving this problem called "dysgraphia," there must be some added thoughts on this matter of *reversals*—a problem touched on too casually at several points in this book. A recent lecture by a person who is internationally considered to be one of the few top authorities on dyslexia, its accurate diagnosis and specifications, brought out several details now accepted by numerous investigators. The first point he made was discouraging: dyslexia is still a great mystery and there are as many definitions as there are investigators. How can any determined attack be made if no one can agree on what the problem is? His second point was even more disturbing. He insisted that dyslexia and several of its primary evidences were usually caused by heredity and genetic factors. He reported numerous cases where aunts, uncles, and grandparents were dyslexic, but he failed to explain how they were scientifically tested for dyslexia since in most instances they were either geographically distant or dead. The greatest disturbance came when this speaker listed reversals as one of the primary symptoms of dyslexia and went on to state that the inability to write numbers and letters properly was also genetically determined.

At the present level of intellectual ignorance among both genetic and behavioral scientists, there is a great majority consensus that although *how* a person learns may be impacted by heredity, *what* a person learns is impacted much more emphatically by the individual's motivations, the environment in which one finds himself, the opportunities found, the experiences one enjoys, and the needs one has to learn whatever the situation offers. It is difficult to accept any notion that one's writing ability is determined by ancestral genes, and the problem of reversals is certainly greatest and most obvious in the act of writing numbers, letters, and words. This book is making the major point that deficits in the ability to perceive and produce symbols is based in visual-motor coordinations and the special movement patterns the individual develops for himself regardless of his ancestry. A somewhat detailed report from a group of teachers in a rural community school will be directly relevant and of considerable interest here.

The principal of this school was deeply concerned about the large number of 5th and 6th grade students still struggling with reversals in all areas of their classroom assignments. Here were students four to six years beyond the time when such problems should have been solved by the individual. These students, many of whom had already repeated one or more grades, were still exhibiting the confusions in number and letter formations with frequently noted "reversals" in their thinking and speaking. Having been introduced to the developmental concepts about the learning processes being presented here, this principal called the physical education teacher, the music teacher, and the art teacher together and invited them to brainstorm the existing situation. Each of these teachers also reported observations of reversals among these students and had the same laments about not being able to successfully assist them in the elimination of these problems. They decided to approach the problem developmentally instead of pursuing the usual academic methods.

The physical education teacher introduced a program in which these students would have to consciously explore and practice both general and special movement patterns—with full and insistent visual guidance and control as they moved about the gymnasium. The boys (in the great majority, as usual) were introduced to ballet movements and every possible balance and counter-balance activity in which there would be prominent demands for visual judgments and visual decisions. This teacher's greatest surprise came over the gross clumsiness of the best athletes in the group. These students were given extended practice in the refinements of movements and dexterities with individual assistance by the girls in the group.

Much to the surprise of the music teacher, most of the students had little or no "sense of rhythm" and could not keep time with even the most basic 4/4 rhythm. In spite of their numerous pocket radios and the constant presence of the music of their choosing, most of the students could not keep step with march music and could not keep in step with each other, with or without music. The first practice sessions were devoted to learning to keep in step with nothing more than a drum beat. As the students could demonstrate a beginning awareness of rhythm and a degree of "music appreciation," the simplest dance steps were introduced. Since most of these youngsters had potentially good singing voices, choral singing was also emphasized.

The art teacher was not surprised, however, to discover that none of these students could make the simplest pictures to represent the simplest stories. The art lessons started with life-sized murals depicting the activities they had just experienced in the gymnasium. Even though many of these contained little more than stick figures the murals began to illustrate some of the very simple movement patterns the students could then talk about as they described their murals. These murals eventually (actually in a very short time) took on many perspectives of sizes, shapes, and distances in the actions the students were exploring. As the visually-directed general movements developed, the visually- directed special movements developed, and the murals took on representations of spatial orientations, time and space sequences, and continuity of time and spatial events. Understandably, the art teacher was the most excited member of this team as she saw "symbolic masteries" developing, skills that would undoubtedly be relevant to many other academic tasks.

This teaching team then decided it was time to make more experiential applications of the new abilities they were seeing in these youngsters who were still demonstrating "reversals" in too many of the academic tasks. They were introduced to square dancing and then asked to expand and elaborate their murals in the art class. In a very short time these students, who had been struggling with all sorts of reversals in almost every aspect of academia, were no longer having these problems. It became apparent that an "allemande left," when it should have been an "allemande right," brought emphatic social confrontations with seven other individuals—and new and expanded concepts of directionality, spatial positions and distances; and all manners of spatial relationships became foundations for the same skills in the area of symbols. The visually guided and monitored movements integrated with the auditory appreciation of the relevant and applicable spatiality of rhythm brought concepts and under-standings of position, sequence, and continuity that was then applicable to the discriminations, interpretations, and applications to numbers, letters, and words. Here was a group of almost 20 students, for whom all academic exercises had failed to solve the reversal problems in five and six years of school, who had now solved the reversals in just a few weeks of reviewing the developmental organizations they needed.

One must not even begin to assume that the teaching team or I now advocate square dancing as the panacea for reversal problems. Those intimately involved with this project knew how to establish foundations so that reversals need not turn into the inevitable frustrations and discouragements they become when someone assumes "these will disappear when this child becomes a little more mature." How much more constructive one can be when all of the developmental components of spatial relationships are thoughtfully considered.

One most interesting aspect of this entire problem of "dysgraphia" and "reversals" appears in children who start out in cursive writing instead of manuscript printing. These youngsters almost never have to struggle through the confusions and frustrations of reversals. There are now more and more primary teachers becoming aware of this who are helping children into cursive writing as early as possible. Parents of children who are still struggling with writing problems that include reversals of numbers, letters, and words should be aware of ways in which they can help their children avoid these frustrations. These will be quite extensively discussed in a later chapter.

Some Labels Now Used More Frequently

ADD

One label now so popular that it is appearing in almost every student's file is ADD—Attention Deficit Disorder. This is a spectacular example of the lengths to which some evaluators will go to find confusing terms which supposedly identify a student's problem. What in the world can this label possibly mean? First of all, if one is unfortunate enough to have a "deficit" of some sort, one would probably want to have a "disorder" in it! Wouldn't a "deficit" with a "disorder" in it be preferred over an "ordered" or "organized" "deficit?" Or, if one had a "disorder," wouldn't it be preferable to have a "deficit" in it? It certainly seems it would be much more understandable to simply state that the individual had an "attention span deficit" (ASD) or an "attention disorder" (AD).

This label has been even more confusing because some professionals have decided to expand it to the ADD Triad. This has come out of the evaluation that identified attention span difficulties in both visual and auditory abilities. Since there is now recognition that two learning modes are involved here—the visual and the auditory—and since most of these individuals also demonstrate signs of frustrations and discouragement by more wriggling than is thought to be acceptable, the third component—hyperactivity—has been added. Now it becomes a clinical "triad," and the student has even more labels added to those already appearing in the school records.

Hyperactivity

Even more disturbing is the tendency of the clinicians to almost automatically turn to the administration of drugs as the solution to the "hyperactivity" problems. There is more and more research contradicting the broad use of these drugs, and it has always been well known that such prescriptions have no influence on the *reasons* for the hyperactivity; there is only some reduction of the *symptoms* in *some* children.[30]

The facts are now well established: the majority of the students who demonstrate what the teachers and clinicians now call "hyperactivity" only demonstrate these symptoms while required to stay at academic tasks in which there is the frustration that arises from a lack of understanding, or from the disappointment of knowing that mastery of the task is not within the realm of their capability. When, in contrast, these same individuals are on tasks in which they can succeed and which they understand, the alleged hyperactivity is noticeably reduced or totally absent. When these same students are observed while engaged in activities of their own choosing, ones they enjoy and complete with pride, the symptoms of "hyperactivity" are absent. These children are not much different from adults put into the same stresses of incompetence. The adults will show the same irritability, the same "distractibility," and the same signs of "hyperactivity." The difference lies in the fact that the adult can usually refuse to stay in such circumstances, and either delegates the task to another, discards it, or even gets another job. The child, who has been put into a required curriculum, is not allowed to simply quit or walk away from the task, and the hyperactivity and distractibility continue to disappoint all concerned.

As has been so frequently stated or implied, the critical need is the recognition of the levels at which the child needs help. There have been no real gains coming out of the reduction of number or length of assignments, the substitution of activities, and/or extended emphasis on the subject matter that is causing the stress. Further, it becomes more and more important that before any student is labeled as having ADD or the ADD Triad, careful classroom observation should be made by *someone other than the teacher* and then judiciously discussed with all involved. This is especially true for the student who is being considered as a candidate for drug therapy.

These may all be quite emphatic statements for a behavioral optometrist to make. The very careful clinical evaluations of these individuals' visual and peripheral sensitivity has brought pertinent clues to the problem. This aspect of the problem was alluded to briefly while we were discussing visual attention span in an earlier chapter. There was neither space nor reason to fully expand the discussion there, but it is important enough for some further consideration here. Back in the late 1960s, there was more than a little concern over the number of students in a private school who were being classified as "hyperactive to the point of causing classroom disruptions." Continued observations of these same youngsters outside the classroom did not fully support the label being given them. However, at that moment there was a most popular solution. This was the carrel—the isolation booth for each child in the classroom. These carrels were constructed as partitions from floor to ceiling, with a surface at desk height and another shelf above for personal belongings. The student was seated facing into the booth with only a view of a cinder block wall 18 to 20 inches in front of him. This carrel was constructed so the student could see nothing except the material directly ahead, and with enough depth to greatly reduce the noise generated by students working in adjoining carrels.

Unfortunately, this arrangement completely eliminated any possibility of eye contacts between student and teacher—eye contacts long recognized as being so important to student-teacher communication. In addition, the lighting in these booths was usually extremely poor, and the student's head and body frequently shadowed the materials on the shelf-like desk at which he was seated. The common result was more, rather than less, hyperactivity. The student had to turn almost a full 180 degrees to accurately receive instruction from the teacher. This whirling dervish behavior was an added distraction, and fewer and fewer learning activities were completed.

At this time, a behavioral optometrist from Australia was serving a three-month residency at this private school and expressed a desire to make a further investigation of the classroom conditions, the students involved, and the apparent problems.[31] His first move was a careful appraisal of each student's visual development with extended clinical attention given to the visual peripheral sensitivity of each student. These evaluations revealed, as expected, that each of these youngsters had an extremely fragile organization of visual periphery that would bring distraction to almost any movement off to either side of the student during academic task completion. This peripheral visual sensitivity was heightened in proportion to the stress of the task. This was no surprise since this is a situation that often applies to any individual frustrated by lack of understanding or reduction of personal accomplishment.

This particular group of students was then given optometric vision therapy that emphasized the organization of visual periphery—what is generally known among behavioral optometrists as visual identification of peripherally located stimuli. Twenty- one of the originally selected youngsters completed the study. Four of these were the control group that received training on tasks unrelated to visual peripheral experiences. This training included practice in laterality, form perception routines then popular in special classrooms, hand-eye coordinations, body image and spatial orientation procedures. The second group of six students received training that especially and particularly emphasized visual peripheral awareness and the recognition of bold geometric patterns in the student's periphery. The third group of five students received this same specific practice but had opportunities to include the use of their hands to verify their visual judgments. The fourth group of six students had the specific peripheral visual training, but also were given opportunities to explore and practice all sorts of peripheral judgments like tossing beanbags into containers while central visual attention was maintained on a target directly in front of the student. This group was encouraged on self-improvement, and was given the opportunity to monitor the performance of other students as well as to critique their own progress.

	Improvements	No Changes	Losses
Group A (4 children)	5	9	2
Group B (6 children)	11	3	2
Group C (5 children)	11	0	5
Group D (6 children)	15	1	0

Figure 6. Teachers' appraisals of changes in students' classroom performance following training program designed for "hyperactive" children.

The chart (Figure 6) shows the teachers' judgments on 16 criteria of classroom performance on these 21 students. Please note the significant differences between Group A and Group D, where the major differences in the training program was the inclusion of the peripheral visual training and the self-motivation of the students. Group A had all the usual routines so generally used in special classrooms and conducted according to the usual instructions given. Group D had the emphasis on the visual tasks plus emphasis on their individual participation and judgment of their progress. These results become even more interesting when one realizes the teacher had no idea which children were in which group, and what visual training procedures were being used with each group. Of course, the rigid statistician will insist that this project is faulted by too small a sample and too little control of variables. The most significant aspect of it all, regardless of any statistical faults it may have, is the fact that 16 of the 17 students in Groups B, C and D no longer needed the daily use of drugs and their "hyperactivity" was no longer an interrupting problem. Yes, this is much too limited a study but it has been repeatedly verified by the clinical experience of many behavioral optometrists who have been providing this sort of vision care to literally thousands of children since this study was done back in the early 1970s. Like all such clinical explorations—whether or not these can justifiably be called "research"—when there is observable, acknowledged improvements in cultural performance, there must be something of value in the program. Just as every insightful teacher practices his or her profession, if any method of helping students "works," it is worth repetition, expansion, and further study.

No one would think of asserting that the procedure just described is the panacea so many are searching for. There can be no question about some children who are so constituted that they are in constant movement and action. There is a possibility, of course, that some children demonstrate a degree of energy overflow that will repeatedly interfere with any of the restrictive desk programs of the classroom. Nevertheless, even these "hot-wired" youngsters should be given the benefits of the sort of evaluation now available from the alert and informed clinicians who have a developmental frame of reference for their clinical appraisals. There can be little dispute over any procedure that brings reductions in the problem instead of masking the problem by the ingestion of drugs, which may be addictive.

What some clinicians are calling ADD and hyperactivity are problems to be prevented and are problems that can be almost entirely preventable by the alert parent and the informed nursery school teacher. Preventive procedures have already been suggested, but further details will be helpful. First of all, we all must recognize that the young child has little reason for a long attention span. The preschool years are so full of new and exciting things and events, the child wants to respond to all possible stimuli. Thus attention will constantly be shifting, and only the most attractive items will be given any extended attention. From a strict developmental perspective, the vast majority of young children are not physiologically or cognitively ready for the restrictions that the primary classroom places on them. This is another of the reasons some serious considerations should be given to those child care centers that promote themselves as "children's universities." If the programs offered by such centers are too demanding, there can be stresses that may create the germs of an attention span problem. The child who is not ready for such stresses and who is kept on concentrated tasks beyond his developmental readiness can actually learn how to use a short attention span to escape the stress of a situation. This can actually be a process of learning how *not* to learn, and the child takes the "flight" route as a survival technique.

There is a rule of thumb that all adults should keep in mind. Like all "rules of thumb" it is a generality, and the child's individualities must temper the use of this rule. Nevertheless, the rule is: A child should not be expected to hold either visual or auditory attention upon a restrictive task for more minutes than he is years old. If the child is 2 years old, attention should not be expected to exceed two minutes, and so on. This does not mean that the child cannot return to the task, but it certainly does mean there must be some sort of break in the confining aspects of the task. This break can be a release from the pages of a book for a few moments of talk about the story. If a child is having any sort of difficulty maintaining attention, the break should be one that permits some activity related to the story. The most helpful activity in such situations is a trip to the chalkboard to draw a simple picture of the story. The sort of release which comes from this activity bleeds off the pent-up energy that would otherwise explode into the "hyperactivity" that can become a deterrent to the entire learning situation. Almost any active participation in the story can be a contribution to the process, and parents can create the sort of situations that lead the child into Level 7 of the learning sequence just recently discussed.

"Normal"

There are two more words appearing in reports and consultations that need a few thoughts. The first of these is the word "normal" so frequently used when contrasting the performance of one child against statistical means and averages. One of the weekly television productions spent a third of its hour visiting a school of "learning-disabled" youngsters. On the whole, this was a splendid example of what can be done to help the youngsters so identified to reach their full potentials. This particular school has an enviable track record, claiming that 90% of their graduates who were discarded by public schools go on to successful performance in colleges. It was disturbing, however, to hear these children labeled as "disabled learners" after all the reports of the successes they were experiencing. The big shock came when a boy of 10 or 12 was interviewed, and he made this statement: "I cannot write as well as all those *normal* kids." Normal kids? Does this boy appraise himself as being *sub-normal* and *ab-normal* in this comparison of himself with "... all those "normal" kids"?

What about this word "normal"? Somehow the statisticians' studies in the hard sciences have so influenced us that we have concluded there are normal humans, and there are those who are not normal. If an individual has had a pulse rate of 65 all of his life, is he *sub-normal* or *ab-normal*? If a person consistently runs a body temperature of 98.0 instead of 98.6, is he *sub-normal* or *ab-normal*? Shouldn't we begin to recognize the individuality of each person, and instead of drawing rigid comparisons with thousands of others, compare him with himself? The thoroughly trained and insightful medical clinician recognizes these variations from what was long ago thought to be "normal" and fully recognizes the individualities of each patient. Why has recognition that the word "normal" is a trap not spread over into the development of our children? Why is this youngster with the lack of writing skills allowed to compare himself with all those "normal kids?" What incentive is there for this youngster to work for improvements in writing when he is already convinced he is not "normal?" Which of us is the *normal* person? There are all those characteristics that mark us as members of the human race and characteristics that allow us to resemble each other. It will always be the multitude of individualities and differences in these several resemblances which will be the sources of our unique skills that will let each of us reach for the mastery of the world and its contents. It certainly is the time to look more at the positives in each individual and completely forget the variations from the "norm" that hinder and delay so many students.

"Handicapped"

The second of these two worrisome words is "handicapped." The dictionary defines this word as "a deficiency, especially an anatomical, physiological, or mental deficiency, that prevents or restricts normal achievements; the disadvantage of disability." (There are those words "normal" and "disability" again!) Certainly, by now the message should be coming through loudly and clearly enough that these words need not even be discussed. Like all the rest, if used at all, they certainly must be used in the proper context, and even then, must *never* be used to set limits that will hinder the progress the child should make.

If the future can ever be reliably predicted on the events of the past, there will be new and even more esoteric words invented to describe the problems of school children. This will especially be true if we adults continue to search for ways to excuse our failures in the developmental guidance of our children. Further, the longer we continue to employ programs of rote memorization of facts that children might need sometime in the future, the more the smart children will be failing in the classroom. The revolution needed must bring programs that help children think—to explore the learning process and the consequences they will experience—so every child will move up to the great potentials that lie in every one of them who survive infancy.

Chapter V—The Appraisals of Learning Abilities from a Developmental Perspective

Adults who are striving to understand the learning problems so many children are demonstrating find themselves faced with added confusions that arise from the testing procedures and the training methods now available. Literally dozens of testing instruments have been designed and utilized in the attempt to find and provide the most appropriate help for each child. Unfortunately, too many of the designers have been test engineers, and how widely these tests and materials are used depends greatly on the stature and enthusiasm of the author/designer. Among these enthusiasts have been the biochemical engineers who have insisted that all learning problems come from a biochemical deficiency and can be solved by ingesting the "proper" drugs. There are the genetic engineers who insist that the presenting problem can be traced to some ancestral gene and that millions of dollars of "controlled research" will find some more definite explanations. There are the pathology engineers who urge that there is some sort of "organic defect" and the only solution will be to find a compensatory or substitutive ability that will allow the learner to bypass the problem as if it did not exist. There are the behavior engineers who insist that self-discipline and environmental controls will lead the learner out of the problem. There have also been some developmental engineers who maintain that if all of these youngsters would be immersed in developmental procedures long enough and often enough, the problem would disappear. Every one of these perspectives has suffered a kind of tunnel vision *ad extremum*—the blind worship of anything that can be quantified by standardized testing and the proper statistical treatment that will provide a black-or- white view of the entire issue. But, in every one of these perspectives, there is still a lot of space in the middle between the black and white quantifications, and too many students have slipped through this gray crack.

The devoted, if misdirected, efforts of these test engineers have brought us tests specially designed to find the specific details of the problem that has placed students into the categories discussed in the previous chapter. As already indicated, the students who have been unable to keep up academically with their age or grade group have been given at least one of the general labels, and when a student would eventually fall two academic years behind, he was then sent for more specific testing. It has all been similar to taking a balky car in for a tune-up. The car (or the youngster) would be given a battery of tests offered by one of the engineers in the attempt to find exactly which part is malfunctioning. Sooner or later these tests of supposedly very specific functions or abilities are expected to identify the exact part not functioning as it should, so that exact "curative" actions can be recommended by the engineer running the tests. Too frequently, however, these tests only put another specific label on the specific problem and fail to indicate the interwoven mediating procedures the individual needs.

When all of these tests are carefully appraised, we find that many of them do no more than verify the observations and conclusions already made by an alert and experienced teacher. A number of these tests do no more than provide some diagnostic labels that are considered acceptable under Public Law 94-142[6] for the placement of a child in special classes, especially if the child has sagged at least the specified two years behind on academic test scores. Some of these tests have obviously been designed from an economic perspective so insurance companies will pay for them. Insurance companies have no problem reimbursing for blood tests, brain scans, injections, and other medical sounding procedures, and the more "medical" the label sounds, the more likely the insurance benefits. Most of the tests have been designed on a pass/fail scoring base and provide nothing more than a student's percentile rank in comparison to hundreds of other students who were used to "standardize" the selected procedures. Regrettably, this standardization has merely established what the educational system has accepted as satisfactory performance in the "perceptual abilities" chosen as the criteria for the skills needed in the classroom. Most of these tests give little if any insight into what specific help the student needs if he fails any portion of the test. The conclusion usually reached is that a particular child has not done as well as expected when compared to what the test designer quite autocratically decided was "normal" performance. Thus, a student is compared to hundreds of other students instead of being appraised as an individual with an individual's unique needs—and this is the student lost in the gray area of almost every test.

Many of the training materials or activities promoted for use by children who have been assigned to special classrooms or "resource rooms" are popular because of the enthusiasm of the designers who insist the children make excellent progress when these specific materials or activities are used as part of the daily classroom program. However, the progress made on these programs does not assure there will be progress in other classroom activities, and these materials are frequently more "busywork" than valid training procedures. A great part of the problem that exists in both the training program and the testing program lies in the lack of a complete understanding of the learning process and how it must help the individual to bring meaning to the symbolic tasks of the curriculum.

This lack of understanding frequently centers on the confusions arising from the words and phrases used to identify each of the perceptual components of the learning process. These same words and phrases appear in most of the tests being used, and some of them receive heavy attention in many of the training materials. These words and phrases will be familiar to every teacher and have been heard or read by almost every parent of a child having learning problems because they appear in consultations and reports, adding to the confusion of most everyone concerned.

Before continuing into an attempt at clarification of the confusing words and phrases appearing in these tests, it is important to comment on what may seem to be a much too critical judgment of tests and training materials. In contrast to what has been written, there are a few of these tests that *do* identify the individual's unique problems, and when properly used, *do* provide excellent information about the abilities the student has achieved and which others need special attention. Sam Kirk, Ph.D., the author/designer of the Illinois Test of Psycholinguistic Abilities, states it very well: "Diagnosis itself is meaningless unless it leads to remediation." Some of the tests actually *do* guide the classroom teacher to the most appropriate training procedures. There are many behavioral optometrists now using clinical procedures that provide much more than a pass/fail score or a percentile rank among thousands of other students. These optometric procedures provide the opportunity to observe and critique the developmental processes the student has experienced and refined, and how these skills are used by the student to meet and master a task that has been presented. One of the differences between the optometric clinical procedures and many of the educational procedures lies in the behavioral optometrist's conviction that the more advanced skills should be used to attack the less advanced ones. Kirk, along with other educators, proposes that the most attention should be given to the inadequate performance areas with emphasis on specific ability training. The optometrist feels the interpretive integrations, which come more satisfactorily when successes overcome failures, are most important, and that the patient in difficulty for visual reasons will probably be more motivated to work on the problem when he realizes there are solutions that can be explored and used to one's own advantage and benefit.

There is neither time nor space nor justification for attempting a full exploration and discussion of all the tests now being used to target children having learning problems. These have greatly varying points of attack on the problems and are usually limited to a particular area of ability that is considered relevant to classroom performance. The title of each of these tests often indicates just which aspect of ability is being probed, and since each of these is so very specific, it gives much more attention to what level of skill has not been reached. Thus, as has been previously noted, the tests tend to measure the product rather than making any appraisal of the process by which the learner reached the product being measured.

The point of this discussion is *not* to critique each of the tests but to move toward clarifications and the elimination of some of the confusions and misconceptions that continue to exist. None of this is done to condemn any of the tests and the "learning materials" which accompany some of them, but to help teachers, parents, and clinicians to better understand the learners' problems, and the learning processes these tests are expected to identify. In this vein, there is one major point to be made. Every one of the dozen or so most widely used tests demands all of the visual abilities and visual skills discussed in the first pages of Chapter II. Thus, it becomes quite apparent that the successful performance on these tests depends most on the adequacy of the sight-vision complex. Since nearly all of these tests are also considered to be quite directly relevant to IQ scores, isn't it safe to conclude that the sight-vision complex has some relevance to intellectual development?

This possibility was frequently discussed, both privately and from the lecture platform, by Ward Halstead, Ph.D., formerly Professor of Experimental Psychology in the Division of Psychiatry in the University of Chicago's Department of Medicine. Halstead was considered the highest international authority on the brain and its function in the

1950s and 1960s. Although his greatest expertise was in the area of brain trauma, his work included extensive study of brain functions in the healthy and untraumatized human brain. Halstead became especially interested in the sight-vision complex and the role it plays in human behavior. He often stated: "The human mind is a black box that we have not yet even begun to open. All we can possibly do is to look at the performance we can attribute to the human brain and assume what is really going on in that black box. We can make good judgments of what the brain does, but we may never fully realize how it does what it does." It is most significant that Halstead considered the sight-vision complex to be a primary component of influence in almost all of the 16 tests of brain- mind competence he designed.[32]

In this regard, Halstead frequently stated his convictions that there is a high correlation between visual performance and intellectual performance. His comment from the lecture platform was: "When you speak of vision and intelligence you are speaking of one and the same." In light of the knowledge we now have, it seems quite safe to think of vision as a significant part of the process and intelligence as the product. This is not to assume that the sight-vision complex is the only process involved in the development of intelligence, but it is quite evident from all the information Halstead has provided as well as a review of all the tests now being used that the sight-vision complex certainly does play a prominent role. A brief review of tests of children's learning abilities will help here.

Thirteen Currently Used Tests

The Bender Gestalt Test: Designed by Lauretta Bender to appraise absence of brain function in children, presence of organic brain defects, retardation and loss of brain function in adults. Here the subject copies nine patterns. It is completely a test of visual-motor abilities.

Detroit Tests of Learning Aptitudes: This is described as "tests of mental faculties" and nine of the 19 tests are fully dependent on visual abilities.

Durrell Analysis of Reading Difficulty: This is described as a test of visual and auditory discriminations but is as dependent on vision as any reading test can be.

Goodenough Harris Drawing Test: The subject is required to draw a person on a blank sheet of paper, and the scoring determines the subject's IQ. This is wholly a test of visual-motor abilities.

Graham Kendall Memory for Designs: This test was designed for the clinical study of patients suspected of having some brain damage. Here the subject views a design and then draws it as remembered. This is, first of all, a test of visualization skills and then a test of related visual-motor abilities.

Otis Quick-Scoring Mental Abilities Test: This is another test of reading ability and thus is dependent on visual skills.

Hiskey-Nebraska Test of Learning Abilities: This was originally designed to test "the psycholinguistic abilities" of the deaf. Every one of the 12 tests are dependent on visual discrimination and the advanced visual skills the deaf person has achieved.

House-Tree-Person Technique: This is frequently referred to as a "Children's Drawings Test." As such, it is another of the completely visual-motor ability tests and has been extended as a criterion of intelligence.

Peabody Picture Vocabulary Test: Although this is described as measuring a child's hearing vocabulary and as an estimate of verbal intelligence, it requires the child to match pictures seen with the words he hears. Here the lack of skills in the sight- vision complex could radically alter the child's "verbal intelligence."

Illinois Test of Psycholinguistic Abilities (TPA): This is a very complex and extensive mix of tests of visual and auditory discriminations. Although the test is heavily loaded with auditory discriminations, there are also many related visual discriminations essential to completion of the test. Thus, many of the results are indirectly related to visual abilities never revealed in the usual sight testing procedures. These are referred to as "visual reception skills," "visual association skills," "visual closure skills," and "visual sequential memory skills." This test is quite unique in that it makes specific recommendations for the enhancement of visual abilities that are related to the reading abilities being probed.

Wide Range Achievement Test (WRAT): This is also a test of reading abilities and thus is heavily dependent on visual discriminations and visual skills.

Wepman Auditory Discrimination Test: This test is primarily described as a way to identify the learner who is not developing auditory discrimination abilities. The examiner is instructed to cover his mouth "so audition is the primary receptive mode." This instruction implies that visual discriminations play a role in auditory discriminations, but there is no reference to the reciprocity that exists between visualization and audition.

Wechsler Intelligence Scale for Children (WISC): This is one of the most popular and widely used of all these tests. It is divided into two sections. There are six "verbal tests" described as using oral language as a vehicle for communication on questions and answers. There are five "performance tests" described as being presented in a visual manner requiring the child to respond by gesture or hand-eye activity. This is a most interesting series of tests and the careful analysis of each subtest leads one to the conclusion that a child must be operating around Level 6 on the learning continuum described in Figure 3 in Chapter II. This test, originally designed to appraise children ages 5 to 16, yields a "verbal IQ," a "performance IQ," and a "full scale IQ." It is most interesting that it scores the subject on a "pass/fail" basis and neglects to identify the developmental level the subject has reached and at which level help is needed.

An Overview of Two Well Known Tests

There are two tests that have had much attention and popularity over the past 20 to 40 years that are not included in the above descriptions. All of these, the 13 just described and the two that will be described next, contain some words and phrases that seem to contribute to the general confusion and misinterpretation of many, hindering the understanding and solution for learning problems. The *Frostig Developmental Test of Visual Perception* and the *Motor-Free Visual Perception Test (MVPT)* have been chosen for special discussion for several reasons. First, their rather specific use of the words and phrases are so widely used in all of the tests mentioned here, and, second, these two tests illustrate many educators' lack of familiarity with well- established sequences and components of human development and with the great importance of the entire movement system, movement patterns, and the "muscle memories" that lay such a significant foundation for all learning performance in the human. Finally, these two tests, like some of the others, do not provide sufficient information on how supervising adults can help the learner make the application of test and material portions for assurance of classroom gains. Ideally, the testing routines should find a way to give full consideration to the desires, the motivations, and the goals of the student. And the individual doing the testing should know about learning processes to find the clues needed in whatever test instrument is being used. There must be quite a lot more in any testing situation than just a standardized score on a standardized test battery as if the children being subjected are also completely standardized.

There is one significant difference between these two instruments. One of these (the Frostig) is completely built around the student's use of a pencil to draw, trace, or mark the test patterns. The other (the MVPT) involves no actions that produce pencil marks on the test pages. This second instrument is described as being "motor-free," and it is, except for the subject's pointing to "one of the four alternative (forms) that he feels is the correct response." This does not totally eliminate the motor patterns the learner has explored, internalized, and refined to skill level in the total learning process. Even if the child did nothing but name the diagram or line drawing chosen as an answer, there would be a motoric component. This interesting fact will receive further discussion as subtests of both of the instruments are explored.

The two test instruments chosen are of special interest to me because they both place emphasis on the role that vision plays in testing and training of the learning processes directly related to academic achievement. This importance is evident in the labels given to each of the subtests. These are: *visual-motor* perception; *visual* discriminations; *visual* closure; *visual* memory; and the words and phrases that heavily imply visual participation—*figure-ground perception; perceptual* constancy; *spatial* orientations, and *spatial* relations. The majority of other available tests also place emphasis on auditory abilities, but these two direct almost all attention to vision development, visual skills, and visual performance. In addition to the visual aspects of these two testing instruments, they also illustrate the possible confusion by many on what vision is and how it differs from the simple and basic *sight* actions of the end organs—the eyes.

The similarities of these two instruments can best be presented by listing the subtests. These are:

Frostig Test	MVPT Test
Perception of Spatial Relationships	Spatial Relationships
Perception of Position of Space	
Figure-Ground Perception	Figure-Ground
Perception Constancy	Visual Closure
Visual-Motor Coordination	Visual Memory

The only real differences in these two instruments lie in the subtests: Visual-Motor Coordination in Frostig and Visual Memory in the MVPT. These last two subtests are an excellent place to start the discussion of what the labels really mean and what the tests really are probing.

Visual-Motor Coordination

This phrase is discussed first because it appears frequently in these two test procedures and receives emphasis in almost all of the training materials used in both the usual classroom and the special classrooms of the contemporary educational system. Over many years, visual-motor coordination has also been identified as "eye-hand coordination." Whatever it is called, it is the visual guidance of the hand/pencil activities that lead to greater understanding of the diagrams, words, or numbers filling the worksheets presented to students as exercises in the learning process. Every single activity a learner is given in which there is a crayon or pencil required is practice in visual-motor coordination and the integrations of motor and visual perceptual development. Almost every preschool and kindergarten activity can be considered as eye-hand coordination procedures, but these become more *visual-motor* activities when the task involves more of the symbolic details such as drawing and writing in the more advanced classrooms.

As already stated and implied quite often in these chapters, this activity is the preparation for and genesis of all symbolic perceptions. (Remember, please, the word *perception* is used in this book as the synonym for the word *understanding*.) Thus, any activity that can be described as visual-motor is part of the total process of establishing the internalized motor patterns and muscle-memory traces so important to both the production and recognition of *any* symbol—be it a diagram, a number, a letter, a word, or an abstract formula. It is this internalized pattern of the direction of hand/pencil movements required, for example, to manuscript the letters *"b"* and *"d"* that allows the learner to know the differences so well that there will be none of the confusions known as reversals. In fact, if these motor patterns for these letters are not fully internalized, reversals will plague the learner until the motor patterns are firmly established. Further, the internalized movement patterns—the muscle memory patterns—that differentiate a square and a rectangle are very supportive to the visual recognition of the slight differences in these two geometric forms. The early learner will frequently demonstrate the inability to correctly name these two forms on visual inspections—and then immediately name them when permitted to trace the shapes with a finger. Thus, the seemingly simple visual inspection of printed patterns and the decisions on similarities and differences will be greatly influenced by the motor patterns the learner has mastered and internalized early in the total process of mastering any symbolic representation of the movement pattern.

The experienced, observant teacher has long known that diligent practice on printing and writing symbols and words is a major contributor to the "sight recognition" of these symbols. If the youngster being tested is asked to point to a test pattern, there is movement involved even though it does not overtly appear as a hand/pencil action. It is, nevertheless, a motorically determined response at the *covert* level of thinking it all through to the correct answer. In fact, there is now a surprising amount of agreement among developmentalists, neurologists, and students of the human brain and mind, that *thinking* is a "motor act." As a result of all this developmental progression, no test of perception can be considered completely "motor-free" if there is overt performance of any degree. Such a response will be based on motor experiences and the internalized organizations of movement that are appropriate to the task at hand. If none of these motoric responses are present, there will be no perceptual ability to be tested.

In sharp contrast, the other test battery being explored here brings important attention to the role of visual-manual coordination in this total learning process. Examples from each of these two instruments will illustrate the point being made here. Figures 7a and 7b show how closely coordinated visual discrimination and motor action are. Figure 8 shows that these test designs cannot be completely "motor-free."

Another statement must be carefully considered. "... while motor and visual perceptual skills are often closely associated, they can also be very separate abilities. An individual with a motor problem does not necessarily have a visual perceptual problem; many children with cerebral palsy, for example, evidence no visual disorders whatsoever. These tests (referring to pencil/paper tests) of 'visual perception' in fact assess visual- motor integration and, therefore, are suspect as measures of visual perception." The determination of the absence or presence of a vision problem, or a "visual perceptual problem," depends on the adequacy of the tests being used, and the concepts of vision the examiner holds. The "evidence of no visual disorders" indicates the absence of the most basic tests of vision and visual performance.

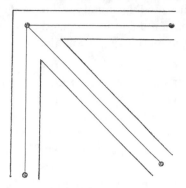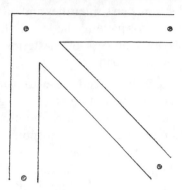

Figure 7a. This is not a duplicate of any of the Frostig materials used for practice in "visual-motor" activities. However, it is a sample of the sorts of materials recommended by the Frostig program. The child is instructed to connect the dots by drawing over the lines between the dots, and to keep his pencil line in the middle of the two border lines. There certainly is no question about this being a visual-motor exercise, but many of such patterns in varying directions and curves provide no real experience with spatial characteristics that visual-motor practice must have if such practice is to be translated to other activities demanding visual-motor discriminations, decisions, and actions.

Figure 7b. As stated on Figure 7a, this is not a pattern that duplicates any of the Frostig materials. This pattern represents what Frostig considered a more advanced visual-motor task because there was no middle line to trace, and the child is expected to connect the dots and keep his drawn line centered between the border lines. Again, this certainly is a visual-motor activity, but unless the visual discriminations and the motor actions practiced here can be translated to other activities, these patterns are little more than "busywork" and practice in drawing lines. Ways must be found to guide the children into making similar sorts of visual discriminations of spacing, directions, where to start and where to stop, and then making judgments of the product for practice in the appraisals of consequences. Just drawing lines will not, in and by itself, provide the skills that visual-motor practice should provide.

There is a suggestion here that there may be a somewhat limited understanding of cerebral palsy. Clinicians with a breadth of experience with these palsied individuals will confirm the statement that there are many limitations in the interpretations and comprehensions of numerous visually-centered experiential situations when there is an absence of the usual motoric signals. However, neither can one possibly defend the notion that cerebral palsy victims are completely devoid of the proprioceptual signals usually experienced by the non-palsied individual. There is every possibility that the cerebral palsy victim obtains *more usable muscle signals* out of *limited movements* than does the individual having none of the palsy interferences. It is

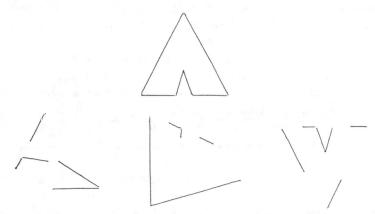

Figure 8. Like the two previous illustrations, this is not a duplicate of the patterns found in the pages of the test materials of either of the two procedures being discussed here. However, this diagram does provide a pattern that is similar to some of those considered to be "motor-free." The instruction for an activity similar to this asks: "If you finished drawing one of these patterns, which one would then look like the one at the top of the page?" The student could not possibly answer this question if there was not some motor pattern for drawing lines somewhere deep in the student's previous experiences. Such a series of patterns actually present a task that demands visualizations, visual discriminations, and the motoric imagination needed to complete such figures. Such performance, even in the imaginative stage, would be impossible without acquired motor abilities.

well known that individuals without the full and usual use of an information processing system make up for some of the loss by learning to more carefully and explicitly interpret those signals that *do* get through the disorder. It is possible for the cerebral palsied individual to integrate those motor signals that do come through with whatever visual interpretations can be made so some of the very same visual-motor perceptions occur for this person that are achieved by the non-palsied person. These may not be to the same amplitude that they occur in the well person, but they may expand to a definite degree of perceptual validity.

Without doubt, the most appropriate example of visual-motor coordination is the act of writing. Writing can only be described as a very refined activity completely unique to the human and observable as the visually-directed and monitored movements of an arm and hand in the very complex process of graphically producing the learned symbolic patterns of numbers, letters, or words while the fingers grasp a crayon, pencil, or pen. More simply stated: writing is the visually steered dexterous movements of a hand to put symbolic marks on paper. Writing will be discussed at length later, but the acquisition of writing skills is so important to the mastery of our language that it cannot be casually passed over. An individual can lose all hearing and speaking abilities yet communicate with ease through writing. Further, writing (or drawing, as the ancient caveman learned) is a time binder and the best way the human can give permanency to his thoughts and expressions and insure that they will be passed on to another human. Speech is instantaneously present and just as instantaneously absent. We now find that our electronic culture has made extensive and expansive ways to record and retain speech for later listening. One wonders if all these recorders were not made necessary because so many individuals could not write—just as the computing cash registers have become necessary because so many individuals could not accurately do simple addition and subtraction. And, worse yet, computers are now being credited with electronic intelligence so the individual does not need to learn to evaluate problems that arise, an example being the sophisticated gear on naval vessels that identifies a passenger jet as a fighter plane because some of the signals are the same. Is it really becoming an era in which a person need not develop those perceptual integrations nor the underlying visual-motor coordinations out of which human intelligence arises?

At this moment of review, another editorial comes in the morning newspaper. It is titled "Reading, Writing and Batteries." It is a discussion of recent requests from teachers' associations that calculators be allowed in class and to be used on tests because this full-scale inclusion "should not diminish the acquisition of computational skills by students." The editorialist writes: "This ... statement is a little bit like endorsing the concept of going barefoot outside in winter 'as long as it does not diminish' the warmth of one's feet. The argument being advanced is that children should not, once they 'understand' the concepts involved, be prevented from continuing to more complicated concepts." The editorialist then asks: "How are they ever to improve their ability to do these manipulations or, for that matter, to see why these manipulations are worth learning if they don't ever have to 'use' them?"

The writer extends his comments to the recognition that the calculator question is relatively simple, and, yes, there are skills involved in using them—skills that can lead to higher-order kinds of expertise. He allows that math teachers can then guide the youngsters on how and when to use calculators if the students grasp the basics and if the teachers can control the more crutch-like uses to which calculators are so frequently put.

The final paragraph of this editorial makes significant points. "But basic math tables are important for a larger reason, and it has to do with more than understanding the rules of multiplying, adding or subtracting. Once they are firmly learned—and this happens after a certain amount of drudgery—they give a sense of the quantities of things, of whether eight times five is a lot or a little less than nine squared, or whether a cake recipe is likely to call for 47 cups of flour. Just as numbers flashed on a digital clock offer an idea of time that is radically different from hands on a circular face, a little square of numbers on a calculator cannot give any serious understanding of magnitude or comparative scales. Even aside from the usual arguments against exclusive reliance on a calculator—what will happen if the battery goes dead, or if, heaven forbid, the individual is caught without one? These kids are going to grow up with a much bigger power shortage where it really counts."

These paragraphs cannot possibly be read without the feeling that this editorialist has some very sharp insights into the development of the totality of the learning process and the importance of the visual-manual integrations.

An 8-year-old boy was recently referred for an optometric evaluation that would find and identify the "visual-perceptual" reasons why he has been having so much difficulty in "reading and language arts," so much difficulty that he is being retained in second grade. The school reports stated: "Ted is a child of high average intellectual ability. No significant processing deficits were revealed through our evaluation. Academic achievement is within the average range but not necessarily consistent with his measured intellectual potentials." This report went into detail regarding five different standardized tests now being used by school psychologists, and in each instance scored Ted's performance "above average for his age" with significant visual perceptual strengths showing in all tests. It is particularly interesting that one of the tests being discussed here was given high credence, and was interpreted as follows: "Ted's visual perception appears well developed for his age. He attained an age equivalent of 8 years, 8 months, and a perceptual quotient of 109. He performed best in areas of visual discrimination and visual short term memory." This test was done when Ted was 7 years, 7 months old, thus giving the impression that Ted was a year ahead of most children his age. Of course, since this test prevents all writing and all hand movements other than pointing, any judgment of the basics of visual-motor coordination were unfortunately overlooked.

Another of the popular tests used by most school psychologists reported: "This (test) suggests well developed visual motor integration skills." The very next sentence states, "When copying designs, Ted made errors in rotations and perseveration of design and distortion of shapes. These errors are expected of a child Ted's age." Ted's performance on these tests actually showed he was having great difficulty in the visual-motor integrations needed for putting his visual discriminations onto paper; yet this problem was passed off as being "expected" for a child Ted's age without any added thought that since he was already showing positive intellectual potentials, this copying difficulty might well be an interference that needed immediate attention. Here is a youngster whose handwriting was later (more than a year later, at the end of a second year in second grade) appraised as being adequate for beginning first grade, and whose visual memory scores are still only adequate for mid-kindergarten. Here is a youngster who has been trying to communicate to everyone concerned, "My hand cannot draw what my eyes can see, and I am remembering very little of what I do," but for some reason his message was not being received.

The school report gives further information regarding the inadequacy of the tests that were run on Ted, and the question arises about why the results of these tests give the impression that Ted is a year ahead of "average performance" while he continues to have critical problems in reading and language arts. Again, one must wonder why tests that do not probe perceptual abilities needed in the classroom are even considered and thought to provide relevant information. After all of the tests were used and Ted's scores were established, some recommendations were given. These were:

1. Give Ted immediate feedback concerning his performance. Be positive and encourage persistence.

2. Avoid confronting Ted with a large amount of work at one time. For instance, cover a page of problems, allowing only two or three to be seen at one time.

3. Color code board work to aid Ted when he is copying from the board.

4. It may be best to present information sequentially rather than simultaneously since Ted may have difficulty processing several

stimuli at once.

5. Both the school and home environments should be aware of the effect of high expectations on Ted. Balance expectations with a focus on persistence and doing one's best.

How should these recommendations be interpreted, and what reflections are they casting on Ted's abilities? Let's take them one at a time and explore the possibilities:

1. Give Ted immediate feedback concerning his performance. Be positive and encourage persistence.

Does this recommendation imply that Ted has little confidence in his performance and needs much praise to keep him motivated? Does it also suggest that Ted has poor work habits—that he does not stay at his school tasks and needs reminding to get the work done? Does this recommendation suggest any ways to help Ted *understand* the tasks?

2. Avoid confronting Ted with a large amount of work at one time. For instance, cover a page of problems, allowing only two or three to be seen at one time.

Is this recommendation suggesting that a whole page of problems confuses and discourages Ted—thus, only a couple of problems will not seem such an insurmountable task? How many math problems are there on a single page of the first grade workbooks Ted was facing at the time of this testing? If more than a couple of problems overwhelm Ted, might there be a visual-motor coordination problem interfering with the amount of work Ted is expected to complete?

3. Color code board work to aid Ted when copying from the board.

This is an interesting recommendation. How will color coding assist Ted in the mechanics of copying? It certainly might help him find and keep his place in the process of looking back and forth from board to workbook and back to board again, but how will the colors enhance the visual-motor actions involved in writing?

4. It may be best to present information sequentially rather than simultaneously since Ted may have difficulty processing several stimuli at one time.

Is the evaluator suggesting that conceding to his memory difficulties will help him to develop these abilities? Is the classroom teacher expected to give Ted information in a manner that is quite different from the way in which the information is presented to the rest of the class? Is it possible that Ted's difficulties in visual memory and visualization skills are the underlying problems that need attention? Shouldn't Ted be given help to master the problems he faces rather than being given ways of circumventing his inabilities?

5. Both the school and home environments should be aware of the effect of high expectations on Ted. Balance expectations with focus on persistence and doing one's best.

Can these comments be interpreted to mean that neither teacher nor parents should expect too much of Ted—that, in spite of his "above average abilities," he really will not be doing too well, and no one should hold out too much hope for his success in the classroom? Is this comment suggesting that Ted's parents should be cautious about too much encouragement and too much challenge towards achieving the learning abilities Ted needs? Does this comment mean that all adults in this situation should be completely satisfied with a performance that is obviously less than Ted's potential seems to promise?

Where in any of these five recommendations is there any suggestion of how to help Ted *learn to learn*? Which of these five recommendations provide any clues to the basic instructional and/or guidance methods that could help Ted explore, expand, and enhance the developmental aspects of the learning process? Where in these five recommendations is there anything more than ways to get the work done whether or not Ted understands any of what he has been doing? Is it possible that the frequently repeated comments about Ted's "above average abilities" would cause the parents more confusion when Ted is having so much difficulty in reading and language arts that he must repeat second grade? Is it possible that tests like the one in which he was judged to be performing at an 8-year, 8-month level even when he was almost a year younger in chronological age, are confusing the educators as much as the parents? Is all of this confusion and misunderstanding the result of using tests that test how well the child might do *on the test* and still provide no clues to whether or not the child has the abilities the classroom tasks will demand?

As a result of all of this lack of understanding of child development and the learning process, Ted is now being given tutoring in reading and being retained in the second grade to improve in language arts. His parents are deeply concerned that another year in the same grade will be little more than repetition of the same experiences without the attention that must be given to the *reasons* for his difficulty.

On the other hand, Ted is fortunate in not being passed on just because he is an alert child, passed on to compound his learning problems and his perceptual problems for greater difficulties in later grades. Here is another of those youngsters who is "smart in everything ... except school" with parents (probably labeled "overly concerned" and "too pushy") who know the test reports have not really identified Ted's needs. I will refrain from asking readers to predict this intelligent boy's future if the help he needs is not made available to him. It is the nature of the human to find the easiest and most economical solutions to problems. Therefore, the odds suggest some very definite disappointments and some undesirable escape behaviors in Ted's future if he cannot be taught how to avoid failure in situations where others less intelligent than he are succeeding.

The optometric evaluation of Ted's visual abilities that are directly related to his perceptual development has been most revealing. At age 8, he still cannot put his name on paper without extreme stress and confusion over the shapes and sequence of the letters. He is still having much difficulty making a "9" when asked to write the numbers from 1 to 10. All of his pencil and paper performance is so slow and so tedious that fatigue and frustrations rise much too quickly. In all of these tasks his developmental delays in visual-motor coordination are vividly obvious. The explanation of the teacher's reports (that Ted cannot copy from the chalkboard) can be found in the fact that he has to take so much time on the sheer mechanics of number and letter forms that he loses his train of thought and loses his place when looking for the next item on the chalkboard. His writing abilities—the ultimate example of visual-motor coordination—are so undeveloped he needs an excessive amount of time to complete the simplest quantity of such work. No wonder he needs hours, instead of minutes, to complete his homework assignments. His confusion on letter shapes is still so great that at the end of second grade he has limited success on the combinations of letters that make words. The fatigue and discomfort arising from the pencil and paper tasks is so great it erases all possibility of the visualizations needed for reliable visual memory. All of Ted's responses and performances on the series of vision development tests did verify the potentials that all of the school psychologist's tests suggested. Because there were consistently repeated evidences of Ted's desire to learn, there is every reason to believe some excellent progress will be the result of the special program of assistance being given. One may certainly anticipate gains in the language arts as Ted finds that he can achieve the visual-motor coordinations he needs for all of the writing this area of the curriculum requires.

Visual Memory

The second of these two test batteries includes a subtest for visual memory and introduces it in the accompanying manual by stating: "This involves the ability to recall dominant features of one stimulus item or to remember the sequence of several items." This is the educators' description of this ability that is so unique to humans. Experimental psychologists and the behavioral optometrists usually call this ability *visualization*, and these clinicians are cognizant of how extensively this ability influences all human behavior. The clinician realizes the significance of the role that visualization plays in all degrees and levels of the interpretations and comprehensions of every aspect of visual inspections and understandings of *all things* visible, and, in many daily instances, those things previously seen but later invisible. Further, these clinicians are vitally interested in the part that hands play in the development of visualization skills. Thus, visual memory is much more than an ability to recall a dominant feature of one stimulus item, or to remember sequences of several items.

Many children clearly demonstrate their use of hands to "visually" explore objects they cannot see, and this behavior is usually present by early school age. In fact, a test designed by three behavioral optometrists[33] allows observations of the success an individual will have in identifying invisible geometric forms by use of hands for manual explorations of them. This same test discloses that if a youngster has not achieved the visual-manual ability to draw a geometric form in a simple copying test, he will most likely *not* be able to visualize and then draw or name the form from memory. Once again, we come face to face with the importance of the visual-motor coordinations as these influence mental images in the act of visualization. Likewise, we are reminded that any test of visual memory may be tainted if the subject is not permitted to use hands to support the visual discriminations and decisions such a test demands.

There has already been discussion of the development of this visualization ability, and it is being redundantly discussed here to again emphasize its importance to classroom success. It not only plays a significant role in the "ability to recall dominant features of one stimulus item," it is tremendously important to the magnitude of comprehension that evolves out of the mental images the reading material is supposed to create. If a story is so poorly written or told that the reader or listener cannot create appropriate and matching visualizations, the story is discarded and not remembered. In addition, no communications will have been established.

There is still one more aspect of visual memory and visualization to be considered. The *meaning* one can bring to a word, pattern, or number will also have great influence on the magnitude of one's mental imageries. Again, we must remember Mr. Gray's comment about "not getting meaning *from* a word but bringing meaning *to* a word." "A picture is worth a thousand words" only if the viewer has the thousand words in his vocabulary. This ability to bring meaning to the mental picture is just as critical as it is everywhere else in the learning process. Thus, any test of this ability will be influenced by how nonsensical or abstract and unidentifiable the test patterns are. The individual who has not achieved any degree of skill in visualization will demonstrate a need to verbally label or describe a pattern in order to have success in identifying it. In contrast, the individual with an advanced degree of skill in this area may be able to duplicate almost any test pattern regardless of its abstractness. This ability has been labeled "photographic memory," and extensive research has shown that such ability may well allow the individual to recall details to an amazing degree. However, it often seems to be a splinter skill that does not translate into a contribution to comprehension or communication with other persons. This strange ability frequently explains the gray areas where students' real problems are misinterpreted because they achieved a "good" score on a test that has little or no relevance to classroom tasks. When such a test is used, its inherent irrelevancy would almost certainly eliminate any possible validity as a test of classroom performance. If, on the other hand, the test included both those items that could be quickly labeled and those that could not be so easily labeled, the student's developmental levels could be determined, and more reliable judgments of the student's personal achievement levels could be made. The great importance of visual memory abilities and the tests that appropriately probe them cannot be overlooked. In the contemporary culture and usual classroom where visualization skills are so essential, a much better understanding of this ability must be acquired by every person who has any concern for the learning abilities of our children and youths. This is especially true when the absence of visualization skills is so epidemic among the 60 million illiterates in the United States.

Perception of Spatial Relationships

Perception of Position in Space

Spatial Relationships

These subtest identifications are found in both of the two test instruments chosen for further discussion here. These are being discussed in group fashion because the manuals for these two instruments describe them in much the same way, and with many similar examples. All of these subtests and training procedures are directed to the contents of the printed test pages and it may appear as if the learner has little need to bring personal experiences to the processes being probed or trained.

Frostig presents these tests as they relate more to the understanding of the words that describe one's spatial positions, i.e., in, out, up, down, etc. These are excellent words that represent spatial decisions because the individual must have moved about in the surrounding environment enough to know what movements these words describe. Frostig then goes on to state that the spatial relationships are pertinent to the abilities needed to correctly make letters like *"b"* and *"d"* and words like *"on"* and *"no,"* or any of the words in our language whose correct spelling depends on the spatial relationships of the letters required. Frostig also makes special references to the confusions such words too frequently generate, and blames the "reversals" that happen on the individual's lack of spatial perceptions. It must be noted, however, that *"b"* and *"d"* and words like *"won"* and *"now"* also involve differences in the direction and sequence of movements needed to inspect and discriminate all of the letters involved as well as the movements required to write these symbols. We are immediately returned to the discussion of visual- motor coordinations and the fact that if the special movement patterns have not been established as a result of the movements through space, there will be deficits in the judgments now being probed or trained as perceptions of spatial relationships.

The sequencing of movements required to make or differentiate the contents of a word brings in another aspect of the entire visual- motor complex. Only the very skilled reader can visually grasp a whole word in one single visual inspection. The unskilled reader needs to make carefully directed and controlled ocular movements in the left to right direction for inspection of our culture's symbolic arrangements. Where "b" and "d" can be differentiated with a quick, single sight-vision inspection, words of any length must be scanned in a fully controlled sequence of very refined sight-vision movements that are neither innate nor easily learned. The longer words thus demand a very advanced sort of spatial orientation that includes knowing where to start a movement and where to stop that movement. It is this "packaging" of the visual-motor movements that must also be fully considered whenever any discussion of spatial relationships is applied to the symbols the students must learn to be a successful reader.

The MVPT test comes somewhat closer to what spatial orientations are all about and describes its test section as a probe of the "ability to orient one's body in space and to perceive (interpret and comprehend—my parentheses) the positions of objects in relation to oneself and to other objects." This definition is much closer to the interpretation the experimental psychologist and the behavioral optometrist put on this phrase. The MVPT test then goes on to state: "An example of a spatial relationship task would be the perception of pictures, figures, or patterns that are disoriented in relation to each other." The informed clinician offers the idea that these "disoriented" pictures, figures, or patterns are only disoriented in relation to each other *if* the viewer recognizes them to be in a position that is somehow in conflict with the viewer's spatial position. The behavioral optometrist defines spatial orientation as "knowing where the world and its contents are from me, *and* knowing where I am from the world and its contents." Thus, if a pattern of any sort is flipped or rotated in some fashion, the judgment the viewer makes *first of all* is: where is it *now* from me, and where *now* am I from it? Only when such judgments are fully completed can the viewer make the correct decisions about the relationships of patterns, pictures, or figures to each other. These decisions must be made from what is rather esoterically called a person's "egocentric locus," that is, "me as the center of all judgments I make about the locus of the world and its contents."

All of this may certainly seem to complicate this entire issue beyond necessity. However, there must always be a discriminating and interpreting person participating in all of this or the phrases now being discussed will have no purpose in the attempt to understand the learning process, the tests of it, and the materials that are offered to help the student understand space and the intellectual organization of all the symbols used to express space. There certainly must be a very clear understanding of what phrases like *spatial relationships, position in space* and *spatial orientations* include and imply if the academic relevancies are to be understood. This is certainly true if there is to be full comprehension that numbers and mathematics are the *language* of spatial directions, distances, sizes and shapes, as well as quantities.

How does one learn the language of numbers? How does anyone learn any language? A story told to me back in the early 1960s is worth retelling. This account came from what the media calls a "very reliable source"—an individual with whom I was discussing the visual problems the astronauts might be facing. There had been a frantic search for mathematicians with the concepts and "number expertise" needed for the space program paperwork. Finally, 19 such experts were found who were judged capable of coping with the problems then existing. The biographies of these 19 revealed that 17 of them were products of the rural, one-room schools that were so much a part of the educational system in the early years of this century. This single fact did not really impress the searchers except to make them realize that the original one-room, rural school did have some very special characteristics and educational advantages. Further analysis of the candidates' personal backgrounds brought attention to the extra-curricular activities of these individuals. All walked the distances between home and school and, in so doing, undoubtedly explored every possible route and details of the space in which they lived and moved. These students would know the shortest and quickest way to get to their destinations in sub-zero weather. They would have learned that it took fewer long steps when they hurried than it did when they could make the same journey at their leisure in spring-fever season. They learned that six long steps could take them farther than nine short steps, that the number 6 could sometimes represent a space that was larger than that represented by the number 9, that numbers could have a useful conceptual inconsistency. In all of the routes available to them between home and school, they had the opportunity to understand the differences in the time it took to make the same trips—how to count out more time if one wished to be tardy, or how to count out less time if there was something special at the end of the trip. Thus, as Einstein so emphatically expressed it, space and time were relevant and numbers were the language of both time and space. Probably without even realizing what they were doing, these 17 youngsters were learning the meanings and applications of the numbers to which they were being exposed in arithmetic class. They learned that addition was the expression of moving forward in space, that subtraction was the expression of moving backward in space, that multiplication was the expression of moving forward in groups, and that division was the expression of moving backward in groups. They discovered in the daily visual-motor experiences of traversing and exploring real space, how to understand and manipulate the symbols of the abstract space that NASA needed to master.

About this time, several first and second grade teachers came to me to discuss a classroom situation that had caught their interest. These were capable, experienced teachers who had been involved with this age children for a number of years. They reported that their students were rather suddenly showing what these teachers considered to be spectacular gains in arithmetic concepts—that the children were doing math problems with ease and understanding not previously observed. One very noticeable gain was evident in the children's comprehension of subtraction. Not being a classroom teacher, I could not offer any reasonable explanation. However, knowing that children of this age usually played games that frequently included applications of what they had experienced in the classroom, the suggestion was made that the teachers go out with the children at recess to see what they were doing. There were groups of children playing astronaut, standing still while they counted: "10-9-8-7-6-5-4-3-2-1- BLASTOFF!" and then running their races. It then occurred to all of us that playing astronaut was an application of using numbers backward instead of the already familiar counting forward. Here were the experiences that let the children learn how numbers can also express directionality, and this greater understanding of the language of numbers then brought them greater understandings of the arithmetic lessons.

This entire matter of spatial relationships and spatial orientations is so very important to intelligent and productive behavior that time and space can be given to one more example. The spatial orientation abilities of a 44-year-old *totally sightless* businessman can bring broader understanding to all readers. Jim Kibben was the owner-proprietor of a successful specialty hardware company, a company that supplied the unusual and more elaborate hardware to designers and builders of showplace homes. This business demanded that Jim travel to many parts of the nation so he could be sure he was obtaining the type of hardware he wanted. Since he could not choose these items from catalogues and felt he could not fully depend on a salesman's verbal description, Jim insisted upon personal *touch* inspections of the pieces he wanted.

Jim had been totally blinded by the ingestion of a wrong medical prescription in his mid-20s, and chose this business because he could use touch to be confident every stock item was exactly what he wanted and what his customers were ordering. It is important to remember that Jim had 20-plus years of usual sight-vision development, during which time he had achieved excellent skills in visual-motor coordinations, visual spatial judgments, and visual memory. Although the wrong medications destroyed his *sight,* it had little negative influence on the *visual* abilities he had achieved. In fact, when he was faced with the hard fact that he could no longer see, he was intelligent and determined enough to go on with his life as if he could see just as others did. He expressed only one complaint—he did not have a glimmer of brightness that would assist him in his orientation to his surroundings.

I met Jim at a convention of the South Dakota Association for Retarded Children in Rapid City, South Dakota, where I was lecturing on the importance of visual-perceptual development in all children and was illustrating my lecture with projected diagrams and pictures. One of these challenged the audience to make interpretations from clues that were not singularly obvious (see Figure 5 in Chapter III). The picture shown demanded the ability to get the most visual information from the fewest visual clues. Suddenly, a gentleman in the back of the auditorium spoke out: "Hey, give me some verbal clues. I cannot see that picture at all." I could not understand the wave of laughter that followed this man's comment. After the lecture, Jim came forward to express his appreciation for having heard some explanations of why he could "see so well" when actually he could not "see anything." This serendipitous meeting resulted in a friendship that brought many extensions to an understanding of spatial orientation. Jim became a "research project" for two intensive weeks in the Ohio State University Experimental Psychology laboratory of Professor Samuel Renshaw. Here, hour after hour, Jim permitted a group of 26 behavioral optometrists to study and probe the visual abilities he had achieved *because* of his total blindness. The greatest interest and the most observations were directed at how Jim could so successfully interpret the environment in which he found himself. How could this man travel all over the United States by himself on his buying trips without a companion or seeing-eye dog? Jim finally explained that he would never have a dog because that would be admitting the dog would know the way around better than he would! The many hours we spent with Jim gave us the secret to Jim's unusual travel abilities.

This particular group of optometrists, who spent time each summer at the Ohio State University for study and research, stayed in the Deshler-Wallich Hotel in downtown Columbus. It was necessary to walk through a complex arrangement of lobby and front desk areas to reach the elevators to the guest rooms in the Wallich Tower. This involved a number of turns and several sets of steps to several landings to a passageway from the hotel to the tower. Jim asked to be slowly led through this maze when we first arrived at the hotel. He could be observed going through the process of visualizing and organizing a "mental map" of the route that had to be taken by all of us. The very great difference in the behavior demonstrated by Jim and the rest of the group was obvious to all. We individuals with the usual sight abilities unthinkingly steered ourselves through this maze using basic *sight* signals while Jim was using a tremendously efficient *visual-motor* organization to move safely and quickly through the same areas. We would try to lead Jim through a different or a wrong route, but we were completely unable to trick him. Here was a vivid example of spatial orientation ability developed to a high level of skill and reliability. Here was an individual who had so well integrated his directions and distances of movements, his visualizations of the spatial characteristics of the areas through which he had to move, and all of the bits of information he could gather and integrate from tactual and auditory inputs, that he had built an exceptional skill in spatial orientations. Here was an individual who knew and understood his surroundings better than those of us who took all of these integrations for granted because we had the primary guidance clues from a fully intact sight-vision complex. Jim repeatedly demonstrated to us, in numerous ways, what spatial orientations were really all about as we observed him in the actual process of "reading" and organizing all of the information he needed to achieve the mastery of the space he occupied. He clearly showed us the relevancies that must exist between an individual's egocentric locus and the contents and characteristics of the spatial environment. Here we discovered the secret to Jim's ability to travel all over the country—it was his splendid visual memories that he held after being guided through a locality once by another person, a person who probably did not "see" the locale as well as Jim did!

What Jim taught us—probably better than many other things he taught us—was that spatial relationships are much, much more than mere placements and positions of objects, diagrams, numbers, letters and words in relation to each other. There must be a person in this process who is making discriminations and judgments about the relationships that must exist to him if spatial mastery is ever to be achieved. Certainly, *position relationships* or *locations* may exist between inanimate objects or symbols, but *orientations* cannot develop without the participation of a live, thinking, and analyzing human being. Further, no illustration of object or letter *positions* can be a reliable probe of *orientations* unless the viewer has achieved orientation skills by moving through, visually, tactually, and auditorily inspecting and discriminating all these bits of information for the final decision on the values and use of this information.

The only difference between Jim and the mathematicians was in how they acquired their primary clues. The space math experts used their own sight inputs while Jim had to use the sight inputs of a companion. From that point on Jim and the mathematicians developed and enhanced their abilities of spatial orientations by primary experiences of visual-motor discriminations and decisions, by primary experiences in the process of developing visual memory and the enhancement of these in the ultimate process of applying them to everyday life situations. Jim and the math experts—and even the first and second grade children—again prove that if the background of spatial experience is not there, the simplistic test patterns will not have any value as criteria of an ability that is so important to classroom performance. In other words, any ability to make judgments of spatial relationships existing among patterns on paper must come out of an individual's primary experiences with spatial relationships and his spatial orientations in the real world and the magnitude of the individual's integrations and internalizations of these experiences. A youngster's ability to "see" and accurately identify the similarities and differences in simplistically drawn, meaningless patterns on a test sheet will not necessarily reliably relate to the skills needed for spatial mastery. Much to our regret, there are youngsters who are test and classroom smart and environment and life "dumb." Unfortunately, there are too many students in this latter group coming out of our present educational system.

Figure-Ground Perception

It is most difficult to determine how and why this aspect or quality of the total perceptual process has come to such importance in so many of the tests and training materials being used now. Actually, *figure-*

ground perception is *not* a separate and isolable component of the manner in which the human learns; it is very simply one of several contributors to the interpretations one makes of the world and its contents. And, in the same breath, one must note that it is a very complex quality one brings to the conclusions one reaches in his visual and auditory perceptions of the world and its contents. It certainly is not easy to evaluate because it, like the words one must interpret, depends so much on what experience and knowledge the individual brings to a particular situation. It is a quality and result of the feedback (which was discussed earlier in this book) that one's interpretations bring to the situation rather than just what the contents of the current stimulus might be. Further, since it is such a personal quality that comes from personal discriminations and interpretations, it is not something that can be trained in isolation! It can only be positively and constructively influenced in the overall process of developing and internalizing visual-motor skills, visual memory skills, and all of the qualities and skills of spatial orientations.

Most of the misconceptions surrounding the figure-ground component of the interpretive process have come from the original illustrations appearing in almost every basic psychology textbook. The most common of these is Rubin's Figure (see Figure 9).

Figure 9. This is the well known Rubin Figure, frequently used to illustrate "figure-ground perceptions." Developmentally-oriented optometrists and psychologists know such a figure as an ambiguous figure since it will be perceived as the viewer wishes to interpret it, and is, in reality, an illustration only of the figure the viewer chooses.

The explanation always states: "If you look at the white part of this picture, making it *figure*, the black part becomes *ground*, and you will see a vase or a candy dish; or if you look at the black parts, making these *figure*, the white part becomes *ground*, and you will see two profiles facing each other." First of all, what one does see here depends completely on the viewer's knowing what a vase or candy dish looks like, and what the profiles of two faces look like. The inexperienced child, unfamiliar with candy dishes, vases, and profiles, does not see any of them in this illustration in spite of the fact that an experienced adult (other than a native of the African jungles) will agree that these items are represented by this illustration.

Almost every skillful photographer knows there can never be a choice between figure and ground. These are not separate entities in any picture and have a ratio of influence on each other in making a picture that will assist the viewer to "see" it as a "good" picture and that will influence the viewer to bring his interpretations of reality to the picture. What may be chosen as a back-*ground* for an uncompli- cated family portrait, for example, might strongly influence the viewer's appreciations of the portrait—the figure in this instance. The novice with a camera quickly finds that his picture of the Grand Canyon, taken while he stood at the railing on the very edge of the South Rim, was not nearly as interesting as the picture taken a few feet back from the rim. In this latter picture, a tree or a retaining wall gave fore-*ground* to the picture, making the whole canyon view a more attractive *figure*.

An example of all this can be found in the story of a seventh grade geography teacher who decided her photographs of the Western United States would be of greater interest than the geography book pictures. Of course, this example will be much better appreciated if the reader has personally experienced North Dakota (where the teacher was to show her pictures) and Royal Gorge, Colorado (where the pictures were taken). The picture she felt was best of all was taken from the bottom of the Gorge, looking up at the crevice in the canyon wall where the cable car runs up and down at a very steep slope. This was a pretty picture, but when it was projected on the screen in the North Dakota classroom, its composition was almost a duplicate representation of a roadside ditch along a North Dakota highway. The cable car track was a splendid figure in this picture, but it was taken from such a position that it did not have the ground which would suggest the verticality of the canyon walls. On the screen all this looked horizontal because the ground in this picture was too similar to that represented in the interpretations the seventh grade students brought to the picture. The teacher looked at this picture with the perspectives her visit to the Royal Gorge were giving her. The students who had never been there could not possibly find the depths of the canyon or the slopes of the cable car track in this picture. The picture's contents did not present the clues the viewers could translate into anything more than the perceptions they could bring to it. The figure-ground ratios of influence were present in the picture for the teacher but not for the children, and probably not at all in the visualizations of any reader who brings no background of experience to either of the geographic areas detailed here.

Further confusion has been generated by the assumption that a printed word on a white page of the textbook is figure and the rest of the words on the page are ground. Figures 10 and 11 are examples of this confusion. These samples also illustrate the fact that if a scene, a picture, or a drawing contains unknown, unrecognizable, or irrational details, the viewer will find the entire scene or illustration confused and difficult to interpret, and this confusion will contaminate the results and the discriminations of the viewer.

A splendid example of how figure-ground perceptions can be influenced by figure-ground relationships in a picture can be found in the two pictures included. Please, to get the full impact of these examples, do not look at the second picture until you have given the

Figure 10. The daisy at the top of this picture will be disturbing to most who view this picture of lovely snow-capped mountains. The down-growing flower detracts from the viewer's appreciation of the scene and must be ignored or seen as something "wrong"in the picture. Here the daisy takes on figural importance that negatively influences all of the rest of the picture. Print courtesy of STEREO OPTICAL COMPANY, CHICAGO

first picture careful visual inspection. In Figure 10, you will see what appears to be a mountain scene, and your inspections will find a flower growing downward from the top of the picture in a fashion that is not usual for such a flower. The more one looks at this picture the more one must either try to accept what appears to be a daisy growing in a completely unnatural and thus unacceptable manner, or one must completely ignore the daisy and eliminate or suppress it from one's interpretation of the picture. If the viewer can ignore the flower and its surrounding plant growth, this is a lovely picture of a high altitude meadow with snow-capped mountains in the background. Like all such pictures, it takes on added vistas and beauty if the viewer can bring a background of previous experiences from having been in such a locale. But the longer one visually inspects this picture, the more disturbing the daisy becomes because one's familiarity with how daisies grow continues to interfere with the appreciation of this picture. In fact, if the viewer cannot completely suppress the daisy, there is enough discomfort to make one decide to terminate visual inspections of the picture. This can be interpreted as the influence of a *figure* on its contribution to the *ground*.

Now, please look at Figure 11. Here is the same picture but it has been rotated 180 degrees and the daisy with its surrounding growth are at the bottom of the picture, growing as daisies are supposed to grow. Instead of a conflict between a figure on the ground, as there was in the first picture, now there is the full compatibility between figure and ground. Now the picture is seen as a much better view of a reflecting pool that contains the image of the snow-capped mountains that make up the background of this picture. Now, the same picture with the rearrangement of the figure-ground components and the influences that now match one's referential framework become an illustration in which the viewer will interpret more depth and perspective. Careful visual inspection will reveal that these two pictures are exactly alike in every detail. They are exact duplicates, yet the pictures are seen as being very different because the figure-ground relationships have been altered by what is actually a change in the interpretations by the viewer.

These two pictures clearly illustrate the influence that *figure* can have on *ground* and these two demonstrate that there must be a ratio of relevance between them. One might describe the first picture (Figure 10) as having relative values of *figure 7* and *ground 3*. In the second picture (Figure 11) *figure* and *ground* are both balanced out at

Figure 11. Most viewers will immediately recognize this as the same picture presented in Figure 10 that has merely been rotated 180 degrees so the daisy is now in the position daisies should be in when seen as part of the foliage. Notice now, please, how much more perspective the viewer puts into this picture, and, thus, how much more "real" the picture seems to be. These two pictures illustrate the influence figure can have on ground and what happens if the figural effect is disturbingly incompatible with the viewer's experience. Print courtesy of STEREO OPTICAL COMPANY, CHICAGO

5 each. *Ground* can have even greater influences upon *figure* and usually does in all of the human's interpretations of tridimensionality—"depth perception" as it is illustrated by both the artist and the expert photographer.

Figure 12 is an excellent illustration of the impact *ground* can have on *figure*. Look carefully at the two number 3's in this picture. Which of these is larger? Now, carefully measure each number 3. Here, the *"field forces"* that *ground* provides for this picture and the individual's ability to put tridimensionality into a bidimensional picture bring interpretations of differences that do not actually exist in the picture. Again, it becomes very evident that figure-ground is in the mind of the beholder and cannot be simplistically represented by either ambiguous figures, or in what might more accurately be identified as overlaid patterns.

Now that there has been this clarification of what the phrase *figure-ground* really refers to in the overall visual interpretations of both pictures and the visual world surrounding all of us, there is a need to

Figure 12. This photo illustrates the impact of ground upon figure, and this can be seen in the apparent sizes of the two number 3's. If one carefully measures both 3's, they will be found to be exactly the same size. If the perspective one puts into this picture can be suppressed (by masking or turning the picture on its side) the numbers will appear to be the same size. Once again, it is not what one sees but how one interprets what one sees. Print courtesy of STEREO OPTICAL COMPANY, CHICAGO.

give some attention to the practice materials and test patterns that the programs under discussion contain. As is evident in the examples shown in Figures 13 and 14, both programs are like the mountain pool scene (Figure 10) where the daisy is confusing because of its irrelevance to the total picture. In both Figure 13 and Figure 14 there are so many overlaid patterns that the actual pattern the youngster is supposed to see is difficult to find. Neither of these two are good examples of figure-ground relationships. However, these are splendid examples of several other aspects of visual interpretations that could give vital information on the magnitude of the viewer's visual skills if the person using these materials has an understanding of these visual skills. Both of these samples demand the skills of shape and form constancy—what the behavioral optometrist calls *visual shape constancy*—the ability to see the hidden shape in spite of all the perceptual confusion and scatter that has been added by other forms and other shapes laid over the pattern the viewer is expected to decipher and decode.

Figure 13 brings in another factor of the visual shape constancy that

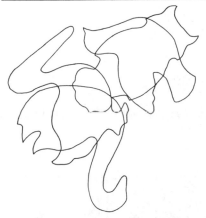

Figure 13. This is not an actual page out of the Frostig program, but it is an illustration of the sort of diagrams used by Frostig as an exercise in the discriminations of what mistakenly has been identified as "figure-ground perceptions." The challenge here is to find a particular figure in spite of the overlapping and interwoven lines that might confuse the viewer because these are considered to be ground.

needs comment. As in several of the actual Frostig practice pages, there are shapes with which many children have had no experience. There is one of the original Frostig pages that contains drawings of hats, one of which is a Russian Shako style hat. Not only is this sort of hat completely strange to most young children, it and several of the others are not in the positions in which hats are usually pictured. Thus, the child's ability to recognize these hats might be so influenced that the entire page is confused. The visual shape constancy needed to recognize these hats, in spite of their unusual positions, is another probe of the visual skills the child has or has not achieved. Figure 13 illustrates such a situation by having a swan as one of the patterns. Not only is this bird in a position not usual for swans, too many young children have no familiarity with swans, and the confusion inherent in this page denigrates all of the visual discriminations and interpretations the child should be bringing to this material. Instead of an exercise in figure-ground recognitions, such pages could be exercises in confusion.

Very interestingly, the alert child will find a novel solution to all this confusion, especially if a teacher has outlined one of the objects to illustrate what the child is expected to do. The alert child will note that if he puts his pencil on any one line, traces it without stopping or turning at any intersection of lines, his pencil will eventually return to the starting point he chose and—lo and behold—he has "found" one of the patterns. Thus, through movement, he can search out and outline each of the patterns without ever really seeing them as individual patterns with other patterns overlaid. Again, he completes the busywork without any practice in the visual shape constancy, or figure- ground factors the page designer thought it contained.

Figure 14 illustrates possible confusions in test materials, confusions

Figure 14. These patterns are not duplicates of any of the test pages, but do illustrate the sort of patterns presented as "figure-ground perception" tasks. Please note that the comparison sample in the middle of the bottom three is near enough like the given pattern (the top one) to challenge the size and shape constancies the viewer might have achieved. The instructions for such test items are: "Look at the top picture and then find where it is hiding in one of the bottom squares." The overlaid lines in the bottom three pictures have been added to provide the scatter that can confuse and distract the viewer from the answer the test designer hoped this sort of test page would elicit as a "measure of visual perceptual" skills.

that really do not test either figure-ground interpretation abilities or the visual constancy skills.

Although my primary interest is in the visual aspects of all the popular tests of perception, it should also be made clear that there is a consistent consideration of the intimate relevancies that exist between vision and audition. Since these two information processing modes are the only long-distance receptors the human enjoys, their influences upon each other are very important in any discussion of figure-ground relationships. Vision is the more accurate function of the two because it operates on line-of-sight where repetitions of inspections are possible. Audition operates in a more general way where locations and discriminations must almost always be quite instantaneous. In spite of these differences, these two abilities have many similarities and figure-ground perception is one of these.

Auditory figure-ground perceptions play a strong part in every waking moment in this noisy world. There are developmental factors in auditory figure-ground that are evident in early infancy. The infant may not establish the sleeping patterns everyone desires in a vacuum of total household silence. There frequently needs to be some of the usual and common household noises as background, and many infants have difficulty sleeping through a time period that is too quiet. Many parents have found that the commercially-available imitation of the mother's heartbeat gives a fussy infant a figural detail within the background of household noises that assists the infant to calm. A ticking clock in the infant's bedroom provides a background noise allowing a figure-ground pattern the infant's auditory system can hold, dismiss, or "turn off" as desired. Some adults become so fully adapted to figure-ground balances, there is usually no interfering problem or confusion. However, the individual who is habituated to the steady business machine noises of a busy office frequently cannot work efficiently in that same office when all of those machines are silent. These individuals complain of its being too quiet to get any work done. One of the gross deficiencies of the carrels designed to "cure" distractibility and hyperactivity in some children was the way they disturbed the auditory figure-ground perceptions the children needed to maintain attention on the schoolroom tasks. When the task is seen *directly in front* of the child and the teacher's voice is coming from *somewhere in the back* of the child, the dislocations can be very distracting. Then, there is the student who has the radio tuned to a music station while doing homework. Is it possible this music supplies a background that eliminates the many home noises—noises of high personal interest, noises which distract, while the music does not?

The Bell Telephone Company conducted some interesting research in this area about 45 years ago. The researchers built a completely soundproof room—a room so completely baffled that the walls, the floor, and the ceiling absorbed 100% of any noise produced in this room. It was so sound absorptive that voices literally "died" in it, and one person could not hear a word spoken by another person. What it led to was the knowledge that a certain amount of background noise had to be put into the telephone lines so there would be a ground against which the voice of the speaker would be figure, thus bringing the best possible transmissions of telephonic conversations. If one listens carefully, a faint sound can be heard between the words being spoken by the other person on the line. This is the noise the telephone engineers put into the line after they found the best figure-ground ratios to give the general population the auditory comfort and the clarity of speech the line is expected to carry.

There is now too much indisputable evidence that the tests used to judge a student's school performance will have to be designed carefully enough so they are realistic probes of the abilities needed in school. Even more important perhaps, the authors/designers of these tests should have a solid background in human development and especially in the development of the learning process. Even then, such tests must be judiciously used to ascertain what *abilities* the individual has achieved instead of simply totaling the number of *mistakes* made as compared with thousands of other students' performances on these same tests. The most critical need is for tests that will compare each of the components of perceptual development with all the other factors of physiological development so the individual's personal needs are fully identified regardless of any esoteric label used to categorize this individual.

Perceptual Constancy, Visual Closure

Although each of these perceptual abilities is treated quite differently in these two tests, there are many similar interpretations given to them. These two labels are being used to describe the visual abilities an individual has in recognizing shapes, letters, words, or numbers, no matter what spatial positions they might occupy or that these same items can be correctly recognized even though parts of them are missing. The visual ability supposedly tested here is what the behavioral optometrist and the experimental psychologist call *shape and size constancy*. The clinicians just mentioned use this phrase to imply that the individual has an interpretive model so well established that no matter how the object or its representation appears, it will be recognized as if it were being viewed in its usual and "correct" position. Some clinicians refer to this as "stenciling," the mental act of comparing or matching with a "stencil" or a pattern one carries in one's mind. For example, no matter how the letter "a" might be rotated or flipped, one's perceptual constancy would bring the immediate recognition of it as an "a." Or no matter how small a friend will appear when standing a city block away, one knows he really is six feet tall. No matter how completely a face fills the cinema screen, the viewer knows this is a usual-sized face belonging to a usual- sized person. This shape and size constancy is not inherent, and the infant will repeatedly demonstrate the learning process that must be fully experienced to establish such a skill. It becomes a very important part of all classroom discriminations and decisions when mastery of all printed symbols is required.

The most common challenges to these abilities are found in the parlor game of charades and the popular television shows, "Wheel of Fortune" and "Win, Lose or Draw." Now also gaining popularity is the game "Pictionary." Each of these games provides some clues, and the viewer is challenged to complete whatever the clues suggest. Another similar activity popular with youngsters are the "hidden objects" pictures in children's magazines where many items must be found hidden in the drawing. The greater the perceptual constancy and visual closure skills the viewer has achieved, the quicker the answer will be found with the least number of clues. The constancy factor is that degree of reliability one can exhibit by his familiarity with shapes, numbers, letters, or words regardless of omissions or distortions. The closure skill is exhibited in the speed and accuracy in recognizing an incomplete shape, letter, or word from the least number of clues. How quickly can one fill the gaps in the puzzle? Once again, the ability the viewer has achieved will be a derivative of primary experience and learning in each of the perceptual areas already discussed in the preceding paragraphs of this chapter.

These skills are much more useful in life than just for playing games. The very process of learning how to think depends on the reliability of one's accumulated knowledge—or constancy factor—and the conclusions one must reach when all of the information needed has not been provided—the closure factor. Taking what bits of information have been gleaned, thinking these through with confidence that this information is reliable, then projecting this information into the possibilities that may exist, thinking on through to a conclusion, and then the result—is what can properly be labeled intelligent behavior. The design of some tests and some test materials contain so many clues, the student being tested may not have to do much thinking to get the "right" closures and hence the "right" answers. This is especially true of test pages in which the test pattern is constantly present for the student's repeated visual inspection. In such instances, the supposedly "hidden" pattern is easily deciphered even by the student who may never have seen anything like it before. The immediate comparison of patterns that are fully visible makes the matching quite easy—the "answer" is provided by "stenciling" with the test pattern. This is similar to so many verbal questions put to students that include the answer in the question. For example: "This is a picture of a horse, isn't it?" The alert student quickly learns to listen carefully for an answer within a question. In such instances, the student need bring neither perceptual constancy nor closure to the task. However, when the question is: "What do you see in this picture?" the viewer must explore his background of picture constancies and come to closure out of his experientially based conclusions. Whether it is a visual question or a verbal question, if the clues are too obvious, the student need spend neither time nor energy thinking about it. The evaluation of much of the primary grade testing materials shows this error in design and the absence of any need for thinking on the part of the student.

There are 11 pages of patterns in the MVPT package that are offered as tests of visual closure. An example of these is shown in Figure 8. Here a complete drawing is given and the student is expected to choose one of the three incomplete drawings that will be the same as the test pattern if and when the lines are extended so as to complete the drawing. Since this is a "motor-free test," the student is not allowed to actually draw these lines; it is to be done mentally as if the lines were being drawn. Here there is another perceptual trick available to the student being tested. It is an ability called "perceptual filling" by many research psychologists and is the ability to visually fill the spaces between unfinished lines as if the lines were there. This is the visual result experienced when one looks at a dotted line and instead of seeing that it is a lot of dots, interprets it as a solid line. There is some significant research that strongly suggests the human retina has neurological structures that are especially capable of this filling to complete the signals the retina then sends to the brain.[18] Thus, the completion of unfinished drawings is not so much a process of understanding the test pattern as it is a result of an inherent neurological function, and this does not then actually prove the thinking processes called closure.

There are two related abilities upon which visual closure skills must depend. One of these is the motor patterns established in the visual-motor coordinations previously discussed, and the other is the visual memory skills the learner has developed. It would then seem likely to follow that these two labels are just another two names for the same processes. Is it possible, then, that if one were well enough informed and alert enough to the nuances of the observable performance of an individual, that reliable judgments of these abilities could be obtained in one probe—one that is sensitive enough to avoid subjecting a youngster to still another test that does not tell anything new about the performance being judged? If this is a reasonable possibility, what performance might provide such information?

There have been frequent, and rather pointed, references to the act of writing and the skills involved in it. Numerous optometric clinicians, after many observations and discussions, and with the very carefully conducted studies of Darell Boyd Harmon, educational psychologist (see Chapter VI), have come to the conclusion that careful analysis of an individual in the act of writing will hold the clues to all of those abilities discussed thus far in this chapter. In addition, what the individual actually gets down on paper brings significant clues to the skills of perceptual constancy and visual closure. As a starting point in this analysis, let us take a look at *how* an occupant of the usual primary classroom gets into the action called writing.

The majority of youngsters in today's classrooms are given pencil and paper and then are immediately expected to make the various marks on paper that represent the letters of the alphabet and the basic 10 shapes we know as numbers. There is no time spent showing these young students how to hold the pencil so there will be none of the "white-knuckle-cramped-fist" grip that interferes with the muscle movement patterns needed for perceptual constancy. It is well established that the ubiquitous "white- knuckle-cramped-fist" grip brings stress and fatigue that almost immediately prevents or eliminates perceptual motor organizations and comprehension of what is being done. These are the very perceptual organizations of the graphic patterns the child should depend on for both shape and size constancies. The youngster who has not learned the "feel" of the *"b"* and the differing "feel" of the *"d"* is the youngster who has to spend extra time pondering how to produce each of these letters correctly. Too frequently, this is the same youngster who continues to "reverse" them as a result of the confusions being experienced.

This confusion is always much more evident while the youngster is *drawing* manuscript letters, partly because of the "line and circle" similarities in so many of these *printed* letters. Somehow, someone with a very limited understanding of the learning process, and even less understanding of the developmental process within the learning process, "armchairized" that it would help children learn to read if the letters the children put on paper looked like the letters in their readers. If these "armchairizers" had thought it through more carefully, they would certainly have realized that shape and size constancy is what gives the learner the ability to recognize letters and words, regardless of the distortions they might contain. They should have realized that it is the meaning and context of the sentence that actually determines what words the reader sees. If this were not true, the great, and frequently horrible, variations in people's handwriting would never be deciphered. We all have the daily experience of being able to decipher someone's scribble by first deciphering the message the writer is sending. There is undeniable evidence that cursive letters hold more individuality and shape/size distinction than do the manuscript "line and circle" letters. This same evidence shows there are few, if any, of the confusing "reversals" that plague the learner thrust into drawing manuscript letters. The cursive *"b"* and *"d,"* the cursive *"p"* and the cursive *"q"* are excellent examples of the differences in the visual-motor perception patterns that help the learner avoid "reversal" mistakes. Interesting, isn't it, that so many youngsters who attended Catholic parochial schools a generation ago, who were immediately introduced to the proper way to hold a pencil and the proper way to write cursively, very seldom experienced the confusions of reversals?

There is still another aspect of cursive writing needing attention here. If it is properly taught, according to the original instructions of Mr. Palmer and the Palmer Method, the whole arm is involved in the smooth and fluid movements that make the letters. As a result of this whole arm movement and the proper grasp of the pencil, the muscle sense of the distance and direction of the movements required for each letter or number are more distinctly established for perceptual constancy. And this muscle sense with its muscle movement memories then becomes a great contributor to the visual-perceptual complex so fundamental to the visual memory and the visualizations for visual closure.

Inspection of the written materials produced by a student will certainly provide many clues to the adequacy and quality of the visual closure skills. Please look at the following example (Figure 15) of the handwriting of three girls in a "standard" sixth grade classroom. The teacher was told by the curriculum director it was time to move the students into "creative writing" in the language arts classes. Recognizing that many of the students in the class were having extreme problems with any activity that demanded creativity, the teacher struggled with ways to fulfill this curricular assignment. Finally, he came up with an idea he was confident would challenge the students to write and would challenge their creativity by challenging them to outsmart the teacher. These sixth grade students were told they could write as many notes back and forth to each other as they wished as long as the teacher did not catch them doing it. If they were caught, their notes would be read aloud to the entire class by the teacher. Thus, it was a game of doing something usually prohibited and at the same time beating the teacher in his own game. The following notes were passed on to me without being read to the class.

Even just a quick look at this handwriting discloses the absence of the motoric skills for writing. Where are the visual-motor coordinations a student should have? The inconsistencies in the size and shape of the letters discloses the lack of perceptual constancy. Where are the perceptual constancies that should have been achieved in learning to

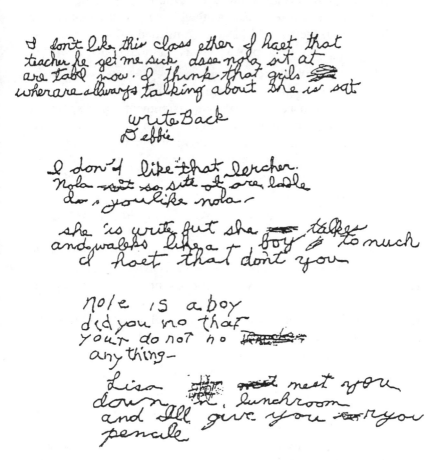

Figure 15. Samples of the writing done by three 6th grade students in a standard classroom.

write? These absences are most evident in the first, third, and fifth notes "written" by the same student. These qualities are also absent in the fourth note showing that a sixth grade student is still printing in manuscript letters. The second note shows the incompleteness of the letter forms which certainly indicates an incompleteness of the motor memory patterns for those letters. Where is there any evidence of visualization skills in any of the five notes? Note, please, the number of words written from a phonetic base that still come out differently each time such words are used. Finally, even the briefest inspection of these notes will certainly bring the conclusion that these three sixth grade students lack some of the thinking skills so extremely essential to their success in communication. Surely, these three youngsters do not vocalize words and sentences as they have put them into these notes. If they did, they would have been hustled off to speech and language therapy. Yet, there probably was no thought about writing therapy for these three girls.

A second sample of sixth grade writing is a page written when this same group was given a creative writing assignment. Since so few of the class could come up with any idea about what they could write, the teacher suggested they write a paragraph about "The Dog Who Lost His Bark." Here in this example (Figure 16) we note that this student lost his train of thought in the stress of trying to "write" the words this paragraph should include.

A columnist by the name of Rehmke, writing in a Los Angeles newspaper, touches all of this issue very well. He wrote: "To think clearly, write clearly. The act of writing down ideas and beliefs often plays a major role in forming them. It forces us to refine our ideas into succinct, logical messages. When friends or associates send us thoughtful replies to our letters, analyzing our views on things and suggesting their own, it furthers our intellectual growth." One would certainly hope that all about which Rehmke wrote will someday happen to these students. If it does not, what is their future in a world that demands such abilities in every aspect of our culture?

In spite of scribbles, the misspelled words, and the terrible sentence structure in these samples, they give excellent insights to all of those visual perceptual qualities and factors the two tests being discussed here are expected to explore—except perhaps those figure-ground qualities that cannot be derived from either the handwriting or the printing so laboriously completed. The alert, informed educator and the alert, informed clinician from whom vision development help is sought will certainly find many clues in this elaborate task that demands advanced skills in visual-motor coordination. Observation of children in the act of writing will reveal how much postural and visual stress is present as they strive to complete such a task. The analysis of the graphic product will provide a wealth of information about the children who must spend so much time completing workbook pages. There is increasing evidence that handwriting practice and the resulting achievement of handwriting skills can be the major contributor to the development of almost every perceptual ability the learner needs. Handwriting cannot be the panacea of all learning problems, but it cannot be overlooked as the major key to the mastery of our language and the communication abilities so essential to success in our culture.

There are three other clinical procedures that can provide many more insights to the developmental levels a child (or an adult) has reached

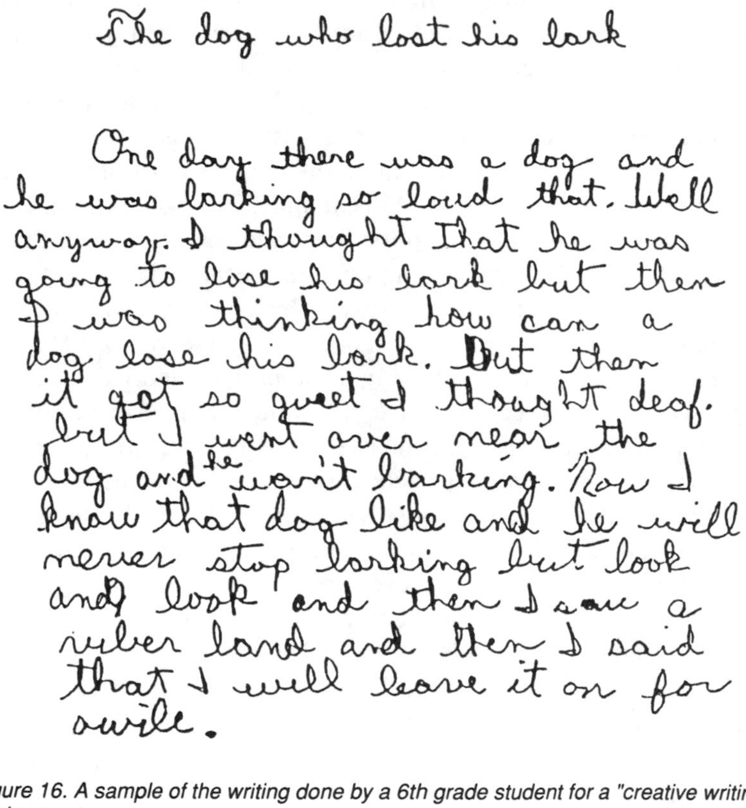

The dog who lost his lark

One day there was a dog and he was larking so loud that. Well anyway. I thought that he was going to lose his lark but then I was thinking how can a dog lose his lark. But then it got so quiet I thought deaf. but I went over near the dog and he wasn't larking. Now I know that dog like and he will never stop larking but look and look and then I saw a ruber land and then I said that I will leave it on for awile.

Figure 16. A sample of the writing done by a 6th grade student for a "creative writing" assignment.

and to his readiness for the academic and cultural tasks he must face. These are not so widely used as those just discussed but they need to be explored here because of their clinical values in providing immediate clues to the interpretive skills of the subjects. Also, these three are specially designed to disclose the manners in which the subjects arrive at their answers. Thus, these procedures give much more attention to the *observable performance* of the individual than they do to the conclusions the examiner reaches in his personal *interpretations* of the performance observed. As a result, the clinical biases of the examiner are more frequently avoided and a truer picture of the subject's abilities is reached. Finally, these three provide excellent examples of the cooperation and communication among clinical disciplines out of which much greater benefits come to the individuals in need.

The first of these three is the *Southern California Sensory Integration and Praxis Test* developed by A. Jean Ayres, Ph.D., for occupational therapists who are now more widely involved in the evaluation and treatment of children identified as having learning problems. This battery of tests has been "standardized" for children ages 4 through 10 and for the "learning-disabled child with average intelligence." It does contain some tests that fall into the same categories offered by the Frostig and MVPT tests and therefore contain some of the minor discrepancies already discussed. For example, the Space Visualization Test, the Figure/Ground Perception Test, and the Position in Space Test are all presented as being "motor-free" because the subject does not "use a pencil to draw his answers." This is a surprising aspect of this battery since its designer, as an occupational therapist (OT), had primary interests in the motoric organizations of the individuals being tested. This designer seems to have fallen into the same trap as others in thinking that because there is no need for pencil drawings, there are no backgrounds in motor experiences on which the subjects' perceptions are based. On the very positive side, 19 of the 22 tests in this battery demand overt, observable performances of the subject in situations that can immediately reveal the level of motoric skills which have been achieved. In all but the three subtests, judgments are made of the actual movement skills achieved rather than on the examiners' interpretations of the subjects' interpretations of pictures and diagrams that are only visually inspected.

The expressed concepts behind this battery of tests are pertinent to this chapter on methods of appraisal and evaluation. In spite of the emphasis on "dysfunction" and the use of these tests to find out what is "wrong" with the youngster, there is a very positive point offered in the definition given to "sensory integration dysfunction." This definition states: "Sensory integration dysfunction (occurs) when the brain essentially is not organizing the flow of sensory impulses in a manner that gives the individual reliable and precise information about self and surroundings." The added comment is made: "Sensory integration dysfunction is to the brain what indigestion is to the digestive tract." The appeal in this statement is the clear implication that the lack of intermodal integrations is the cause of the problems instead of giving credit to the symptoms, which are too frequently stated as the cause. In addition to this, there is emphasis placed on what the child can actually accomplish in each of the subtests. In spite of the fact that each child is scored against national standards, there is the constant emphasis on the clinical observations of overt performance and the developmental histories of each child.

There is one portion of this battery that will certainly attract the attention of many optometrists. This part contains tests of eye movement abilities, ocular pursuit skills, convergence ranges, and "quick localizations" or what the optometrist identifies as "saccadic fixations." These are tests originally designed and widely used by optometrists and generally considered as optometric "property." Here are a number of optometric tests being conducted by members of another clinical group, and some optometrists will wonder what the OTs' reactions would be if their tests were being used by those who were not OTs. The optometrists who are disturbed by this would claim "trespass and encroachment" and would demonstrate some of the same resentments being expressed by some members of the medical profession who feel their "secrets" are theirs alone and are not to be used by anyone who has not had medical training.

On the other hand, there are a number of behavioral optometrists who feel there is more and more need for interdisciplinary exchange of concepts and procedures as long as all involved understand and make proper applications and interpretations of the performance being evaluated. A. M. Skeffington, O.D., who has been widely recognized as one of the greatest single contributors to the development and the clinical progress of the optometric profession, frequently spoke to this point. "If another profession can use optometric concepts and procedures so patient benefits result, then these procedures were not the private property of the optometric profession in the first place. If optometrists can use concepts and techniques from other clinical disciplines with proper insights and applications so there is patient benefit, then these concepts and techniques were not the private property of the other profession. The issue is not to whom the knowledge belongs but how can disciplines cooperate and communicate for the greatest welfare of the public and especially the child in trouble." Many behavioral optometrists are happy to share knowledge if it will be used properly and thoroughly in the appraisals of the problems now being clearly recognized by a number of disciplines. If, on the other hand, there are confusing interpretations being made and inappropriate conclusions being reached, the confusions about children's performance can be multiplied instead of eliminated. Here again is the express need for communication among disciplines and the most effective programs for the ultimate benefit of so many individuals.

Whatever the present situation may be, or what the near future will bring in this reach for communication between professions, the fact remains that this entire series of tests used by occupational therapists brings more attention to *abilities* than it does to *disabilities,* and this sets it out as one that should be given much more consideration in the total search for understandings and solutions.

The second procedure that is becoming much more widely used and now gaining greater respect is the *Structure of Intellect Learning Abilities Test (SOI-LA).* This has been designed by Mary Meeker, Ed.D., and Robert Meeker, Ed.D., and should be thoroughly investigated by every clinician and educator having *any* responsibility for the education of children.[34] This test is best described by using statements taken directly from the test manual. "The basic philosophy of the SOI-LA is that all students have intelligence. The task is to assess 'what kind' not just a global 'how much.' Therefore, every student entering school can benefit from comprehensive assessments of strengths and weaknesses in the many facets of cognitive functioning." The strong emphasis here on the "abilities" and "strengths" certainly attracts me. Further, the subtests are so carefully and cleanly designed that the manner in which the subject completes each subtest gives information that can be immediately applied to his needs in the classroom. (See Appendix C.)

This test of learning abilities is heavily based on the many years of work by J. P. Guilford of the Psychological Laboratory of the University of Southern California from 1950 to 1968 as well as studies by numerous other researchers into human intelligence. This battery of tests has been thoroughly standardized, as required by the statisticians who seek the "normal" behavior levels of large groups of individuals. Of much greater interest to me is the opportunity this battery provides for the immediate clinical observations of the processes by which the subject solves each of the tasks presented. Further, I appreciate this procedure because there is no confusion about the sort of demands placed on the subject being tested, and there are no suppositions about what sort of perceptual or cognitive processes are being expected of the subject. Full recognition is given to the role that vision plays in the total learning processes. The prologue in the manual for the special assessment of vision and its development states: "Vision, like the rest of the brain, also grows, develops, and changes." It is refreshing to find an educator with Dr. Meeker's background who recognizes vision for what it really is and for what it contributes to how the human learns.

The major manual of the SOI-LA briefly discusses the major operations it includes, which are: Memory; Evaluation (critical thinking); Convergent Production ("the process of finding correct answers to problems involving more than just retrieval of information—it is 'rigorous thinking'"); and Divergent Production ("the generation of information where the emphasis is on variety and quality of output, conveniently accepted as creativity. The contrast between convergent and divergent production is the difference between zeroing in and expanding out.") It states: "A final point about operations in the Structure of Intellect model should be made. Because the SOI-LA subtests are pencil-and-paper measures, the mode of the decoding is almost completely visual. Therefore, the operations are visual in nature. The responses required of students, however, may involve visual-motor skills or auditory memory on a few subtests. One justification for emphasizing visual operations is that classroom learning is predominantly based on visual stimuli. Even if directions are presented vocally, they typically are given only once, and then activities move on to books, printed exercises, chalkboard presentations, and other visual experiences. It should be noted that the emphasis on visual attributes among the subtests did not affect the factorial validity or basic structure of the interrelatedness among subtests." (See Appendix C.) It is exciting to find a recognized authority on learning and the development of human intelligence making the point that vision is a significant part of this entire process. This is quite a contrast to those self-appointed authorities who continue to insist that "vision has nothing to do with learning."

There is another reason this SOI-LA test is of value to the theme of this book. It brings added verification of the work by Lyons and Lyons in the early 1950s, which demonstrated statistically the positive effects of optometric visual training on measured intellectual development. Their reports, fully verified by qualified statisticians, show significant increases in intelligence quotients as measured by pre- and post-visual training programs.(35) (See Appendix D.) Here in documented studies from 1962 to the present, the SOI-LA tests show the same sort of gains in intellectual performance.

Here again, the cooperation between educators and optometrists have brought benefits to both professions and through them to a great number of teachers and children. Pre- and post-evaluations of children who have had optometric visual training (vision therapy) have brought significant evidences of the benefits of such clinical care. This continuing interdisciplinary research is already having great impact on many children who have been wrongly identified as "learning disabled." As more and more behavioral optometrists and informed educators communicate and cooperate, more and more children will have the help they need.

The more one studies this SOI-LA test the more evident it becomes that here is a method of judging what the subject is capable of accomplishing rather than itemizing all the failures and the disabilities present. It is much more positive, and as a result, it provides guidance for appropriate assistance, which makes it extremely valuable. It should be thoroughly investigated by all who are striving to help children reach their ultimate achievement levels. It is readily available to every qualified clinician and every educator from Western Psychological Services[36] or from the authors in Oregon.[37]

The last of these three procedures to be given this added consideration is at present (with others interested) used only by behavioral optometrists who are searching for learning-related vision problems. These optometrists do not diagnose nor treat learning problems as such since they are not fully qualified as educators or educational psychologists. As clinicians specifically trained in the evaluation of vision problems and those clinical procedures needed to mediate such problems, they do not use the standardized psychological tests unless they have completed the necessary courses in the use and interpretations of these. In the vast majority of optometric offices, there is the sincere feeling that a full understanding of vision problems is a full-time responsibility.

The battery of probes now being used are not considered as tests for which there are "pass" or "fail" scorings. These routines provide opportunities to make direct and instant observations of how the patient uses his visual abilities for the inspections, discriminations, and decisions needed to complete the tasks presented. Further, these routines offer the patient the opportunity to use manual and verbal abilities as supports and reinforcements needed to complete the task at hand. All this allows an immediate view of the system integrations the patient has achieved, and, thus, is somewhat similar to the sensory integration evaluations provided by the Ayres battery just discussed. It also allows expanded communications between other clinicians and optometrists with the advantages that arise from observations of the same human behaviors without the duplication of non-optometric tests and the possibility of misinterpretations of another discipline's routines. Thus, the informed optometrist can determine what abilities have been achieved, where skill levels are not yet adequate for the tasks the patient must face in daily activities, and what optometric assistance the patient needs to move on into the further development of the visual skills needed. These clinical programs—optometric visual training—are never prescribed as complete solutions to learning problems. They are specifically and individually designed and prescribed to reduce and/or eliminate the visual problems that might be interfering with learning progress.

The developmental optometrist does not assume he is attacking "reading problems" as such and is fully cognizant that "reading problems" are the domain and responsibility of the educator. However, the developmentally oriented optometrist is fully aware of the great possibilities that exist when abilities of visual inspection, visual discrimination, and visual interpretations are enhanced to a higher skill level so that there may very well be improvements in all of the performance related to mastery of the symbols of our culture. Readers are reminded of the discussion of the sight-vision complex in Chapter III.

The greatest plus offered by this uniquely optometric procedure is its reliability in identifying the visual needs of the patient. Here again is a series of observations of abilities and skill levels the patient has achieved in each of the tasks presented. Here, the speed and accuracy of the patient's performance unequivocally indicates the visual abilities this individual is able to bring to the task for the best responses in the least time. Likewise, if the performance is slow, tedious, or confused, the informed optometrist can quickly diagnose the inadequacies so the best clinical help can be achieved from the clinician best trained to provide it.

It is my sincerest hope that this discussion of methods of appraisals and evaluations so widely used—and sometimes so widely misused— can bring about many extended interdisciplinary communications now so critically needed. Such communications will surely allow all concerned to reach for greater successes in meeting the needs of the thousands of students now having unnecessary academic problems and to move into the real basics of learning how to learn.

Chapter VI—"Back To the Basics"

Thereare now many educators and educational columnists urging a "return to the basics," and their recommendations are most intriguing. Since more and more studies are strongly indicating that the primary curricula are too symbolically advanced for primary children, this cry about getting back to basics becomes more interesting until one discovers that the "basic" programs now being touted are still very academic and intensively abstract for the multitude of children arriving at the classroom door without the developmental readiness they need. On the definite plus side is the growing awareness that many changes must be made as quickly as possible.

A conference called by former Labor Secretary Ann McLaughlin and former Education Secretary William Bennett, with the support of former Commerce Secretary C. William Verity, brought educators, government officials, and business leaders together to look at the facts surrounding the gap between what our young people are learning and what they need to know for success in the economic world. Interestingly, not one of the 50 or so participants offered a serious challenge or solution to the report's gloomy thesis. The columnist reporting this forum commented: "No doubt this was partly because the evidence is controvertible, partly because no one was singled out for the blame." Would finding someone on whom the fault could be laid have been considered an incontrovertible action?

The report from this forum further contends: "The problem is not that the schools are less competent than they once were, but that the work is more complex than it ever was." This conclusion sounds to me like a cop-out, or a way to avoid bringing about changes in what the schools should be doing to bring students up to the qualifications needed by a "more complex" workplace.

"Computerization has caused five jobs to be melded into one. What used to be a succession of simple tasks calling for 'specific and splintered knowledge' now requires people with good communication skills and the ability to analyze customer needs; to understand several types of information and to deal with non-standard requests." The question immediately arises: Were the schools of the past better because they trained "specific and splintered knowledge" in which no communication abilities were needed? Or another question: Was it completely adequate that earlier graduates were not trained to have a broader understanding of "non-standard requests" made of them in the workplace? Are these forum participants admitting that the schools are not responsible for the development of thinking skills needed for "broader understandings" required outside the classroom?

A survey of the business executives contributing to this report found two-thirds of them find current job applicants lacking in the baseline skills in reading, math, communication, ordinary problem solving ability, and basic attitudes and work habits. The comments from these executives include:

> "Writing skills continue to decline.... This is the area where we have had to do the most remedial work in the past five to 10 years at all levels."

Hopefully, readers will remember the exchange of notes by 6th grade girls reported in the previous chapter.

> "Understanding numerically controlled manufacturing processes is a major problem area. Employees must be able to understand and use computer-controlled machine tools."

This statement raises two questions about 1) the lack of basic math concepts, and 2) the wide justification of putting computers into kindergarten classrooms.

> "We notice a problem on follow-through ... the inability to think through and take over ownership of the problems they unearth. Such employees tell their customers they cannot help them, or refer the customer to their co-workers, who might know even less than they do."

Here again, one wonders what was left out of classroom explorations of concepts and the conclusions the students were challenged to reach. There is also a huge question about the students' willingness to take risks in the process of developing self-confidence.

> "There is a widespread attitude of 'that is not my job'. Workers need to overcome such attitudes. They are too dependent on specific, explicit instructions."

Isn't this still another indication of students' lack of self-confidence and the inability to think for themselves?

This report continues by quoting Albert Shanker, head of the American Federation of Teachers. Mr. Shanker pointed out that the problem is not that the schools are ignorant of the requirements but that they have not yet figured out how to impart these basic skills to those individuals who will constitute the bulk of the nation's work force. Is Mr. Shanker saying the educational system does not know what the required basic skills are, or that the educational system does not know how to teach these basic skills? Is he saying that the schools cannot meet the developmental components of the total learning process, or that they still have not designed the educational process so it will fit the inherent learning continuum of the human? Doesn't all of this add up to the failures in trying to make the student fit the classroom instead of making the classroom fit the student? How do all of these conclusions provide anything more than another summary of the vast problems that exist? What *really are* the basics to which the educational systems will return in reaching for the solutions to the problems identified by the participants in this conference? The final comment made by Mr. Shanker was: "What is needed is a complete restructuring of American schools." Will this restructuring include a return to the real elemental basics of child development and the learning process, or will it be just another reorganization of class-rooms and curricula so more children pass the tests and look better when compared to the national average scores on these tests? It appears the real question is: Just what is meant by the phrase "back to basics" and what does the educational system think the "basics" are?

" ... a complete restructuring of American schools." If Mr. Shanker had said, " ... a complete restructuring of the American *classrooms*," he would have hit the exact center of the most basic of all basics lying outside of the individual child! There are 999 chances out of 1,000 that he did not even begin to realize what he was saying in that short sentence. If the reader will return to Figure 1 in Chapter I and look at the extreme lower left corner, two words will stand out: *Environmental Energies*. These energies constitute the environment through which every child moves in all of the dynamics of individual development and all of the elements of the learning process. These have had only the slightest mention here because all attention has been directed to the human being we can observe and somehow measure. All of these environmental energies can also be observed and measured but they are so subtle and commonplace they are grossly ignored—except in the contemporary workplace. These energies are especially ignored in the classroom where the usual school architect gives attention only to room size, shape, "adequate" lighting, and "proper" ventilation. If the space allowed is large enough for an average class of 28 to 30 students, has room enough for the teacher's desk and some storage cupboards, has ample lighting and proper ventilation, it is considered totally sufficient by the school board who will finance it. Isn't it interesting that business and industry are spending hundreds of thousands of dollars on the design and manufacture of chairs, desks, adjustable walls, light intensities and arrangement of sources, colors, room temperatures, background music, and programmed rest breaks while the environment in which our children spend so many stressful hours each week is almost totally ignored?

The past few years have brought a "new" cultural science called "ergonomics," now defined as "biotechnology" in recently printed dictionaries. This comparatively new discipline has burgeoned for several reasons. First, the discomforts and reductions in productivity now being blamed on the computer, which predictions place in front of 90% of the work force by the year 2000. Second, the millions of dollars these problems are already costing the business world. Third the thousands of dollars in actual clinical costs the employees attribute directly to the impacts of the negative environmental conditions that surround them. The attention now being given to ergonomics can be totally credited to those adults who emphatically complain about their discomforts, or to the adults who are responsible for the productivity of the work force being supervised. The dollar signs speak very loudly! More loudly than classroom failure does!

It is long past the time for some serious thoughts about the environmental influences that impact upon children who, in their inherent biological flexibility, plasticity, and adaptability, do not so emphatically vocalize their discomforts and the adaptations their bodies make to relieve the stresses, aches, and pains they experience. It is in these critical areas of physical, physiological, and mental development where most of the deleterious adaptations are made that are unseen until the problems become clinically obvious. Research done by educator Darell Boyd Harmon in the late 1930s and early 1940s must be recovered and very carefully studied.[38] This research was done under the auspices of the Texas State Department of Maternal and Child Health, the Texas State Teachers' Association, and a half-dozen other closely related groups. It provides indisputable evidence of how *basic* the classroom environment is to the welfare of all students and especially to those in their most formative years in the elementary grades. Look, please, at the following data on the incidence of organic, functional, clinical, and subclinical difficulties found in the 16,000 children Harmon studied who spent five days a week in 4,000 ergonomically *incorrect* classrooms:

Visual difficulties	53.3% of the students
Nutritional difficulties	71.3% of the students
Postural difficulties	30.2% of the students
Possible chronic infections	75.2% of the students
Possible chronic fatigue	20.9% of the students
Dental difficulties	92.0% of the students

These data, with much, much more, were published in 1949 by the American Seating Company for the American Institute of Architects under File Number 35-B and was copyrighted by Dr. Harmon. Extensive follow-up studies of the children who continued in the control classrooms (those not completely remodeled) brought even more alarming data. Generally, the number of students in difficulties did not greatly increase but each student progressed into more and more serious problems. These same extended studies showed the students with dental difficulties progressed into serious malocclusions; those with nutritional difficulties became more seriously malnourished with severe chronic illnesses; those with visual difficulties demonstrated much more serious problems of progressive myopia and astigmatism; and those with postural difficulties progressed into spinal distortions that became structured into permanent "back problems."

Lamentably, the environmental stresses and the cultural pressures are many times greater now than they were 50 years ago when this significant Texas study was done. The informed, developmentally oriented optometrist of today is increasingly alarmed about the visual problems now being demonstrated by so many children. For example, 50 years ago nearsightedness (myopia) was not an epidemic sight-vision problem until youngsters reached high school or college levels. In fact, it was then first categorized as "school myopia." Today, there are many—too many—children in primary grade levels demonstrating rather extreme nearsightedness. If such problems are found by the alert optometrist, to what extent are all of the other problems existing among today's classroom occupants?

Here was a fully designed and carefully completed ergonomic study done by a state department of health years before anyone thought of the presently popular buzz word for such research. Here was a study far more complete than any being run on adults at that time. Although 50 years have passed, and this tremendously significant data has been lost in the confusions of academia, something must be done to bring as much attention as possible to the basics which have such an impact on the performance of the learning systems of the child who must succeed in the classroom environment. Every primary level teacher attempts to decorate the classroom so there is a constant academic aura to which the children are expected to respond either overtly or subliminally. What is now so sadly overlooked or ignored because of budget constrictions is the biological and psychological influences of proper lighting; the color of the walls, floors, desk surfaces and chalkboards; temperature controls; and most important of all, desk sizes, all of which were fully described in Harmon's publication *The Coordinated Classroom*.[38] If one would walk into 100 classrooms today, *one* may be found in which the desks can be and have been adjusted to fit the various sized children who occupy them. But in the vast majority of classrooms, there will be big youngsters striving to do their work in desks too small for them and other children attempting to finish their workbook assignments in desks too large for them. In both instances, the stresses and discomforts will obviously be interfering with these children's productivity, and eventually there will be physical and physiological problems that not only deter the learning process but that will undoubtedly contribute to hyperactivity, shortened attention spans, perceptual confusions—and the ultimate result—greater absenteeism. All of these negatives exist simply because someone has neglected to adjust each desk height to each child's size. "For want of a nail, the shoe was lost, etc." How long would business and industry put up with such negatives and the obvious results?

If all these statements sound excessive or incredible, please look at the hard, proven, indisputable evidence from the Texas study. The following five charts taken from the original report speak for themselves.

COMPARISON OF SOME HEALTH PROBLEMS FOUND AT BEGIN-
NING AND END OF THE SIX-MONTH EXPERIMENTAL PERIOD

November, 1942 and May, 1943

Becker School, Austin, Texas

PROBLEM	Percent of cases found in November 1942	Percent of cases found in May 1943	Percentage change during six-month period
Visual Difficulties.......	53.3	18.6	-65.0
Nutrition Problems........	71.3	37.2	-47.8
Chronic Infection.......	75.2	42.6	-43.3
Posture Problems.......	30.2	22.4	-25.6
Chronic Fatigue.......	20.9	9.3	-55.6

*Children entering school after November, 1942 eliminated from this table.

Figure 17. It is important the reader understand that the experimental group of children spent these six months in classrooms where all ergonomical conditions were changed to be physiologically and psychologically correct from a developmental perspective. The desk sizes were correct for each child; the walls and ceilings were proper colors and reflectances; temperatures were carefully controlled; lighting was designed to provide the best illumination without glare; and simple body movement freedoms were designed into the desk seats for each child. The curriculum in all classrooms was carefully maintained so there were no variations in this aspect of the academic program. The change was made only in the learning environment, and the environmental energies to which each child responded at subliminal levels.

COMPARISON OF VISUAL DIFFICULTIES FOUND AT BEGINNING AND END OF THE SIX-MONTH EXPERIMENTAL PERIOD November, 1942 and May, 1943 Becker School, Austin, Texas Shown Graphically in Figure 20			
GRADE LEVEL	Percent of cases found in November 1942	Percent of cases found in May 1943*	Percentage change during six-month period
ENTIRE SCHOOL	53.3	18.6	-65.0
Grade 1A	30.7	7.6	-75.0
Grade 1B	35.7	21.4	-40.0
Grade 2A	38.4	23.0	-40.0
Grade 2B	46.1	23.0	-50.0
Grade 3A	58.3	8.3	-85.7
Grade 3B	61.5	15.3	-75.0
Grade 4A	66.6	20.0	-70.0
Grade 4B	72.7	27.2	-62.5
Grade 5A	71.4	21.4	-70.0

*Children entering school after November, 1942 eliminated from this table.

Figure 18. These reductions of visual difficulties came because of the same changes described for Figure 17. The major influences that can be noted for these splendid reductions of visual difficulties can be directly traced to physiologically correct desks, physiologically correct lighting, and physiologically correct desk tops, walls and chalkboard colors. The reductions of the deleterious environmental stresses become even more important when one reconsiders the role that vision plays in the total learning process.

COMPARISON OF NUTRITION PROBLEMS FOUND AT BEGINNING AND END OF THE SIX-MONTH EXPERIMENTAL PERIOD November, 1942 and May, 1943 Becker School, Austin, Texas Shown Graphically in Figure 20			
GRADE LEVEL	Percent of cases found in November 1942	Percent of cases found in May 1943*	Percentage change during six-month period
ENTIRE SCHOOL	71.3	37.2	-47.8
Grade 1A	57.1	57.1	0.0
Grade 1B	53.3	13.3	-75.0
Grade 2A	80.0	33.3	-58.3
Grade 2B	80.0	66.6	-16.6
Grade 3A	71.4	28.5	-60.0
Grade 3B	85.7	21.4	-75.0
Grade 4A	73.3	33.3	-54.5
Grade 4B	84.6	30.7	-63.6
Grade 5A	57.1	28.5	-50.0

*Children entering school after November, 1942 eliminated from this table.

Figure 19. The emphasis on adequate and proper nutrition is much greater today than it was in 1943 but the fact that even the most adequate nutrition may be negated by the environmental stresses must be given much more attention. When one realizes that nutritional problems can almost immediately lead to chronic illnesses and greater absenteeism, one can comprehend the importance of the learning environment that is most conducive to the learning process. The pediatricians who contributed to this Texas study were agreed that the proper desks, the proper lighting, and room temperatures were the primary factors in the nutritional aspects of this study.

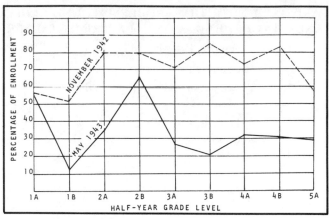

Comparison of visual difficulties found at the beginning and end of six-month experimental period (November, 1942 to May 1943) at the Becker School, Austin, Texas

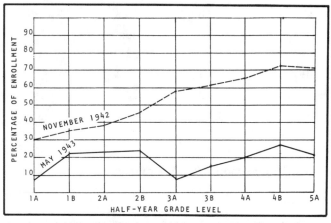

Comparison of nutritional difficulties found at the beginning and end of six-month experiment period (November, 1942 to May, 1943) at the Becker School, Austin, Texas.

Figure 20. These two graphs merely present the same data in a more visible form.

   Since this book is an attempt to bring fullest attention to child development and dynamics of the learning process, there is another chart from the Texas study that the reader must examine carefully. This is the report on classroom progress of those children who had the ergonomically correct classrooms in which to learn. Comparing the experimental school to the control school shows that the children in the experimental classes made academic gains more than twice those of the children in the control classes.

ACHIEVEMENT GROWTH BY MONTHS OF EDUCATIONAL AGE DURING THE SIX-MONTH EXPERIMENTAL PERIOD

November, 1942 to May, 1943

Becker School, Austin, Texas

	Range of growth	Mean change	Median change	Model change	Percent changing 6 mo.or less	Percent changing less than 6 mo.	Percent changing 6 mo. only	Percent changing over 6 mo.
	Months	Months	Months	Months				
Experimental School	0-32	10.2	10.0	10.0	24.0	16.6	7.4	76.0
Grade 1A	0-18	9.8	9.0	9.0	25.0	18.7	6.3	75.0
Grade 1B	0-21	10.8	11.5	10.5	14.2	14.2	0.0	85.8
Grade 2A	4-19	10.9	9.0	8.3	9.0	6.0	3.0	91.0
Grade 2B	4-17	9.4	9.0	9.0	26.6	20.0	6.6	73.4
Grade 3A	6-24	11.7	11.0	10.9	10.5	0.0	10.5	89.5
Grade 3B	2-32	13.5	14.5	14.5	16.6	11.1	5.5	83.4
Grade 4A	5-25	10.9	10.0	10.0	15.3	7.6	7.7	84.7
Grade 4B	4-27	11.8	12.0	11.0	26.3	21.0	5.3	73.7
Grade 5A	3-15	8.9	10.0	11.0	24.1	20.6	3.5	75.9
Control School	-8 to +18	6.8	6.0	6.0	66.6	44.4	22.2	33.4

Figure 21. If one has the courage to ignore all of the physiological facts this study presents, the academic facts cannot be overlooked. The achievement growth (academic gains) of the children in the experimental program was almost two and a half times that of the children in the control groups. Remember, please, the academic programs were exactly alike for all these children in both the experimental and the control groups. The changes were in the learning environment in which the children spent their school hours. It appears that "mastery of the environment" must be achieved by the child before "mastery of the academics" can evolve. Making the environment more supportive and less stressful frees the child to more positively respond to all the teacher presents in the daily lessons.

There is a footnote in the original 1949 publication that must be included here without further comment: "The data and material presented up to this point digests the substance of three of the writer's so-far-unpublished papers: 'The School Environment as a Factor in Growth Deviation,' read before the Sixteenth Annual Meeting, American Academy of Pediatrics, Dallas, December 10, 1947; 'The Classroom as a Factor in Growth Deviation,' presented to the Ninety-Seventh Annual Session, Scientific Assembly, American Medical Association, Chicago, June 24, 1948; and 'Light on Growing Children,' read before the Mid-West Area Meeting, American Academy of Pediatrics, Milwaukee, June 29, 1948, and the Western Area Meeting, American Academy of Pediatrics, Seattle, September 14, 1948."

More than one reader will comment: "How can our classrooms be changed now in these times of such major financial problems in every school district? How can anyone expect that every learning classroom will be completely remodeled with better desks and all the better learning conditions described here?" Please note that the size of the classroom desks has had a lot of emphasis in this chapter. There are several reasons for this. First, almost every desk in every elementary classroom can be sized to fit the child who occupies it each day. All this takes is a few moments of the janitor's time spent while the child is sitting at the desk.

The child is instructed to sit with both feet on the floor and lean slightly forward. Have him bend the preferred arm so the elbow is pointed at the desk. Instruct the child to now swing the arm so the point of the elbow just passes the front edge of the desk. The proper height of the desk for each child is where the elbow just barely flicks the front edge of the desk as the arm is moved across it.

It is also most beneficial if the seat or chair of the desk can have height adjustments. Again, ask the child to sit comfortably with both feet on the floor. The teacher or the janitor should just be able to slip a flat hand under each of the child's legs at the front edge of the seat. If there is too much space between the child's legs and the chair edge, the child will be postured backward with too much pressure on the tailbone, and this will bring discomfort and fatigue that will contribute to restlessness and the resulting loss of comprehension and productivity. If there is none of this space between the legs and front edge of the seat, the child's legs will be strangled, and this will add to the stresses of the desk work.

The proper desk height is more important than just the benefits provided to classroom productivity. The Texas study showed, beyond any doubt, that improper desk sizes were too frequently the early causes of back problems demanding the clinical attention of chiropractors, osteopaths, and orthopedic specialists. The children who have been seated in desks too large for them will characteristically show growth patterns that eventually end up with one shoulder considerably higher than the other; the high shoulder will be the one on the side of the non- preferred hand. Such problems can be serious later in life, and the primary cause can be traced to the wrong sized desk.

Orthodontists also find too many youngsters with a crooked bite, and this, too, can be traced back to the tilt of the body and head when the child is seated in the wrong sized desks during those important growth years between second and sixth grade. To experience this problem, lean forward as if you were seated at a desk. Tip your head to one side and let your mouth and jaw go slack. Now slowly close your mouth, and you will probably find that your teeth do not match. Imagine your child sitting in such a position during the classroom hours, and you will have one of the reasons for what the orthodontist calls malocclusions.

The changes in the classroom that can be immediately beneficial cost nothing more than the teacher's and janitor's attention!

The careful evaluation of these data provides some further details that cannot be overlooked. Some review of the inherent biological characteristics of the human will bring a fuller appreciation of these points. When the human body gets into any sort of "unwellness," one or more defensive systems come into the situation to either neutralize or eliminate the difficulty. If it is an infection such as the common cold, the blood-lymph brings changes in body chemistry to neutralize the pathologic organisms. If this "get well" process is not effective, the difficulty becomes a problem that extends beyond tearing red eyes, runny nose, and dry throat. When the situation reaches the problem stage, external chemical agents are ingested to assist the body chemistry. If the usual over-the-counter "cures" are not effective, the individual finally seeks more extensive clinical care, and eventually the "wellness" process wins out, and the desired healthy status is recovered. This is the "get well" process the entire human body goes into when the difficulty can be internally mediated by the inherent coping systems of the human. The bottom line is that the body will always move toward the optimum level of "wellness" to function the best it possibly can.

There is a contrasting situation that arises, however, when the causes of the difficulties are external in origin, and the body has no internal system with which it can neutralize the sources of the difficulties. These are the situations reported by the data in the above charts. In these circumstances, the body can only make changes in those parts most emphatically impacted in an attempt to make adaptations or compensatory adjustments to the stresses encountered. The most common example of this is the epidemic increase in nearsightedness demonstrated by adults who must spend intensive hours on the computer, or the young children now being thrust into excessive extended near-centered visual stress in academia. In both these instances, the stressor agent is external, and the body has no coping system except adaptations in function and, eventually, in structure. Here the original difficulty raises ocular discomforts, fatigue headaches, and occasional blurriness. When this progresses to the problem stage, there are fewer headaches but more constant blurriness, especially on distant points of view. If glasses are prescribed simply as a "correction"—actually only a compensation—for this distance blur, they are nothing more than a concession to the symptoms. On the other hand, if glasses are judiciously prescribed to reduce the stress that has been instigated by the external influences, and the sight-vision system can then move back toward more effective functions, the "wellness status" is recovered, and the nearsightedness (the adaptation) is controlled, reduced, or eliminated. What is now greatly disturbing the alert behavioral optometrist is the increasing prevalence of nearsightedness that can be almost directly traced to the added stresses which come from the glasses prescribed to temporarily reduce the inconvenience of the sight-vision adaptations to the stress (distance blur). Such glasses are more a concession to the problem than they are a neutralization of the stresses, and the adaptations continue instead of being neutralized. However, because the stresses were ignored and only the symptoms attended to, the distortions increase and become more complex. Again, the bottom line for the deleterious stresses that arise externally are similar to those which arise internally in that the clinical attentions must be directed at the original causes of the difficulties rather than limiting attention to the resulting adaptations and some sort of compensatory remediations. Again, if the functional systems within the human being are given the proper support and assistance, there will be a move back from the less desirable adaptations to the more efficient and effective functional qualities inherently present.[39] All five of the charts from the Texas project show the reductions of the difficulties observed when the external causative stressor agents were eliminated. In several instances, the recovery of "wellness" was very significant.

Please review Figure 20. The solid lines on these two graphs show the increase in visual and nutritional difficulties over a six- month period among the children in the control group where the stressing environmental influences were *not* removed. As reported, the continued observations of these children that extend beyond the specific time period of the research project showed that individual problems became greater and greater. In contrast, the broken lines show that when the traumatizing external conditions were eliminated, there were significant trends back to the "get wellness" stages which, undoubtedly, were more conducive to better academic performance. Even more striking, these data show that if the traumatizing influences were not present the deteriorations would have been *prevented in the first place.*

With fully admitted biases toward vision development and the vision care that is known to bring more adequate visual skills and advanced levels of visual performance, I cannot pass this point without comments about Figure 18. When the children had the advantages of the more beneficial environment, there was a 65% reduction of visual difficulties. This makes an emphatic point—65% of visual problems demonstrated by children in the first five grades—the developmental time when the entire child is more plastic and adaptable—could have been prevented by early elimination of those external causative stressor influences. Since the classroom is so predominantly a visual task, such gains in visual "wellness" should influence academic growth. Figure 21 shows exactly that! When 65% of the visual difficulties were eliminated (along with the other gains in "wellnesses," of course), there were *no* regressions among the experimental group while there were regressions of as much as 8 months among the control group. Individuals in the experimental group showed as much as 30 months' academic gain while individuals in the control group showed no more than 18 months' gain. In summary, there was a 76% academic gain among the children in the experimental group while the children in the control group showed only a 33.4% academic gain. All of this in only six months of the project's time! Since the entire theme of this book is a reach for greater understanding of developmental sequences and the learning process and how these can be most positively influenced, this Texas study seems to be worthy of more than passing notice. How can there be continuing disregard for this fully validated information if there is to be any return to the basics about which there is so much talk?

Unfortunately, this superb report, *The Coordinated Classroom*, has been out of print for a number of years. Of course, it can be found in the Library of Congress, and there are quite a number of behavioral optometrists who have highly treasured copies in their private libraries. Parents are urged to seek out the clinicians who might have a copy so it can be more thoroughly perused. Reading this entire report can provide extensive insights to the impacts of the environment in which children are now placed by our school systems. The outcry about asbestos and disinfectants in school ventilation systems might profitably include the consideration of these even more general environmental problems. While we wait rather hopelessly for some miracles in the classroom, parents can gather beneficial details on study centers in which their children can do their homework more effectively and successfully.

Neither I, nor any parents, have the prerogative to greatly influence the other external environment our children face—curriculum. This is entirely and rightfully the domain of the individual properly trained for it—the teacher. There *is* a domain, however, that is completely under the supervision of the parent and open to suggestion from the clinician. This is the area in which each child should find the concrete meanings and applications of all the teacher has offered. This is the internal domain the previous four chapters have been discussing. Here is where the roles of the "extra-curricular" contributors become so important.

As previously noted, there is no possible way this chapter can fully discuss all of the opportunities open to parents for their guidance and encouragement of the learning processes. Since the most attention has been given to the achievement of manual skills, visual skills, and verbal skills, these will continue to be the focus of all the guidance recommendations. Again, these will be presented in the order of their usual development in the youngsters' "learning how to learn" activities.

The Manual Skills

Before suggesting even one activity to enhance manual abilities to desired skill levels, there must be the reminder that special abilities are derivatives of general abilities. Thus, a few general movement activities must be reviewed and refined before moving into manual activities. The emphasis need not be on general transport (walking, running, jumping) "exercises" but should be much more intensely directed at the movements that demand bilaterality and variations of it into thrust and counterthrust of unilaterality as in skipping and hopscotch. If these seem too juvenile or kindergartenish, there is always the jump-rope routines of the world champion boxer or the ballet of the Super Bowl football player. The goal is much more than time spent in childish routines—the ultimate goal is movement and body balance skills that lay foundations for the arm-hand activities that are completely free and available for the manual skills the learning process must have.

There certainly is no point in suggesting that all children get into sports, but there is one sport activity that provides the greatest opportunities for this basic bilaterality and balance of the supporting structure—the total upright body. This activity is soccer. The very fact that the rules demand no use of hands, that ball control must come out of the use of feet and legs, head, shoulders, and sometimes hips, presents situations in which the player is in visually directed and monitored movements while constantly maintaining the best possible integrations of bilaterality and equilibrium. Of course, ballet training will do the same, but not at the same levels of basic and primitive organization provided by soccer. Add to the elements of bilaterality and balance all the controls of stopping, starting, and the changes and sequences of visually directed movements, and there is a full background for the much more advanced developmental factors of time, intervening space, and the geometry of space in which the child must perform in the efforts to avoid the goalie and still put the ball into the net.

As soon as general movement abilities begin to indicate some skill attributes, every child should be introduced to the more specialized movements of arms and hands. After observing and training hundreds of youngsters over the past 40-plus years, I am completely convinced that a large chalkboard provides learning opportunities unavailable anywhere else. The word "large" in this instance means eight feet in horizontal length and four feet in vertical height. If there is no wall space available for a chalkboard this size, it must not be any less than four feet in horizontal length. Just as in all other areas of skill development, larger general movements must precede the refinements to the smaller, more complex special movements leading to the manual skills of drawing and writing. Thus, the chalkboard must be big enough for the procedures in which full arm and hand movements can be practiced. The sense and concepts of directionality are most emphatically instigated by the signals that arise in rotary joints such as the shoulder socket for the upper arm. Only the rotary joints provide the exploration of *all* directions of movement. The wrist has some rotary movement flexibility but nothing like that available from the shoulder. The large chalkboard provides the surface area on which the full range of multidirectional visually directed and monitored movements can be practiced. If parents have any desire that their children will learn to write, for all the reasons previously discussed in Chapter IV, they will make the large chalkboard available where their children can use it easily and frequently.

Obtaining a large chalkboard need not be a major problem. The big commercial boards are quite costly, so the homemade chalkboard solves the dollars problem. If the full size board is possible, a full sheet of tempered masonite or tempered pressboard provides the very smooth surface needed. Green chalkboard paint is available at many paint stores and will supply the gritty- textured surface the board should have. The regular chalkboard paint must be frequently stirred and several coats are desirable. The board should be painted while it lays flat so the paint does not ripple, or if the board has already been put on the wall, the paint must be carefully brushed out to avoid any ripples. This surface should not be washed! Good erasers and soft cloths will pick up the dust and allow corrections. If this surface is washed with soap and water, it will soon lose the surface texture that makes it so beneficial to the looks and the feel of whatever is chalked upon it.

It is important to note the characteristics of the wall-supported chalkboard as a training and guidance device. The erect posture unique to the human is achieved after 12 to 15 months of practice and experience in all the general movements of infancy. Thus, a chalkboard on the wall provides a surface for performance that is most suitable for a child because it contributes to and matches the child's concepts of directionality that have evolved in the process of gaining the erect posture. This erect posture frees arms and hands so they may become the tools of performance.

Figure 22. Ideally, and to be physiologically most correct, this chalkboard should not be flat on the wall. It should have a 12 to 15 degree slope that puts the bottom of the board slightly away from the wall and closer to the child using it. This is quite important, but if it is not possible because of room design or space restrictions, the chalkboard on the flat wall is still very important to the child's mastery of all the basic movement patterns foundational to drawing and writing. The vertical center should be at the child's eye level. The large pictures produced while your child is standing at the chalkboard assist in establishing directions of hand movement that will make artwork in the classroom more expressive of your child's primary experiences.

The vertical plane of the board is conducive to full arm movements with the child's shoulder as the primary pivot for vertical, horizontal, and diagonal lines. The elbows and wrists enter into the action for the extension and retraction of the hand as it moves over the chalkboard surface. Wrist rotations and finger motions in holding and using the chalk complete the full sequence from the whole arm to the distinct finger control.

The great problems children are having in learning to write are directly due to the stresses and tensions arising from the lack of arm and hand freedom of movement. Thus, most horizontal writing surfaces, such as desks and tables, are cultural in origin and only in recent years have been adapted to a child's body mechanics. There are still far too many classrooms where the desks have not been adjusted to children's sizes and postures, and this is also a major contributor to scribbling. Practice at a chalkboard as described can greatly assist in overcoming the stresses inherent in the flat desk surfaces. When the pattern of movement for writing a word is established in the entire arm, with the balance of correct body postures, the child's writing becomes smoother, more legible, and scribbling is not established as a deleterious habit.

Retarded children have provided us with another bit of pertinent information. They have particularly illustrated that children learn "up" and "down" with ease when it is expressed in their own total body movements. "Top" and "bottom" are learned through activities with objects, toys, and furniture. All of these they can easily and correctly translate to the vertical surface of the chalkboard.

The difficulty arises in the 90 degree rotation necessary to recognize the "top" of a sheet of paper on the desk as the edge farthest away. Frequently, when children are asked to draw a line at the top of the paper, they place it anywhere on the sheet and insist it has been drawn "on the top" because it is the topside surface. When instructed to draw a line at the bottom of the sheet, they will turn the paper over because "bottom" is "underneath" or it is the "down" side. Repetition of instruction, explanation of top and bottom, and drill on paper may not resolve this confusion. Their concepts of top and bottom have come from their experience in body movements; these are not the same as the adult's cultural concepts, and they have no muscular feelings (kinesthesis) for it in their developmental background. The use of the wall chalkboard, followed by its use when slanted at 45 degrees, or the use of an easel, has cleared up this problem so well that it should be almost routine for all children before they are expected to pick up a crayon or a pencil and start the writing lessons.

The child's work at the chalkboard should be patterned after the sequence of development of movement control, just as all guidance is kept in accord with the expected trend and flow of the child through the time-growth-development learning sequences.

The illustrations here all show a large size chalk. This is definitely recommended for the beginner because there is no possibility the child can hold it with the same white-knuckle- fisted grip so common in the use of pencils. The most desirable is the chalk listed by the Dixon Company as Railroad Crayons, and the most visible colored chalk is yellow. This can usually be found in school supply sources. If this particular chalk cannot be found, a triple-sized chalk can be found in many supermarkets. Parents should make an effort to find this chalk. It will certainly assist children in all of the chalkboard activities recommended as beneficial to classroom progress.

There is definitely a best way to hold the chalk, and this is a preliminary to how the child will also hold a pencil. The chalk should be wrapped with masking tape for easier grip and prevention of shattering when dropped. The exact manner in which the chalk should be held is illustrated in Figure 23, and, once mastered, it will enable your child to practice the basic routines that will help him find the arm, hand, and finger combinations preparatory to all the crayon and pencil tasks of the classroom.

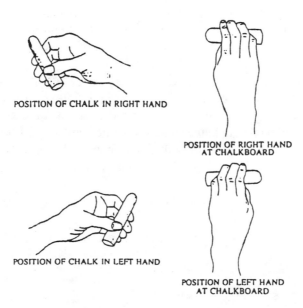

POSITION OF CHALK IN RIGHT HAND

POSITION OF RIGHT HAND
AT CHALKBOARD

POSITION OF CHALK IN LEFT HAND

POSITION OF LEFT HAND
AT CHALKBOARD

Figure 23. Please note that the chalk is held in place across the tips of all fingers by the thumb, instead of held in the usual grasp using the thumb and the first and second fingers, as a pencil is held. This grasp, shown above, allows the full circles without having to "break" the wrist at the bottom of the circles. This grasp, shown here, also permits much more complete proprioceptive signals out of the motor patterns of these circular movements.

1. Bi-manual Circles

The child who demonstrates any degree of spasticity or manual rigidity (which is usually present to some degree in every child having difficulty in school) should work on large circular movements first, using both hands in unison. These should be varied through the developmental directions:

a. Right hand moving clockwise while left hand moves counterclockwise

b. Left hand moving clockwise while right hand moves

counterclockwise

c. Both hands moving clockwise
d. Both hands moving counterclockwise

The use of both hands at the same time in this activity is in no manner intended to influence "dominancy" or "preference" of a hand, but to get all possible control of each hand and to emphasize each in the bilateral relationships. The preference for one hand may well be a product of innate skeletal patterns, as some research has indicated. The eventual preference will come as the child develops more and more hand freedoms and skills and will most likely result from the natural dexterities that come out of movement practice. (There will be some added consideration of "dominancies" later in this chapter.) The important aspect to remember is that the use and development of both hands in basic guidance routines is a prerequisite for any of the more discrete or distinct skills that will then lead to stress-free and fatigue-free writing and refined manipulative actions.

Figure 24. The ultimate goal of this procedure is equally sized and shaped circles, continued and completed while the child holds his visual attention on a chalked spot on the chalkboard that is in the center of the area between the circles. This not only provides the opportunity for the rhythm and coordination of the arms and hands, it provides a constant opportunity for the development of the visual peripheral judgments coming from the control of the circle production. The rhythm and coordination of both hands in the movements of making circles on the chalkboard will be reinforced by the visual judgments of the size and shapes of the circles being produced.

2. Bi-manual Straight Lines

The child holds a piece of chalk in each hand and moves both hands in unison in various patterns of movement as illustrated in the following picture. The bi-manual lines are drawn from opposite letters to the central bull's-eye until all directions of movement are explored and practiced. The letters should be placed far enough apart on the board so your child can reach them with full arm extensions while standing approximately 12 to 14 inches from the board. All of the letters should be placed to complete a spoke pattern that requires the same arm extensions for all starting marks. Movements from the letters to the central target and then movements from the central target to the letters will give practice in all possible variations of directions.

Figure 25. This picture illustrates another physiologically important point. The chalkboard is hung so it is 12 to 15 degrees out of the vertical positioned so the bottom is nearest the user. This slope allows the most efficient posture and freedom of the arms as they rotate from the shoulders. The Texas research demonstrated that this slope contributed to the speed and accuracy of the motor patterns being learned here. A child cannot fully perceive a straight line unless he can also draw a straight line. Bilaterally drawn lines on the chalkboard provide the opportunity to "feel and see" lines like those he will be drawing in his primary workbooks.

Urge your child to explore all possible variations he can find. This experience with diagonal lines will greatly assist the child in the visual recognitions of all the shapes and patterns that are different from circles and squares, and the mastery of diagonal directions is a major step forward in the entire developmental sequence.

Encourage your child to strive to keep all arm and hand movements coordinated so both chalks arrive at their destination at the same time. This not only develops the freedom of the movements but establishes the muscle sense (kinesthesis) of how intimately elated each hand is

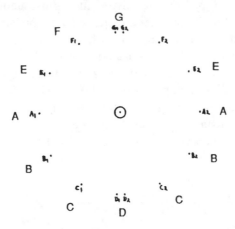

Figure 26. Letters and Bull's-eye Patterns. This illustrates the dot to center point pattern for practice in bilateral control of hands when drawing straight lines.

to the other. When your child starts on these routines, you may note he tends to turn head and eyes to watch and guide the chalk. As freedom of movement occurs, urge your child to keep head still with visual attention on the center target. Urge him to see (be visually aware of) all hand movements "out of the corner of eyes" in a manner that will assist in the development of visual-peripheral awareness. This assists in the widening of visual span for motion, orientation, and the details being searched for on a page of print. This is an important but not commonly recognized factor in many activities. The superior athlete, the safe driver, and the good hunter all have great need for this ability. It is critical in the awareness of what is happening around a person, as well as for the visual inspections of the object at which one is looking.

3. Follow-the-Dots

Follow-the-Dot activity books for children are familiar to most parents. Frequent and lengthy searches of children's book displays have not disclosed many that are suitable for the young child. Either the child does not recognize numbers or the concept of number sequence is not yet established. The ability to connect dots with a line demands the ability to visually anticipate the direction of the line to the next dot. This is not a skill that comes in a happenstance manner and is a visual-manual ability that must be developed by each child.

The usual kindergarten workbooks do not contain enough follow-the-dots activities. These workbooks usually require that some sort of a line be drawn connecting two hats, two chairs, or a word with a picture of the object named. Too frequently the teacher "OKs" the page if the two somethings are connected with a line no matter how circuitous or crooked. This wandering line does not adequately develop the visual anticipations and interpretations of the shortest distance between two items. This is a place where parents can assist their child at the chalkboard.

A dot, or an X, is placed on the chalkboard by the parent, and the child is instructed to place the chalk on this mark. The adult then places another mark on the board in any position and the child is instructed to connect the marks with a line. The child is then instructed to hold the chalk on the second mark so he will be ready to move immediately and accurately to the third mark placed elsewhere on the board. This can continue until the board is full of lines and dots in every conceivable position. Of course, it is important to urge quick, full arm movements that will produce straight lines between the marks. As the child becomes more adept, the speed of the action is increased. Children enjoy this procedure because it can provide a challenging "Fox and Goose Chase" that develops anticipations, visualizations, and speed of visual-manual actions.

With another bit of ingenuity, the parent can so place the marks that the finished sequence of lines will represent a simple outline of geometric shapes or an actual thing. All young children are tremendously pleased when they stand back and view the results and find they have drawn a picture. First grade children can count the marks as they connect them, thus obtaining added experience in what numbers are for and how sequences of numbers are important. Second grade children (and an occasional first grader) can number the marks before, or after, they connect them to utilize and apply number sequence concepts they are learning in school.

Now the child can begin to enjoy the creations of free-hand drawings and spontaneous designs that can be put on the chalkboard. Thus comes the primary skills of movement and direction that will then be applied to the more complex act of writing. The routines given here are the "creeping stones" to drawing and penmanship. If parents would observe the pencil and paper productions of a child before and after these routines, they would be fully convinced of the value of the chalkboard, and no home would ever be without it.

The reasons for all of this extra practice at the chalkboard should be quite clear; it is establishing the foundations on which the more advanced manual skills can be developed, and these are the warm-up routines which should be reviewed—at least briefly—before any of the more advanced routines are practiced. Writing skills are the ultimate goal, and the writing skill levels achieved will greatly depend on the solidity and reliability of the functions that have been achieved.

Take a moment, please, to put yourself into the same situation your child may still be experiencing. Please write (do not print) your name in large letters in the air, using your preferred hand in your habitual writing fashion. Note how freely your arm and hand move, and how little thought you need to give to doing this. This ease comes from your having established a "motor pattern"—a habit pattern that requires no conscious attention. Write your name in the air again, this time using your other hand. You will probably note a very slight clumsiness, but you will have no difficulty completing your name because of the bilateralities in hand actions that you have achieved and the great familiarity with your name. Graphologists have often reported that a motor pattern as meaningful and well practiced as your name will be present even if you try to write your name in the sand with your big toe, and the individual characteristics you have put into this pattern will be consistent no matter how you write your name. For example, if you put a vertical loop in your "t's" before you cross them with your preferred hand, you will put a vertical loop in this letter if you write it with your big toe in the sand.

Next, write your name backward using your *non-preferred* hand. Backward, here, means that you start with the last letter in your name and write it from right to left. This presents a task for which you have not established a habitual motor pattern, and you will find you have to give so much attention to the formation of each letter, and the directions in which your arm and hand must move that you may even lose the sequence of the letters. Suddenly you find you do not know how to spell your name—the one word you have probably written more often than any other.

The child just learning to write faces the same dilemma. So much thought must be given to all of the hand movements involved that the word to be written is overshadowed with the confusion on details. Such confusion strongly interferes with the acquisitions of the motor pattern for each letter, and the end result is confusion in the visual-manual signals that should be contributing to comprehension. Instead, writing, as a contributor to the comprehensions it is supposed to generate and support, becomes a stressful and frustrating deterrent with delays and interruptions in completion of the assignment.

Unfortunately, such a lack of visual-manual skills has brought another of those denigrating clinical words. The child having such difficulties in achieving writing abilities is now labeled "dysgraphic" and the problem is labeled "dysgraphia"—once again as if there were some sort of pathology present. This is another of those clinical buzz words that implies there is some sort of genetic problem or some sort of neurological defect that causes the problem. Thus, it becomes another of those "disabilities" for which substitute abilities are found, and the parents are too frequently told not to worry; their child need not learn to write because he can use the typewriter or computer. Later, in the business world, a good secretary can always be hired to do the writing—all of this instead of a program that will lead the child into the basic programs for the basic development of the visual-manual dexterities that will then allow the easy acquisition of writing skills. The most depressing aspect of this increasingly popular clinical buzz word is the omission of the intellectual development that is known to come out of the ability to *write* one's thoughts. The word "dysgraphia" simply means that the child is without writing abilities, so no parent must allow such a label to prevent his or her child from achieving the visual-manual dexterities innately possible in almost every human.

In all of this turmoil over writing abilities, there is increasing discussion of the advantages and disadvantages of manuscript (printing) and cursive (script) writing. One educators' journal(39) devoted an entire section to this discussion, and good points were made by the proponents of each educational method. It is interesting that the arguments swirled almost entirely around the tactual and kinesthetic aspects of the procedures. Only one presenter casually mentioned the role that visual discrimination skills play in the writing act, and visualization abilities were not even mentioned by any of the discussants.

Where are you now, Mr. Palmer, when we need you so badly?

Many adult readers will remember the grade school hours spent practicing the Palmer Method of cursive writing. Mr. Palmer wanted everyone to write beautifully and legibly, and his first lessons were: 1) how to hold a pencil with straight relaxed fingers, 2) how to move the entire arm so the pencil hand would *slide* smoothly across the paper, and 3) how to do circles, continuing ovals, and push-pulls on paper with ruled lines that were widely spaced. The writing lessons started every day with these circles, ovals and slightly tilted lines until students gained the easy fluidity of arm and hand movements. These patterns were always preliminary to any approach to the letters of the alphabet. Mr. Palmer's method brought excellent results because it completely avoided the white-knuckled fist demonstrated by today's child in the efforts to scribble out each line of each letter in manuscript form. It also brought immediate results in the proper spacing of letters and words on the page since the connections of letters in the words and the spacing between words came as a natural event in this total effort. Further, there is one start and one stop to each word instead of many starts and stops on each letter required in manuscript form. This closure of the letters into one "package" (the word itself) assists the learner to achieve the visual impression of completion and contributes to the total form of the word, which then becomes a specific visual clue that assists in word recognition and word remembrance. This closure into one unit also contributes to the muscle impressions that allow a child to set the motor pattern each word must have.

The careful reevaluations of how children successfully learn to write have brought desirable changes in writing lessons. One of these is a plastic bulb that slips onto the pencil to guide fingers into a more relaxed posture. This bulb prevents the white-knuckled fist so frequently observed in the contemporary classroom. It will eventually replace the three-sided rubber sleeve being used so widely now. The three-sided sleeve does help children to keep the pencil from slipping and turning, but it does nothing to relieve the cramped fingers almost every child now demonstrates.

Unfortunately, these bulbs are not yet commercially available. Parents can obtain sculpturing compound, named Super Sculpey, in a hobby store and make a bulb the right size and shape for their child's hand. The material is first approximately shaped and sized and then as it is held by the child with fingers in the proper position, it can be finally shaped and sized. Figure 27 shows this bulb in a hand, and how it will assist the hand posture.

In spite of all the physiological and logical reasons for cursive writing, the manuscript letter form is still widely used because someone offered the notion that a child would learn the alphabet more quickly and easily if the letters to be written were the same shapes as those in textbooks. Although this is a reasonable assumption, it is not necessarily true. When a child really learns letters and words, it makes

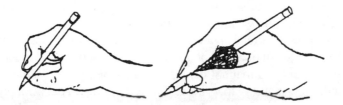

Figure 27. These two illustrations show the undesirable white- knuckled fist that creates so much stress and fatigue that become an interference to writing as a learning act ... and the open hand that Mr. Palmer urged. The right illustration also shows the sleeve that slips onto a pencil to prevent the bent fingers of the fisted grip, and the cramps that too frequently result.

very little difference in what shape they are presented just as long as they consistently resemble those they are supposed to represent. This is the result of the size and shape constancies that underlie the knowledge the child brings to the letters and the words. If this were not true, we would not be able to read each other's writing—as badly scribbled as it so often is by many individuals. When the child *knows* letters and words and brings his meanings to them, they will be deciphered in almost any shape. This is especially true when the child also has the motor patterns and the visualizations that allow the production of these symbols.

Another point in favor of cursive writing is that every child who has not yet achieved directionality skills and concepts and the special movements described here, will go through an expected period of some "reversals" of numbers and letters. These reversal problems are much more common on manuscript letters, appearing most frequently on the letters "b" and "d," "p" and "q." Just looking at these printed letters provides one clue to their reversibility. Each of these letters has the same geometric form—a stick and a ball. The learner has to have visual inspection skills that allow the recognition of exactly where the ball is attached to the stick. Take a moment to write these same letters in cursive form and you will note that each of them has its own distinctive pattern; each requires a distinctive direction of arm and hand movements. The JNDs are much more evident in cursive form than they are in ball and stick letters.

Again, there is certainly no wish to encroach upon the prerogatives of the classroom teacher. However, there are the continuing questions about why educators do not realize the values of writing skills to reading abilities—and to all thinking abilities. The ability to *write* numbers, letters, and words is certainly more beneficial than the mere ability to see, say, or sing the symbols! This question does express a few of the reasons why parents should encourage their children to learn to write. As already stated, "dysgraphia" is *not* a "disability"—it is simply the result of a lack of assistance, instruction, and practice on how to achieve the manual dexterities and the visual- manual skills that underlie the ability to write. If the school system does not provide this learning opportunity, it does fall to the parents to provide it. It is imperative that the *basic* movement skills and the *basic* visual discriminations be achieved one way or another for success in the academic environment.

In spite of the possibility that a child's teacher feels all in- classroom attention must be given to manuscript writing, hopefully there will be no resentment over the exploration of cursive writing at home. After all, the more ways one can do any one thing, the greater the knowledge gained. Actually, there are more similarities in most manuscript and cursive letters than there are differences. The letters "s," "z," "r" and "l" in manuscript are the only vivid dissimilarities. Practice in both kinds of writing will certainly offer more opportunities for the discriminations of the critical JNDs existing therein.

From a completely clinical, physiological, and developmental viewpoint, cursive letters will be the recommended homework. The sequence of the alphabet can be changed to match the patterns of the arm and hand movement sequences of early childhood. It is impossible to determine who insisted the alphabet start with "a" and follow the universal sequence through to "z." From a human development perspective, practice should start with the round letters that are the extensions of the circles the child first learns to put on chalkboard or paper. The rest of the *developmental* sequence is detailed in the following instructions.

The chalkboard is the best practice area, and the letters should be written in large sizes. Letters like "o" and "c" should be at least six inches high, and letters like "l," "b," and "p" should be at least nine inches in vertical size. These sizes will assure the full arm movements so frequently mentioned here and will avoid the scribbling too often seen when the student is writing at the desk. These sizes should not be reduced until there is a definitely observable full and fluid arm movement on each letter. Each practice session should be limited to one of the letter groups shown in Figure 28, and it is very possible the scribbling habits will not allow all letters in each group to be mastered in one session. The recommended sequence should be followed exactly because it provides practice in similarities of movement directions, each new letter using some of the movement directions found in the preceding letter. The *quality* of performance is much more important than the *quantity* of practice. Better the child should practice for five minutes six times a day than for one 30-minute session in which fatigue and frustration can wipe out all benefits of the practice.

Have your child start with the first letter in group 1, and do not allow him to proceed to the second letter until there is no apparent hesitancy in arm and hand movements while forming the letter. Next, have the child do at least four or five of the same letter in connected form so that the continuity of letter-to- letter is practiced. This "sets in" the motor pattern for each letter. When ease and fluidity is apparent, have your child go on to group 2, but review group 1 before going from group 2 to group 3. Continue to review group 1 or 2 after any of the more advanced practicing. Doing so will allow a child to be confident in the establishment of visual-manual integrations.

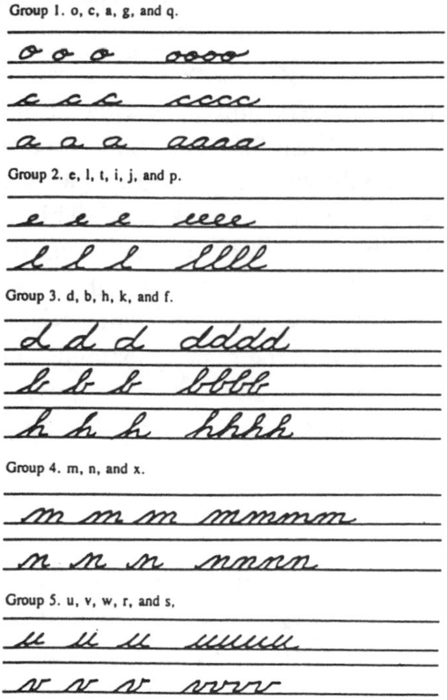

Group 1. o, c, a, g, and q.

Group 2. e, l, t, i, j, and p.

Group 3. d, b, h, k, and f.

Group 4. m, n, and x.

Group 5. u, v, w, r, and s.

Because capital letters are individually more distinctive in shape and size, these should be practiced one at a time, and almost any sequence is permissible. The best results with capitals may be achieved by using letters in family names.

Eventually, combinations of letters should be practiced. By now, it would not be surprising if combinations are quite spontaneously happening in the words your child wants to master. Have him practice the groups

Figure 28.

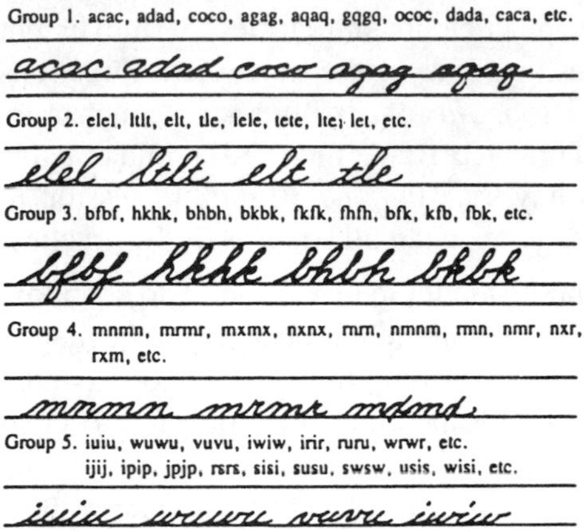

Group 1. acac, adad, coco, agag, aqaq, gqgq, ococ, dada, caca, etc.

acac adad coco agag agag

Group 2. elel, ltlt, elt, tle, lele, tete, lte, let, etc.

elel ltlt elt tle

Group 3. bfbf, hkhk, bhbh, bkbk, fkfk, fhfh, bfk, kfb, fbk, etc.

bfbf hkhk bhbh bkbk

Group 4. mnmn, mrmr, mxmx, nxnx, rm, nmnm, rmn, nmr, nxr, rxm, etc.

mnmn mrmr mxmx

Group 5. iuiu, wuwu, vuvu, iwiw, irir, ruru, wrwr, etc.
ijij, ipip, jpjp, rsrs, sisi, susu, swsw, usis, wisi, etc.

iuiu wuwu vuvu iwiw

Figure 29.

given in Figure 29 to achieve legibility of the letters that have so many similarities:

When all letter forms are produced easily and well, it is time to move to pencil and paper. The sheets of paper should be large enough to allow the same full arm movements learned at the chalkboard. If you cannot easily obtain such large sheets (look in a school supply store for newsprint paper), you can use the classified ad section of the newspaper with kindergarten pencils or felt tip pens. Turning the pages to the horizontal position will make the fine print into a dull background presenting less confusion and distraction. Blank paper is best, however, and worth looking for.

Some children may need an intermediate posture in making the move from chalkboard to desk. If this is the case for your child, have him first stand at the table or desk, letting this erect posture duplicate some of the same directionality experienced at the chalkboard. This will assist the child in learning that the away movements at the desk translate to the up movements at the chalkboard, and the toward movements at the desk correspond to the down movements at the board. Make sure that the child's grasp of the pencil is similar to the open-fingered grasp used at the chalkboard so that there are none of the interfering, disruptive hand cramps. Have the child imitate the grip illustrated in Figure 30.

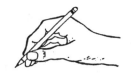

PROPER FINGER AND PENCIL
POSITION FOR LEFT HAND

PROPER FINGER AND PENCIL
POSITION FOR RIGHT HAND

Figure 30.

It should not be inferred that writing skills are the only skills needed, or that writing skills will be the panacea for all developmental problems. There is no need to point out once again the importance of the ability to form the stereotyped symbols that are the expressions of one's creativeness, innovativeness—even one's intimate thoughts. If this writing ability is the only manual skill achieved, there may well still be complexities of problems in mastering the world into which one progresses.

I am taking "author's license" to tell a personal story with several emerging points. A number of years ago I was conducting a teachers' in-service at a special suburban school in the Philadelphia area. All of the values of the chalkboard and the special routines to be used there were being emphasized. Enthusiasm led me to get a bit carried away with descriptions of how most of these chalkboard routines had come out of my personal experience in optometric vision therapy for children having academic problems. I was quite clearly indicating these routines were my inventions.

At the end of the session, the lovely Miss McIntyre, the widely experienced veteran of the classroom, very gently asked if I were familiar with a book by J. Liberty Tadd entitled *New Methods in Education.*[40] When I admitted my ignorance, Miss McIntyre suggested it could be obtained in the Philadelphia Library, and it would undoubtedly hold great interest for me.

This book was obtained as quickly as possible and I was startled to find that Mr. Tadd had extensively plagiarized every procedure and explanation given to the teachers at the in-service—*11 years before I was born!*

Point 1: Pride and humility are like figure and ground—it is essential there be the right balance between them!

Point 2: Here was a book published in 1902 that presents the basics of the total learning process in a delightful manner in the poetic prose of the late 1800s. Tadd wrote: "The first tools to be used and trained are the mind, the eyes, and the hands—the instrumentalities of the organism. To these our chief care should be given. It is of little use that the pupil has built a machine or performed a piece of work by mechanical movements if his own organism is not complete, if his hand is not sure, his eye not true, and his mind not balanced."

Tadd then goes on with his developmental philosophy in which he

First Exercise, Manual Training Drawing
Figure 31. This picture, taken from Tadd's book, shows the primary students practicing their "eye-hand-mind" exercises at the chalkboard in the 1900 classroom.

describes the learning process that many of us have spent all the intervening years trying to understand. Tadd wrote: "Of course, if children or adults have passed the nascent period for this work, extra time must be given to acquiring the desired facility; for few can be found now to dispute the desirability of real manual dexterity for each hand for all boys and girls whatever their future life may be, apart from the idea of drawing as a mode of thought expression for educational purposes, and as a means of correlating all the various studies. I do not think a psychologist can now be found who will not strenuously advocate real drawing and proper manual training as one of the chief means to reinforce 'knowledge,' and to make it 'wisdom.' They will advocate it as a means—through motor movements and touch sensations—of awakening and making still more alert the brain, which is far too frequently made dull and torpid by too much verbal memorizing, too much print, too much 'telling,' and too little doing."

Tadd was a "manual training" teacher. A teacher of the *learning process—manual training.* Today, those same instructors are known as "industrial arts" teachers. Teachers of the *end product*—what Tadd referred to as "building a machine or performing a piece of work by mechanical movements." Even in the 1890s there was an educator proposing that the *process* of learning was more important than the *product* of the mechanical efforts.

A third point to be made in this personal report is that here is a

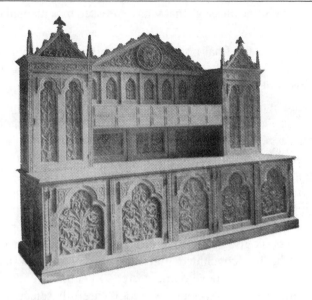

Vestment Case, Carved by Pupils of the R. C. High School.

Figure 32. One has great difficulty imagining present high school students having this sort of manual-visual skills. Have our students lost more than mere carving abilities in this process of overlooking the "basics" that are really important to the total learning process?

textbook for the educators of that era detailing and describing the classroom methods that would explore the basics for the development of the students in both performance and thinking skills. Many of the boys shown in this beautiful old book's pictures went on to designing and carving exquisite furniture for homes and churches. The older girls are shown writing, drawing, and sculpting in a manner only a few special artists can do today. Tadd wrote in 1902, "All recent studies of the cerebrum point to the fact that our intelligence is associated with a union of brain cells one with another, and the more experience we gain through the various senses, the greater will be the structural union and complexity of the brain cells." Exactly as has been detailed by Aoki and Siekevits[28] in their Scientific American article "Plasticity in the Brain Development," in which they write: "We are only beginning to understand how molecular events influence the structure of neurons and how these structural changes are translated into brain functions ....Ultimately the answer will lead to the profound appreciation of how each individual person, in spite of being formed by inexorable genetic processes, is also the unique product of experience." The same message that was expressed by a manual training teacher 90 years ago!

And, of course, the final point to all of this momentary tangential journey—how long will it take to get "back to the basics" in these present levels of confusion?

Once again, it may seem as though another panacea is being offered. Nevertheless, the need for finger dexterity is so great, especially when the "prophets of doom" are insisting that everyone will be faced with mastery of the computer by the year 2000, there must be some attention given to the development of these dexterities. Such basics must be provided outside the classroom where even coloring, cutting, and pasting is being replaced with academic routines. The previously mentioned research by Alan Gottfried, Ph.D., the developmentally oriented psychologist,[21] has revealed some interesting facts. After long study, he has concluded that the three most important contributors to intellectual development are: 1) genuine Tender Loving Care, 2) multiplicity of experiences, and 3) carefully selected "educational" toys. A request to Dr. Gottfried to explain what he meant by "educational" toys brought forth his strong feelings about which toys are really "educational." He especially endorsed those toys demanding visual-manual discriminations and manipulations like those inherent in DUPLO, LEGO, TYCO BLOCKS, and the old reliables like Tinker-Toys and Erector sets (and not "batteries not included" toys).

A morning paper report which arrived as this section of the book was being completed, certainly reinforces Dr. Gottfried's conclusions. The report from several university and college department heads and from officials of the National Science Foundation lamented the disappearance of "hands-on science experiences" in our schools. Most of these concerned individuals mourned the fact that, "The students don't know how to use Bunsen burners, pipettes ... we would expect them to know how to use a balance, buretts to titrate, read volumes, and how to light Bunsen burners." All of these educators "would agree that students don't have very good lab skills." The article goes on at great length to condemn the computer as the culprit for the situations in which finger dexterities were not needed and, hence, not developed. The major point of the entire article lies in its quote of the old Chinese proverb: "I hear and I forget; I see and I remember; I do and I understand." It also quotes Carl Sagan of Cornell University: "What modern science is all about is a succession of counter-intuitive discoveries. It's confronting nature as it is, even if it contradicts your expectations about how things work." This may seem to be a rather abstract statement until one realizes that Sagan is emphasizing the importance of "hard evidence of real events that happen in experiments ..."—the hands-on experience that can only come when there is the manual skill which will permit the experimentations. This news piece ends with a comment from a science coordinator for a county school system: "Students get the idea that whatever is on the computer is correct. In a real laboratory situation, experimental results often differ, and students must learn how to deal with differing results." All of this seems to be pointing up the basic fact that manual skills are very important to the science courses we expect to be the intellect-stretchers for our high school students. One cannot avoid asking if maybe these same manual skills, so critically important to high school students, might not be the extensions of the manual skills first explored and achieved with the educational toys Gottfried found to be important as early as the age of 3. One might legitimately ask, "Is there any relevance between these toys and these science skills and the manual abilities needed for everyday performance in our increasingly complex world?"

Dominance

There is another detail that must not be overlooked. The human comes with two hands that are intended to be a matched pair, a pair that is most effective in assigned purposes if the hands are efficiently used as support and reinforcement for each other. One of the greatest advantages of the toys just mentioned—LEGO, Tinker Toys, and others—is the requirement for the use and integration of the two hands for the bilaterality they offer. One of the most critical problems now existing for so many youngsters is the *unilaterality* and the resulting dependence on just one hand instead of finding the manner in which the two hands support, guide, monitor, and "instruct" each other in almost every daily activity. There has been too much emphasis upon "dominance," as if one-handedness was most desirable. This emphasis on "dominance" of one hand, one leg and foot, one eye, and even one ear has completely ignored the fundamental architecture of a bilateral being with many pairs to be matched and integrated for much greater abilities. This undue emphasis on "dominance" and the insistence that all of the right side components, or all of the left side components, be "dominant" has resulted in restrictions and hindrances in the development of the totality the fundamental design promises. As a direct result, too many individuals are so *unilateral* that the "non-dominant" components are just along for the ride and make less and less contribution as time, growth, and development occur.

There is another interesting aspect of all this dominance issue. Somewhere along the line, in the attempt to explain some of the learning problems being demonstrated, the notion was offered that symbolic confusions were the result of "mixed" or "crossed" dominancies. Quite typically, the youngsters who demonstrated "reversals" (or what was previously labeled "strephosymbolia") would also demonstrate a degree of confusion on which hand they preferred to use, or which eye was the "dominant eye," or which foot was chosen to kick a ball. Certainly, as an individual develops skills in the use of each of these components, there will be a choice between them *when the task requires only one of them.* In looking carefully at all areas of the abilities required for any unilateral activity, one undoubtedly finds that preferences are the result of a well organized *bilaterality*, and the "non-dominant" component is making significant supporting and reinforcing contributions to the action of the moment. Certainly, an individual will hold and manipulate a pencil with only one hand, but if there is the bilaterality the individual was designed to achieve, the other hand will be making its contribution by assisting in posture, position of the paper, and the balance of efforts in accomplishing the task. The child in those difficulties usually attributed to a "lack of dominancies" is more likely to be the child who has not yet established all of the unities and integrations of the two architectural halves that make up the total design of the upright bilateral person who can move and perform with the fluidity, economy, and efficiency the movement skills are supposed to provide.

If one looks carefully at all the evidence, the efforts to establish the dominancies that result in unilaterality have not solved the "reversal" problems. In contrast, the activities that extend and develop the integrated bilateralities have brought gratifying gains in the skills needed for the eliminations of such problems as "reversals" and "sequencing." Please recall the report on the benefits of square dancing and think a bit more about the movement skills and the organizations of the total action system present in the human. Please remember that there cannot be the development of the skills in selected parts unless there is full and interwoven development of the totality. From the developmental perspective, there can be no substitute for those sequences that will organize and elaborate the unity of the totality which will then allow the refinements and extensions of *what seem to be* the independent uses of selected parts. As Gesell stated long ago, "If one attempts to probe any part of the total, he must constantly remember there are many related and connected parts which must also be fully considered."

Hopefully, all of this has alerted every reader on how basic these manual abilities really are in the overall learning process, and the reader will find more and more ways to assure every child of the opportunities to discover the wonders of the two hands and the ways these operate to reach, grasp, manipulate, and understand the world into which the child has come. There are some special advantages to an appropriate hobby that will assist in building manual skills. This must be carefully chosen and encouraged so it captures and holds the child's interest with a real sense of personal accomplishment. Crafts and hobbies are the extension of the toy experiences and not only extend visual- manual integrations and visual inspection and discrimination skills, but carry each child into the more advanced levels of visualization for creativity and production.

The Visual Skills

How can one possibly itemize all of the visual skills needed for the ultimate personal development without writing another book on this subject alone? No matter which particular visual skills are (or are not) discussed, there will be criticism over the choices included here. Just as has been done in the discussion of manual skills, the more pervasive and more basic of all these skills have to be selected for discussion. It is hoped that discussion of the ones selected will provide enough insights that omissions can be filled in by the reader.

Fundamental to any and all visual skills is the development of visual awareness. The students of child development and the behavioral optometrists are quite appalled over the number of children who have, for one reason or another, failed to develop a full and alerting awareness of their visual surroundings. It is easy to blame this on the magnitude of centralized visual attention given to television, but this is only one of several reasons why so many children pass through the exciting, challenging, and attractively designed world with so little interest. A generation or two ago, before life became so rushed and harried, there was much more time to stop and look—"to stop and smell the roses." Today vehicles either move too rapidly through crowded traffic or are too enclosed to allow any time for visual inspections of the environment and its contents. Too, parents try to occupy children with "travel games" that, by their very nature, often restrict the children's visual attention to the game instead of to the constantly changing and challenging environment. A generation or two ago, when children walked where they needed to go, there were many more things to see and inspect. I remember the grade school teachers who challenged class members to find the first spring flowers or the first returning birds or the differences in leaves and blades of grass. Remember the mathematicians? The chances are great these individuals observed much more of their environment than simply the path on which they walked.

The development of visual awareness *must not* be started in the ubiquitous shopping mall! The child who has not yet found out how much the visible world contains can be so overwhelmed in the rushing multitudes that there may be a complete turn-off of all this stimulation purely as a survival technique. The child who cannot turn this visual bombardment off can react emphatically and distressfully in these surroundings.

Like most other preparations for the buzzing, bumbling confusions of the big world, practice for the mastery of such environments must start in the familiar and comfortable enclosures of the home. Here, instead of dodging the hurrying crowds, the child can visually explore many more intimately interesting things. The usual house noises that continue even when the baby is napping will allow the practice on selective cancellations of extraneous stimuli. Making sure the baby can see all of the family actions can encourage the baby to make the first selections of what to attend to and what to ignore. The entire process of the purposeful cancellations of extraneous and irrelevant stimuli has to start with practice in how to ignore visual and auditory signals. The home that is too quiet or too devoid of activity can well contribute to the distress that arises in the much too noisy and busy outside world. Like all other human abilities, the development of visual awareness must include practice in how to profit from it and how to ignore it when it ceases to be a contribution. There should be multiple opportunities for every child to find and develop these awarenesses of all that the visible world contains and all of the signs and signals from which information can be visually derived. The observant child will be the interested child, and the interested child will become the intelligent child.

The more specific visual capacities to which attention will be directed are: 1) the visual discrimination of sizes and shapes; 2) the visual discriminations of spatial directions and distance; and 3) the visual discriminations of just noticeable differences (JNDs). As has been previously stated, visual abilities develop in the very small child "under the tutelage of the active touch." This immediately brings us back to the discussion just completed on manual skills. There is a major difference, however. It is not enough that the learning child merely explore objects to obtain tactual information. There must be consistent and repetitious opportunities for the manual-visual and visual-manual integrations described in Chapter II. This means that every object manually explored must also be visually explored just as carefully so that things that "feel big" are visually recognized as "looking big" and those objects that "look big" are manually explored to understand why they "feel big." Much of this exploration and interpretation occurs normally in the early developmental stages, but it is essential that the concerned adult provide the multiplicity of experiences that also afford the challenges of making all these judgments.

We have already explored the importance of the inspections and discriminations of sizes and shapes in the organization of number concepts and the extrapolations into math concepts. There are numerous aspects of all this evolution of concepts that must be based upon visual discriminations when hands are not available to support and reinforce such judgments. An example of this is the simple task of choosing a container the right size for the objects one wishes to place into it. Later in life, the judgment of a parking space or the space that will allow one's car to pass another car are times when the reliability of one's visual size judgment becomes very important.

Closely related to all of the visual judgments of size are the visual judgments of distances. Experimental psychologists and behavioral optometrists have spent many years in investigations of the human's ability to make reliable visual computations of spatial distances. This is one area of the astronauts' training program that has included many hours of practice. So many of these visual computations are based on movement experiences that we now come back to the importance of the general transport movements that occupy the infant and young child for most of the preschool years. The astronauts have found that when the influences of gravity changed, their visual judgments of both distance and size were changed—in some cases, quite completely distorted to their disadvantage. Part of the training for these space travelers included the challenges of making size and distance judgments while in radically different postural positions. Some of this sort of activity can be a game for the child who has not yet established some reliability in these visual judgments.

More basic and preliminary for almost all children—and especially those having any degree of difficulty with mathematics—are the simpler tasks of making a visual estimation of the distance to an object across the play area, and then stepping it off to verify or correct the initial appraisal. The child must count his steps as the distance is being walked out, so there is the immediate comparison of the estimate with the actual distance. Asking the child to then size his steps to match the estimate made gives valuable experience in both size and distance comprehensions. Please recall the earlier story of the mathematicians who were capable of math concepts needed for the space age and then invent every possible experiential situation that will give your youngster this same sort of practice in making and verifying visual judgments of visible distances.

The third of the visual skills—the ability to recognize and analyze just noticeable differences—is one of the three most basic to all of the visual tasks in the contemporary classroom. The first two contribute to the foundations for many of the academic concepts but the speed and accuracy of visual JNDs will fully determine the student's success in every symbolic task of every classroom program. The part these judgments play in the process of learning to read could be discussed for many pages. A few common examples should suffice to focus our attention on the value of this visual skill.

Our language contains a multitude of words that look alike but are spoken differently, or that are spoken quite similarly but look very different. The words "their" and "there" have identical pronunciations, but the spelling and meaning are entirely different. In "queen" and "queer," the visible difference is slight, but the vocalization and meaning are very different. Most disturbing are words like "quake" and "quay," where the visible difference is slight but the pronunciation is extremely dissimilar. More common are all of those "---ough" words the beginning reader must face, and all of the very accurate visual discriminations that must be made both for spelling and pronunciation.

All of these complexities which exist in our language and which must be thoroughly mastered in the acquisition of reading skills bring us to the significant relevancies which exist between the visual skills and the verbal skills. There must now be the immediate recognition of the dependency each of these two skill areas has with the other. As the manual-visual and the visual- manual integrations become more significant as the basics that must be considered, there are also the verbal-visual and the visual-verbal integrations of advancing importance in the organization of the basic abilities that every child must bring to the classroom of the 1990s and the much more complex classroom of the 2000s.

Preparation for the visual JNDs every youngster will be facing must be provided by the concerned adult in the most concrete and realistic everyday situations. A few years ago the daily comic pages included generally similar pictures in which there were numerous very slight differences the child was challenged to find. The two pictures might be of a mother standing before a stove in the kitchen. On the stove in the first picture there is a deep saucepan, and in the second a fry pan sits on the burner. In the first picture the mother holds a long-handled stirring spoon. In the second picture, she is holding a long-handled fork. In the first picture, the mother's apron strings are tied in a bow; in the second, the strings are tied in a simple loop knot. The mother is wearing glasses in the first picture, but not in the second. And so on, with many little differences the youngster is challenged to find. Such puzzles are excellent practice in the extension of visual JNDs. Similar puzzles (see Figure 33) were found in children's magazines, and now that these have lost their popularity, parents should find ways to help their youngsters make such discriminations and judgments. Family group pictures can be a splendid place to start, especially if the photographer made several exposures of the group to make sure all were smiling, or all had their eyes open. Two similar chairs in the family room can provide an opportunity to examine and find the JNDs between them. The usual home is full of comparable objects, dishes, silverware, pans, canned goods, etc., in which this practice in visual discriminations can be explored. The ultimate reason for all of it lies in the basic preparations it provides for the speed and accuracy of the visual discriminations needed for reading abilities. The return to basics *must* be more than the increased number of textbooks and computer programs.

By this time, every reader will be aware of the need for complete clinical evaluations and the carefully determined visual skills every learner should have. This care is supremely critical for the youngster in academic difficulty. It is no less important for the child demonstrat-

Figure 33. Hidden Pictures. Dick Whittington and His Cat.
In this big picture, find three fish, a barking dog, pipe, light bulb, spoon, snake, foot-ball, bird, frying pan, letter C, pencil, toothbrush, bell. This is an excellent example of the sort of pictures in which many familiar objects are hidden demanding the practice in visual inspections and visual discriminations so many children need. (From the children's' magazine Highlights.)

ing superior performance in the classroom. Both children must have the *protective, preventive,* and *enhancement* vision care that will assure their continued academic progress without the visual and/or perceptual deteriorations that undue stress can bring.

There are now many valid and reliable clinical procedures available for the special benefits of every student facing academic tasks, and for every adult facing the increasingly stressful visual tasks of the "unfriendly" computer. There will be those clinicians who loudly and vehemently disparage the benefits that vision care can bring, probably because there is a great ignorance about it or an inability to provide it. Parents and educators must not allow such unprofessional condemnations to so influence them that full investigations of the available procedures are not made. The best rule is still "get a second opinion" from those who are completely familiar with the clinical services available. It is still the privilege of the parent and the teacher to make the search, ask the questions, and make the final decisions.

The Verbal Skills

Hopefully, every reader now has grasped the point of this entire discussion—that a *return to the basics* must be the development of the learning skills that will prepare the child for abstract classroom tasks. This is even more true in the acquisition of verbal skills. Because the human child is such an excellent parrot and is born with abilities and opportunities to acquire his "native tongue," there is the too frequent assumption that clear and expansive speech patterns are all that are necessary. There have been repeated references to the integrations of the visual and verbal abilities usually achieved by most children, but the frequent comments about the return to the basics demand a bit more discussion of the verbal skills each child should have achieved.

Any indication of speech problems of any magnitude should have the attention of the developmentally oriented speech and language therapist. Baby talk that continues into the school years or mispronunciations that persist in spite of constant parental reminders must not be ignored. Speech skills, which are so unique to the human, are of such significance to all communications that early problems must not be allowed to persist. There are some basic speech opportunities in everyday situations that parents need to be aware of so they can guide and assist their children in verbal practice.

The verbal-vocal-auditory complex has already been discussed in earlier chapters. The infant finds ways to use this vocal-auditory-verbal complex in the first few weeks of life. There is the "I'm hungry" cry; the "I need attention" cry; the "I'm lonesome" cry; the "I need help" cry; and the "I'm frustrated" cry. Every mother learns to "read" these messages quickly, and the infant learns very quickly which parent can meet the needs of the moment. These vocalizations and the auditory discriminations being made so that the proper cry is issued to receive the proper parental responses, lie in the basics that will become more and more relevant to classroom activities. There are a few clinical reports on how specialists in child development have "taught" infants to send up an appropriate cry, and because all this seems to happen so automatically with infants, too little attention has been given to it and its relevance to classroom tasks. These tasks seem too far off in the future to make these connections. Whatever the situation may be, there is a need for parents to recognize their role in the development of these vocal-auditory-verbal abilities.

Most parents already know how important it is for them to do a lot of talking to their infants. Of greater importance is the consistent and carefully planned efforts to have children do the talking, especially about their daily experiences. At the risk of sounding redundant, the ability to express and describe one's actions, observations, or experiences can be the ultimate cue to advanced intellectual development. And, like all other development, there is the critical ability of also making JNDs in vocalizations, auditory judgments, and verbal expressions. The point has already been made that a child "speaks what he hears" and "hears what he speaks," but all adults must be reminded that practice in the appraisals of JNDs can be as basically significant here as it is anywhere else in the developmental sequence.

The place to start all of this practice is in having your child talk about what he is doing while he is doing it. Your child must pay full attention to all details if good descriptions are being verbalized. A parent can make an exciting game of this by closing or covering his eyes and having the child describe what he is doing so well that the parent can visualize what is happening. After several times, have the child close his eyes while the parent does the describing. This not only provides practice in doing and describing; it also provides the extensions and enhancements of the ability to visualize the events of the moment. The visual-verbal and verbal-visual integrations discussed in Chapter II are being extended.

Such conversations should extend beyond the proper pronunciation of the words the child is using. It must include activities where the judgments of noises, sound sequences, and slight sound differences will be recognized by the learner. There is valuable practice in learning how to listen, one of the skills so essential to classroom success. There are a number of toys designed to challenge such auditory exercises. The Wizard, Simon, CopyCat, and other similar toys that present a series of sounds that must then be repeated by the operator are excellent experiences. Eventually, music lessons that demand visual-auditory matchings become valuable, not to assure that a child will become a concert pianist or a symphony instrumentalist, but to practice, in an advanced way, the basic visual-auditory-manual skills. Parents should never simply pass off musical experiences because "My child is not musically inclined" or "My child cannot carry a tune in a basket because his father can't either." Perhaps the lack of musical appreciation is in reality a lack of the basic skills in auditory discriminations—skills to be learned just as any other skills are learned. The many reasons for experience and practice to achieve verbal skills cannot be overemphasized.

The ultimate uniqueness of the human as a result of manual skills, visual skills, and verbal skills which no other creature can achieve brings us back to the recognition of what "the return to basics" must include. Every investigator of human development comes to the conclusion sooner or later that intellectual capacities are not fully achieved by any of us. Further, there is the growing realization that intellectual capacities of *every* child, regardless of clinical label, can be enhanced and extended by the developmental opportunities offered to the child. This amazing process of *learning how to learn,* and the applications of all that is learned, offers all of us a challenge we must fully understand and more fully explore if we really are going to "return to the basics."

Epilogue

Without any doubt, every author is consumed by the conviction that his book is the one that will set the whole world straight, and all problems will then be solved. This most common assumption has been a large part of the motivation for this book. There is one aspect of the entire situation described as "learning disabilities" that has had the primary moving influence on me. This is the fact that all of the hundreds of thousands of dollars scattered across this problem have really made so little positive impact. There is the deep feeling that the major reason for the lack of solutions reached lies in the efforts to "cure" the problem without enough thought being given to the "prevention" of the problem. This is another case of trying to lock the barn *after* the horse is stolen and is so similar to all the efforts and dollars spent on reading problems. If an equal amount of time and money had been spent on how a child learns to read successfully, we could have many more answers about those who have not achieved success in this process. We learn very little from studying failures compared to all we can learn by studying successes.

As one writes this epilogue, it is impossible to put the book by J. Liberty Tadd[40] aside without reviewing some of what he wrote in the 1902 teachers' edition. It is so appropriate here, it must be offered for contemplation 90 years later.

Tadd wrote:

> We should develop a disposition disposed to energetic action or work, in response to stimulating thought a disposition that hungers and thirsts for right action according to the environment. Too often head-learning creates a wish or desire for good without there being sufficient impulse in the organism to prompt the energetic action required to achieve it. For this purpose, energy must be stored in the organism and conserved by a training in action and deeds until a working out of thoughts and deeds grows into a habit. To consume and waste the vital energy by beginning too early with abstract tasks and various forms of thought studies is as needless as it is common. Too often I find the mind enfeebled, the memory weakened, the vitality abused and consumed by studies meant to strengthen instead of methods being employed that would conserve and add to the vitality, at the same time that the mind,

the memory, the judgment, and the imagination are being improved.

In common with this improvement of the mental and physical being, there should be the development of the emotional being through the feelings the love of action, a training of head and eye to obey the mind and execute its orders that fit both head and hand, heart and will, to cope with the problems of life.

Nothing gives greater dignity to man than a complete realization of the power of being able to do. No joy is greater or more lasting than that received by doing well with the complete being brain, eye, hands, will and judgment all tools, God-given tools, to be trained and used.

Largely as a result of imperfect training or wrong methods of education in youth, beauty and high quality of product are too commonly lacking in mechanical industries and in the world of literature and the fine arts. Our people excel in quantity of product, but not in quality. When this (education) is properly done, the rising generations will reach a development in the manner that has heretofore been enjoyed only by the few. Our youth will come out of the early educational process sound in brain and body, strong of purpose, positive in application, trained in the use of hand and eye, with originality developed and judgment matured, possessing an ability and a capacity to use it that will manifest themselves in every art and industry. And this means a building up of character and a recognition of man's duty to humanity, and to God, by which alone are to be fostered the best citizenship, the largest human happiness, and the fullest enjoyment of the marvels of this wonderful universe in which we live.

One cannot help but wonder about the possibility that Mr. Tadd had foresights and premonitions of what the future was to bring in our schools. Here, back at the turn of the century, a manual training teacher, who was an astute philosopher, was warning his colleagues in education with insights on where his profession was heading. Wouldn't Mr. Tadd have been an interesting participant in the conference reported in the opening paragraphs of Chapter VI?

Hopefully, I have clearly expressed and described some of the processes of human development and some of the sequences of learning development that will allow teachers, parents, and clinicians to find some of the ways to assure success and some of the ways to prevent failures! If I have been successful in this venture, perhaps there will be new awareness that there are indeed ways to assist all children to progress more evenly and more successfully through these stages of development and levels of the learning process, in manners that will not cost hundreds of thousands of dollars, and will achieve results in shorter periods of time. There are really only three requirements: 1) that the educational system and all of its personnel take a new attitude of consideration for the development of the individual child and his individual abilities; 2) that parents assume their responsibilities in the guidance and nurturing of their children; and 3) that clinicians will begin to think beyond their self- centered prejudices and become a part of the solutions instead of continuing to be a major part of the problem.

Perhaps this is expecting too much, but is the present situation to be accepted without any further concern? Is the present course of events what we are willing to permit for our children? Shouldn't we hope that all our children could be smart in everything ... including school?

APPENDIX A

Public Law 94-142; The Education for All Handicapped Children Act

The determination of which children would be eligible for the services this law was to provide demanded a definition of "specific learning disability." The following is the first definition established:

Specific learning disability means a disorder in one or more of the basic psychological processes involved in the understanding or in using language, spoken or written, which may manifest itself in an imperfect ability to listen, think, speak, read, write, spell, or to do mathematical calculations. The term includes such conditions as perceptual handicaps, brain injury, minimal brain dysfunction, dyslexia, and developmental aphasia. The term does not include children who have learning problems which are primarily the result of visual, hearing, or motor handicaps, of mental retardation, of emotional disturbance, or of environmental, cultural, or economic disadvantage.

The Report to the U.S. Congress on Learning Disabilities, prepared by the Interagency Committee on Learning Disabilities (1987), states:

As more has been learned about learning disabilities from research, and as people have attempted to apply this definition in a variety of settings, numerous shortcomings of the definition have become apparent. It wrongly implies that learning disability is a homogeneous condition rather than a heterogeneous group of disorders. The use of "children" in the definition fails to recognize that for most people a relative disability persists and affects them throughout adulthood as well. It does not indicate that, whatever the etiology of learning disabilities, the final common path is an inherently altered process of acquiring and using information, presumably based on an altered function within the central nervous system. Finally, though properly recognizing that learning disabilities do not include problems with learning as a consequence of mental retardation, sensory or motor handicaps, emotional disturbance, or socio-economic or cultural disadvantage, the definition does not clearly recognize that persons with those conditions may have learning disability in addition to, if not as a consequence of, their other handicap.

As a result of the advancing recognition of the interdependencies and interrelationships existing between all physiopsychological systems in the human, the National Joint Committee for Learning Disabilities made some revision in the definition. It now states:

> Learning disabilities is a generic term that refers to a heterogeneous group of disorders manifested by significant difficulties in the acquisition and use of listening, speaking, reading, writing, reasoning, or mathematical abilities. These disorders are intrinsic to the individual and presumed to be due to central nervous dysfunction. Even though a learning disability may occur concomitantly with other handicapping conditions (e.g., sensory impairment, mental retardation, social and emotional disturbance) or environmental influences (e.g., cultural differences, insufficient or inappropriate instruction, psychogenic factors) it is not the direct result of those conditions or influences.

This expansive report, published and distributed in August of 1987, is worth study. It marks a definite increase in the recognition of the lags and/or deviations that can occur in the dynamics of human development discussed in Chapter I of this book. In contrast, there is still the attempt to find specific etiologies and specific mediations instead of viewing the individual as a total being in whom any inadequacy in one area of development can impact on all other areas of development. This latest definition is certainly a long step forward and will open some minds to the further understanding of the learning process in the human and the stresses and demands of the increasingly complex future.

APPENDIX B
WHAT IS IT?

With just a few added lines this picture becomes something everyone is familiar with in everyday experience. Now, all of the many other details one "saw," because the new viewer needed to find something familiar, disappear. An astronomic map, a weather map, a duck flying in from the upper right corner, or a brick wall in the lower left portion all disappear and are difficult to recover. Knowing what this picture presents now overrides all other interpretations, and the cow is easily seen in the original picture in Chapter III.

APPENDIX C

The SOI-LA Program

There has been a broadening emphasis by numerous professionals on the critical need for interdisciplinary cooperation if learning problems demonstrated by so many students are to be mediated. The following describes an example of the coordinated efforts by informed educators and optometrists to reach some of the solutions in the epidemic of current problems.

This particular research showed that there could be intellectual growth beyond that occurring in the standard curriculum as determined by the SOI-LA evaluations. This program brought gains ranging from one-half to six and one-half grades when vision enhancement procedures were carefully combined with the most relevant intellectual development procedures. This particular program, now being continued in a number of other cooperative efforts, extended over a period of one year with 29 students participating. There were 20 boys and nine girls: three were second graders, seven were third graders, seven were fourth graders, three were fifth graders, one was a sixth grader and eight were seventh graders.

Table A shows the intellectual growth possible when students participated in vision enhancement programs coordinated with SOI training modules chosen for their relevance to the visual abilities needed in the classroom. The greatest significance of this research was the fact that there were greater gains made by each student than those usually made when either of the programs were used in isolation.

The titles at the top of each column in Table A are quite self-explanatory, and these denote the visual aspect of the intellectual abilities relevant to academic progress. The initials that appear below the column titles need further explanation. These are the SOI initials that identify those aspects of the intellectual complex directly relevant to academic progress.

Col. 1. CFU: Cognition of Figural Units: Scores here are representative of line confusions when reading, letter and word confusions and transpositions, difficulty in recognitions of shapes and sizes, and minimal differences critical to word identifications.

Col. 2. CMU: Cognition of Semantic Units: Scores here are representative of abilities in comprehension of printed material. The manner in which this test is run provides almost immediate clues to a visual problem that can be interfering with academic performance.

TABLE A

	Visual Closure	Vocabulary	Memory Attending	Memory Sequencing	Visual Discrimination	Eye-hand Coordination	Word Recognition	Ideational Fluency Quality	Verbal Fluency & Spelling
	CFU	CMU	MSU	MSS	EFU	NFU	NST	DFU	DMU
RANGE OF IMPROVEMENT	5-6	5-4	5-5	1-5	5-4	5-4	5-4	5-6	1-6.5
AVERAGE GROWTH 2.1	2.8	2.5	2.7	2.0	2.3	2.0	2.6	3.5	
NUMBER OF STUDENTS MAKING PROGRESS	22	20	16	15	19	21	21	19	18

Col. 3. MSU: Memory of Symbolic Units: Scores here represent the levels of visual memory needed for recognition of symbols infrequently encountered in the reading lessons.

Col. 4. MSS: Memory of Symbolic Systems: Scores here represent visual memory for symbolic systems such as multiplication tables, mathematical formulas, and sentence structures. Here, visual attention span and the retention of visually obtained information can be scored and can indicate the need of perceptual-motor testing and training.

Col. 5. EFU: Evaluation of Figural Units: This test probes visual discrimination skills for significant details, and low scores are related to problems of transposing or reversing letters, omitting small words, and errors with beginnings and ends of words.

Col. 6. NFU: Convergent Production of Figural Units: Scores here can relate to numerous visual-motor abilities such as keeping up with demands for copying classroom materials under time pressures.

Col. 7. NST: Convergent Production of Symbolic Transformations: This probes a student's speed of word and/or number recognition and can provide significant clues to the problems of the student who cannot complete reading assignments in the expected or allowed time.

Col. 8. DFU: Divergent Production of Figural Units: Here the individual's ability to translate personal ideas into words and drawings is probed. This test involves visual-motor coordination but also probes creativity and the imagination to complete a task without needing specific instructions.

Col. 9. DMU: Divergent Production of Semantic Units: This is also a probe of verbal fluency and creativity and can reveal difficulties in composing stories and then putting them into symbolic representations when creativity is present and adequate. Thus, it may reveal a lack of skill in the basic visual-motor skills and the concomitant intellectual skills the classroom demands.

It is particularly interesting to note that the parents and teachers of the 29 children included in this project reported: 1) better grades, 2) higher achievement scores, 3) greater motivation to go to school and to do homework, and 4) improved work and study habits.

The nine aspects of the SOI-LA evaluation are but a portion of the total test process and are given here because of the proven and significant relevance to the visual aspects of the contemporary classroom. Again, it is important to quote the Meekers:[34] "The basic philosophy of the SOI-LA is that all students have intelligence. The task is more to assess 'what kind'—not just a global 'how much.' Therefore, every student entering school can benefit from a comprehensive assessment of strengths and weaknesses in the many facets of cognitive functioning." It is appropriate to add to this comment that every student could benefit from the cooperative efforts of the educator and the clinician to assure the student of those visual skills so critically relevant to intellectual skills.

Further investigations of the Meekers' work is sincerely recommended for all who have the responsibility of guiding children to their innate potentials. It is also pertinent to draw the reader's attention to all of this as it goes so far beyond those test instruments previously discussed in Chapter V, where some test designers admitted their procedures had little value in determining classroom abilities thus possibly had no value in determining procedure for the elimination of the problems. The SOI-LA procedures provide both the etiology of the learning problems and the clinical mediations for the problems.

APPENDIX D

LYONS AND LYONS: "THE POWER OF OPTOMETRIC VISUAL TRAINING AS MEASURED IN FACTORS OF INTELLIGENCE.

The relationships between visual skills and intellectual development have been a point of interest for a number of optometrists since the early 1950s. Even then, the non-optometric critics were insisting that any gain in academic performance following vision enhancement activities was due more to individual personal attention (the Hawthorne effect) than it was to any change in visual abilities. Further, the critics were insisting there was no "scientific evidence" of the gains, and the conclusions were based entirely on "anecdotal reports" instead of "scientifically designed research studies."

It seemed quite appropriate to use some of the same instruments to judge the apparent gains that the education profession was using to appraise changes in mental abilities as a result of classroom programs. Thus, the Primary Mental Abilities (PMA) Test, supplied by Science Research Associates, was chosen to test a number of students before and after vision enhancement training (optometric vision therapy). The following chart illustrates the gains of 12 students, ranging in age from 7 to 11 years, in the test categories used in the PMA and the Chicago Tests popular then and now for the appraisal of student progress. The optometric criteria for the choice of these 12 individuals were: age and the presence of school problems not explained by obvious intellectual potentials, and also because these students had sought optometric care for visual problems that might be relevant to classroom difficulties. Only one of these 12 youngsters had an "ocular problem" that could be vaguely suspected of being a contributing factor in the classroom difficulties. The other 11 were without "ocular problems" of any magnitude.

The authors of this report made several emphatic points in their discussions of the vision enhancement procedures and the use of the Primary Mental Abilities Test. These were: "1) We were not conducting a psychological investigation, nor were we concerned with calculations of IQs. 2) We were investigating the levels of visual abilities measured by these tests. 3) When profiled, these high or contrastingly low points of individual abilities provide the design or blueprint for adapting vision enhancement procedures to the individual."

For the information of the reader unfamiliar with vision enhancement procedures, it should be noted here that routinely these are programmed for in-office activity that includes judiciously individualized regimens to establish the basic efficiency of the sight-visual system. This is supported and extended with many activities especially designed to enhance the particular visual perceptual skills the individual PMA testing identified as inadequate for the student's grade level and academic tasks. The students who were reported here were especially guided in those visual skills the contemporary optometrist has determined as being particularly relevant to the cultural tasks the student is facing. It has been undeniably determined that the proper nearpoint lens prescriptions that reduce the stress of the near-distance study task are also important in this process, and Lyons and Lyons made careful note of this assistance in their report.

Every clinician with responsibilities to students "smart in everything ... except school" should make a determined effort to obtain and study the Lyons and Lyons reports.

TABLE A

Test Scores Pre- and Post-Optometric Visual Training in the Lyons and Lyons Program

SRA-PMA Test Results (AGES 7-11) - Gains in Months

child	sex	(date) (1) age (2) grade pre-test	post-test	total train time in months	verbal meaning words	pict.	total	space perc.	reasoning words	figure	total	perception	nos.	total non-read.	total read.
4	M	10-3-52 (1)9.7 (2)4.6	1-14-53 (1)9-10 (2)4.9	2	3	0	3	38	40	6	24	21	15	18	22
5	F	4-8-53 (1)7.8 (2)2.7	6-15-55 (1)9.10 (2)4.9	4	39	56	50	6	56	37	45	40	12	29	29
6	M	4-8-53 (1)10.2 (2)5.8	6-15-55 (1)12.4 (2)7.10	4	48	33	34	10	(-9)	31	14	73	12	38	36
7	M	10-17-52 (1)7.10 (2)2.2	5-29-53 (1)8.5 (2)2.9	4	22	16	16	16	28	7	16	23	6	15	15
8	M	1-11-55 (1)11.7 (2)6.5	6-21-55 (1)12.0 (2)7.0	4	21	15	23	13	45	18	42	37	(-5)	16	22
9	M	1-24-53 (1)9.11 (2)5.1	822-54 (1)11.5 (2)6.6	6	24	32	26	7	15	34	33	25	1	27	30

#	Sex	Date 1	Date 2	(1)/(2) Date 1	(1)/(2) Date 2													
10	M	1-19-53	3-2-53	(1)9.10 (2)4.5	(1)10.0 (2)4.7	2	19	13	7	10	19	7	30	13	8	??	19	
11	M	4-15-53	11-23-54	(1)9.10 (2)5.2	(1)11.5 (2)6.8	8	45	40	47	66	16	0	16	37	30	16	32	

Chicago Tests Ages: 11-17

Gains — (1) months; (2) percentile rank

#	Sex	Date 1	Date 2	(1)/(2) Date 1	(1)/(2) Date 2		Nos.	Verbal	Space	Word Fluency	Reason	Memory
12	M	1-17-53	8-7-53	(1)16.6 (2)11.5	(1)17.0 (2)11.10	2	19 / 15	? / 13	7 / 7	56 / 37	44+ / 53	86+ / 72
13	G	8-14-54	6-10-55	(1)14.10 (2)9.10	(1)15.8 (2)10.16	6	31 / 17	30 / 20	36+ / 30	57 / 41	33+ / 25	21 / 7
14	M	2-19-54	3-23-55	(1)11.7 (2)6.10	(1)12.9 (2)8.1	7	24 / 8	27 / 12	42 / 17	45 / 31	60 / 20	34+ / 27
15	M	11-3-54	5-25-56	(1)11.3 (2)6.2	(1)12.10 (2)17.9	5	46 / 25	23+ / 1	19+ / 5	24 / 7	22+ / 3	89 / 37

Footnotes, Pertinent Publications and Remarks

A search of the literature on child development, intellectual development, and educational methods can be a never-ending process. It is not difficult, however, to pick out references and remarks that illustrate the common thread of opinions and interpretations that run through all the literature. It is interesting that even where there is considerable disagreement on methods of rearing and education of children, there is much agreement on the basic concepts of human development and how it can be hindered or enhanced depending on cultural and environmental influences.

One could fill a large book with such references and remarks. Perhaps a few of these will help every reader of this book to gather a little of the background that has been brought to summation in this publication. The comments chosen are from representatives of education, pediatrics, ophthalmology, psychology, physiology and optometry, with selections made on the basis of pertinence and status of the person quoted. Each will be identified thus: (e) for education, (p) for pediatrics, (o) for ophthalmology, (psy) for psychology, (phys) for physiology and (opt) for optometry. Please note the dates on each of the items since these will give an idea of the long-standing interest in what has been presented in this book.

Life is a succession of lessons that must be lived to be understood. Experience, and not memory, is the mother of ideas. My desire is to impress all with the importance of developing the organism through each of the different sense channels, in addition to the verbal or word centers. The tendency with the present modes of education is to overtax the memory and overload the mind with studied words. Instruction by telling is a feeble mode of impressing the mind. 'Actions speak louder than words.' Only in proportion to my experience can I understand the symbols for things, that is, words. Words are empty sounds unless accompanied by clear ideas or thoughts of the things signified. I can have true ideas or false ideas only in proportion to my experience.

From: New Methods in Education
        J. Liberty Tadd
        Orange Judd Company
        Page 16 (e)

236

The human organism strives to grow, develop and function as an integrated whole. In each of its responses to the forces or restraints in its environment which stimulate it, it performs organically by seeking physical balances with those forces and restraints which meet certain functions on an inherently determined system of coordinates. These responses have a large share in determining the organism's later developments, efficiencies, and well-being.

From: The Coordinated Classroom
        Darell Boyd Harmon
        American Institute of Architects File No. 35-B, 1942
        (psy & e)

Some of the earliest literature on visual-tactual integrations (frequently referred to as "the kinesthetic methods") appeared in the reports of Plato (427-347 BC) in Protagoras. Here he describes the early stages of learning to write. "When a boy is not yet clever in writing, the masters first draw lines, and then give him a tablet and make him write as the lines direct." Quintilian (about 68 AD) recommended: "As soon as the child has begun to know the shapes of the various letters, it will be no bad thing to have them cut as accurately as possible upon a board, so that the pen may be guided along the grooves. Thus mistakes such as occur with wax tablets will be rendered impossible, for the pen will be confined between the edges of the letters and will be prevented from going astray." Quintilian further advised "learning the sound and the form of the letters simultaneously."

From: Remedial Techniques in Basic School Subjects
        Grace M. Fernald
        McGraw Hill Book Company, 1943
        Page 27 (psy)

Perhaps the most important conclusion to be drawn from the extensive researches here reported is that disability of any degree in any of the basic school subjects is wholly preventable. If educational methods were more intelligently adapted to the idiosyncrasies of the individual child, all children would achieve up to their mental level in all school subjects. It is largely for this reason that I believe this book is one of the most significant contributions ever made to experimental pedagogy.

From: Remedial Techniques in Basic School Subjects
        Professor Lewis Terman, Stanford University
        McGraw Hill Book Company
        Page ix (psy and e)

Discrimination is a process of differentiation; perception is a higher level process of recognition. For example, visual discrimination is a prerequisite to the visual perception, or recognition, of the words in the reading process. A pupil who can discriminate between the forms of words is a good observer. Some children, for some reason or combination of reasons, do not make accurate observations regarding the likes and differences between word forms. Visual discrimination is based upon trained observational skills.

From: Foundations of Reading Instruction
       Emmett Albert Betts
       American Book Company, 1946
       Page 330 (e)

Comparable social forces are beginning to define the possibilities and opportunities of professional specialization in the field of child vision. The child specialist in this area will have a basic scientific interest in the nature and needs of child development. He will relate his practice to the broader aspects of family and child welfare, as well as to specific visual difficulties; he will recognize the pervasive mechanisms of growth in his policy of periodic follow-up; he will adjust treatment and guidance to these mechanisms; he will appreciate that vision lies close to the citadel of personality and will so render his services that the dignity of the individual child will be respected. This he will do through deepened insight into the general dynamics of growth which underlie the patterning of individuality in vision.

From: Vision, Its Development in Infant and Child
       Arnold Gesell, et al.
       Paul B. Hoeber, 1949
       Page 294 (p)

It is our belief that motions and perception are inseparably related. The development of perception in the child is the development of motions, and the only valid understanding of perception at any level is in terms of the movements that define it. The organization and stability of the perceptual field depend on movements of orientation, location, and differential manipulations that have become established in the motion patterns of the individual.

From: Perception and Motion
       KU Smith and WM Smith
       W. B. Saunders Co., 1962
       Page 7 (psy)

It should be remembered that biologically the eyes were adapted for relatively simple purposes ... to look for enemies and for food; and although, from long custom, we accept the conditions in which we live today as normal, it by no means follows that the eyes have evolved sufficiently to fulfill the exorbitant demands of unremitting close work imposed upon them by a highly complex and artificial civilization. The more is this understandable when we remember the functional minutiae required for the attainment of accurate vision and the high degree of coordination necessary between the movements of the two eyes so they will fulfill the requirements of binocular vision. It is understandable that this complexity of the visual apparatus tends to make it less capable of withstanding long-continued strain than a cruder and less highly specialized mechanism.

From: Ophthalmic Optics and Refraction
          Sir Stewart Duke-Elder
          C. V. Mosby, 1970
          Page 559 - Vol. V (O)

Visual exercises: We have already seen in the fourth volume of this series of texts that vision includes not only the formation of retinal images by the dioptric system of the eyes and their transference by physiological processes to the cortex (of the brain), but also the perceptual appreciation of their presentation as patterns endowed with meaning. In the interpretation of such patterns the memories of past experience play a dominant part and the ease and efficiency of the process of seeing depends in a very large measure on the facilitation of the cortical processes involved. Orthodox ophthalmology has devoted itself almost entirely to the events occurring at the lower level, and has confined its interest to the means of attaining suitable dioptric images on corresponding retinal areas to the relative exclusion of the consideration of events at the higher level; and it must be admitted that this unequal division of interest is without reason! Difficulties of interpretation at the higher level can be as much a cause of strain as (optical) disturbances at the lower, and in the easement of visual strain the ophthalmologist should give consideration to them both. The facilitation of the processes of seeing is exemplified in a comparison between the efforts of a child who fixes each letter in his early attempts at reading with the practiced reader who can interpret print with a glance which does not require fixation even on each word; it is the difference between the facile ease of the practiced golfer or skater and the strained efforts of the tyro ....Repetitive exercises, by facilitation of the perceptual processes and the provision of an accumulated fund of memories and associations to aid interpretation, are of an immense aid in the art of seeing.

From: Ophthalmic Optics and Refraction
        Sir Stewart Duke-Elder
        C. V. Mosby, 1970
        Pages 575-576 - Vol. V (O)

Therefore, the inherent responsibilities that are assumed by every adult who is guiding children demand that only the best and most thorough care and guidance be given the child. If this responsibility is shirked, or ignored, to any degree in any of these observations, then both the teacher and the child will suffer the consequences. The teacher's daily load will be heavier and less productive and in some cases complete failure! The child's daily load will be more difficult and discouraging, and in time, may become so discouraging to him that he no longer tries to succeed in the visual process of learning to read. The early identification of any interfering visual problem can be the difference between success and failure for both the child and the teacher in the total educational process.

From: The Early Identification of the Interfering Visual Problem
        G. N. Getman in Learning to See and Seeing to Learn
        R. C. Orem
        Mafex Associates, Inc., 1971
        Page 123 (Opt)

Robinson (1953) reported that the only visual scores which consistently differentiated high and low achievers (in reading) involved binocular visual performance. It is interesting to note that Beltman et al. (1967), in their study of dyslexia, reported that 42% of the dyslexics and only 9% of the controls failed their simple foveal suppression tests. Yet, they concluded this finding was not significant. Benton (1973) reports five times the incidence of convergence difficulties in the learning-disabled population as compared to the normal. In the literature on vision and learning one very definite trend becomes apparent. Those who considered the physiological as well as the physical visual processes found relationships to exist between vision and learning. Those who restricted their testing largely to the physical segment found there was little or no relationship between vision and learning. However, all state that they were appraising vision.

From: Basic Visual Process and Learning Disability
        Gerald Leisman
        Charles Thomas Co., 1976
        Page 333 (e)

Vision is developed by the growing child as a result of the child interacting with his environment. The process of this development has been carefully documented by numerous researchers and clinicians (Gesell, 1949; Getman, 1962; Piaget, 1969). Their studies leave little doubt that vision is a learned skill. Its development has been shown to follow the same laws of anatomical, physiological and psychological development as all other learned skills, and therefore is subject to the same developmental inadequacies. Visual system inadequacies can lead to visual problems, which, in turn, may affect the learning process.

From: Basic Visual Processes and Learning Disability
         Gerald Leisman
         Charles Thomas Co., 1976
         Page 393 (e)

The development of vision in the individual child is complex because it took countless ages of evolution in the race to bring vision to its present advanced state. Human visual perception ranks with speech in complexity and passes through comparable developmental phases. Moreover, seeing is not a separate, isolable function; it is profoundly integrated with the total action system of the child, his posture, his manual skills and coordination, intelligence, and even his personality make-up. Indeed, vision is so intimately identified with the whole child that we cannot understand its economy and its hygiene without investigating the whole child (Gesell, 1949). Vision, therefore, may be the key to a fuller understanding of the nature and needs of the individual child. He sees with his whole being. The conservation of vision, particularly in the young child, goes far beyond the detection and correction of "refractive errors." Acuity is only one part and aspect of the economy of vision.

From: Basic Visual Processes and Learning Disability
         Gerald Leisman
         Charles Thomas Co., 1976
         Page 394 (e)

What complicates the diagnosis of the learning-disabled child and what can be accomplished to help this child visually are two questions which must be answered. Confusion regarding vision and sight will continue to exist because many educators, psychologists, pediatricians and others in the medical profession equate vision solely with refractive errors and reduced visual acuity. On the other hand, many optometrists consider a model of vision which incorporates the perceptual, developmental and integrative aspects along with the simple end- organ functions of acuity, fixation, accommodation, convergence and fusion (Rappaport, 1967).

From: Basic Visual Processes and Learning Disabilities
          Gerald Leisman
          Charles Thomas Co., 1976
          Page 405 (e)

Just as there must be a recognition of the interrelationships of the information systems within the total child, there must be a recognition of the interrelationships of the sources of information now available. Just as none of the information systems in the child can be considered in isolation, neither can the information sources be considered in isolation. This concept (of interdisciplinary communication) is not new by any means, but although it is frequently expressed, it has yet to be very frequently implemented because of the reluctance of so many in some disciplines to either listen to, or read, the philosophies of other disciplines. I learned long ago that I eventually profit the most by directing myself to read and examine the comments of those with whom I do NOT agree. If we can all begin to do this, new and positive vistas will be opened to such as those of us contributing to this book ... but more especially to every child we will be influencing, either directly or indirectly (Getman, 1976).

From: Teaching Children with Learning Disabilities
          J. M. Kauffman and D. P. Hallahan
          Charles E. Merrill, 1978
          Page 234 (e)

Departure from the traditional disease model. By dealing with a child's strengths and styles, the pediatrician, or health care professional, deviates from the traditional disease orientation. For example, one might "diagnose" particularly superior motor skills in a child and then suggest ways such an asset can be utilized. This requires a departure from the deficit-oriented medical model.

From: A Pediatric Approach to Learning Disorders
          M. D. Levine, R. Brooks and J. P. Shonkoff
          Wiley and Sons, 1980
          Page 12 (p)

If we confine our attention to activity involving physical interaction with the environment, or objects in it (that is, ignoring such activities as verbal communication), it is clear that vision is the most powerful exteroceptive sense. No one would, I suppose, dispute this. What I want to argue, however, is that vision is also the most powerful proprioceptive and exproprioceptive sense. Further, because of its trimodal power, vision normally functions as an overseer in the control of activity, developing patterns of action, and tuning up other perceptual systems, and keeping them tuned.

From: The Function of Vision in Modes of Perceiving and Processing Information
D. N. Lee
H. L. Pick, Jr., and Elliott Saltzman, Eds.
John Wiley & Sons, 1983
Page 361 (psy)

To help children to learn, carefully prescribed preventive, learning lenses for use in the classroom are irreplaceable. This is the only thing that will satisfy the avoidance response to school-task containment. With the educator using present knowledge of developing visual perception in children, and the behavioral optometrist applying his clinical knowledge to prevent visual problems that interfere with learning, there is the possibility of developing a generation of adults capable of fully utilizing their intellectual endowments. These superior adults will fulfill the exacting demands of our developing technical age.

From: Clinical Optometry
A. M. Skeffington
Optometric Extension Program
Monthly Chapters, 1928-1976 (Opt)

In human society, most information is acquired through the visual system. Uncorrected impairment of visual functioning can prevent the normal acquisition of information through this sensory modality and lead to difficulties in learning. While most definitions of learning disability explicitly exclude diagnosable vision disorders, there may be subtle abnormalities of binocular functioning, accommodation to close visual targets, or higher processing of visual information that interfere with the learning process. Detection of such abnormalities and exclusion of more obvious vision problems at the earliest possible point in a child's development are crucial to the prevention of subsequent learning disabilities that might otherwise ensue.

From: Report of the National Eye Institute (Section of the NIH)
Learning Disabilities, A Report to the U.S. Congress
Interagency Committee on Learning Disabilities, 1987
Page 32

Individuals improve their motor skill through the use of programmed movements only after they have properly understood the behavioral goal for which the movements were used. Movements are learned from past experience if they are recognized as having been successful.

Learning from previous experience thus depends on sensing and moving, not just on sensing. The two processes are facilitated by unceasing communications between sensory and motor systems. One example where this is of great importance is "active touch" or handling objects. Their shapes and textures are perceived better when the objects are actively explored than when they are passed over the passive hand and fingers.

From: The Neural Basis of Motor Control
        V. B. Brooks, Ph.D.
        The Oxford University Press, 1986
        (phys)

FOR ADDITIONAL INFORMATION AND DEEPER INSIGHTS

The four groups that can turn the academic problems into academic solutions are: 1) the parents who know their youngsters' capabilities; 2) the youngsters who still want to learn and succeed; 3) the teachers who want more than standard lesson plans and drill on facts, and 4) the clinicians who want proven solutions rather than more symptoms. There is now literature available to all of these individuals. The following is a listing of the most relevant and pertinent books and video tapes. To assist in this solutions' search, each listed item's primary thrust is noted in parenthesis.

Books

1. Elkind D. Child development and education. New York: Alfred A. Knopf, Inc. (Child Development)

2. Elkind D. The hurried child, growing up too fast too soon. New York: Alfred A. Knopf, Inc. (Child development)

3. Elkind D. Miseducation, preschoolers at risk. New York: Alfred A. Knopf, Inc. (Early education)

4. Getman GN. How to develop your child's intelligence. Box 636, White Plains, Maryland: Research Publications. (Child development)

5. Granger L, Granger B. The magic feather, the truth about "special education." New York: E.P. Dutton. (Education)

6. Grassilli R, Hegner P. Playful parenting. New York: Richard Marek Publishers. (Parents' opportunities)

7. Hallahan DP, Cruickshank WM. Psychoeducational foundations of learning disabilities. Englewood Cliffs, NJ: Prentice-Hall, Inc. (Learning problems)

8. Hoopes A, Hoopes T. Eye power. New York: Alfred A. Knopf, Inc. (Visual training)

9. Kavner RS, Dusky L. Total vision. New York: A and W. Visual Library. (Vision therapy)

10. Kavner RS. Your child's vision. New York: Simon and Schuster, Inc. (Vision and child development)

11. Kauffman JM, Hallahan DP. Teaching children with learning disabilities, personal perspectives. Columbus, Ohio: Charles E. Merrill Publishing Company. (Views on learning problems)

12. Kraskin RA. You can improve your vision. Garden City, NY: Doubleday and Company, Inc. Contact author at 4600 Massachusetts Ave. N.W., Washington, DC 20016. (Visual training)

13. Levy J. The baby exercise book for the first 15 months. New York: Pantheon Books. (Child development)

14. Leisman G. Basic visual processes and learning disability. Springfield IL: Charles C. Thomas. (Learning processes)

15. Levine MD, Brooks R, Shonkoff JP. A pediatric approach to learning disorders. New York: John Wiley and Sons. (A medical perspective)

16. Lyons EB. How to use your power of visualization. Red Bluff, CA: Lyons Publications, 19065 St. Croy Road, Red Bluff, CA 96080. (Vision development and intelligence development)

17. Rowley EV. Enhance your child's development. Published by author, 14461 Woodinville-Redmond Rd. N.E., Woodinville, WA 98072. (Child and vision development)

18. Smith F. Insult to intelligence, the bureaucratic invasion of our classrooms. New York: Arbor House. (Education)

19. Ungerleider DF. Reading, writing and rage. Rolling Hills Estates, CA: Jalmar Press. (Education)

20. Wunderlich RC. Kids, brains and learning. St. Petersburg, FL: Johnny Reads, Inc. (Child development, neurologic and nutritional development)

(Editors Note: No publication dates were submitted with the original manuscript and since this work was published posthumously, it was not feasible to obtain more information from the author. Those readers who wish to obtain any of these books should be able to do so given the above information.)

Video Tapes

1. Sheil ML, Sasse M. The importance of being an infant.

2. Sheil ML, Sasse M. The importance of being 1.

3. Sheil ML, Sasse M. The importance of being 2.

All video tapes are produced by Toddler Kindy Gymbaroo, Pty. Ltd., 4 Selbourne Road, Kew, Victoria, Australia 3101 and are available from Research Publications, Box 636, White Plains, Maryland 20695. Telephone: (301) 645-2224.

References

1. Wheeler RH, Perkins FT. Principles of mental development. New York: Thomas Y. Crowell Co., 1932.

2. Roark AC. Much of education research found to be inadequate. Los Angeles Times, March 16, 1988: page 3.

3. Getman GN. How to develop your child's intelligence, 8th edition. White Plains, Maryland: Research Publications, 1984.

4. Birch HG. Dyslexia and the maturation of visual function. In Reading disability, (J. Money, Ed.). Baltimore: Johns Hopkins Press, 1962.

5. Gesell A. (Director, Original Yale Clinic of Child Development, New Haven, CT.) Personal communications.

6. Public Law 94-142, passed by Federal Legislature, 1967. (Please see Appendix A for definitions of learning problems that this law established.)

7. Gray WS. On their own in reading. Chicago: Scott, Forsman Co., 1948.

8. Smith KU, Smith WM. Perception and motion. Philadelphia: W. B. Saunders Co., 1962.

9. Gesell A, Ilg FL, Bullis GN, Getman GN. Vision: its development in infant and child. New York: P. B. Hoeber (Harper), 1949.

10. Fernald GM. Remedial techniques in basic school subjects. New York: McGraw-Hill, 1943.

11. Sherrington C. Man on his nature. Cambridge, England: Cambridge University Press, 1951.

12. Lisberger SC. The neural basis for learning of simple motor skills. Science, 242 (November, 1988).

13. Renshaw S. Psychological optics. Santa Ana, CA: Optom Extension Prog, 1940-1955.

14. Gesell A. Infant development, the embryology of early human development. New York: Harper and Brothers, 1952. (Also: The embryology of human behavior, a sound film, narrated by Gesell, available from the International Film Library, Chicago, IL.)

15. Roby A, Gottsacker R. Developing vision skills. ESEA Title IV-C, Fountain Valley School District, Fountain Valley, CA, 1982.

16. von Helmholtz, HLF. Treatise on physiological optics, (JPC Southall, Ed.) Rochester, NY: Optical Society of America, 1924. (Note: von Helmholtz was a German physiologist who was credited by all students of vision as the primary authority on the physiological structure and function of the eye. His influence is still great.)

17. Cohen AH. The efficacy of optometric vision therapy. J Am Optom Assoc, 59, 1988.

18. Hubel DH, Wiesel TN. Nobel prize winners in neurophysiology (1981), quoted in numerous articles: Time, Oct 19, 1981; Science, Oct 30, 1981; Sci Am, Dec 1981.

19. Peachey GT. Some observations of the functional relationship of central and peripheral visual fields in a learning-disabled population. Santa Ana, CA: Optom Extension Prog, Research Reports and Special Articles, March and April, 1976.

20. Greenspan SB. Annual review of literature in developmental optometry. J Optom Vis Dev, 7 (4), 1976.

21a.Gottfried AW, Rose SA. Tactile recognition memory in infants. Child Dev, 51, 1980.

21b.Fagan JF, Singer LT. Infant recognition memory as a measure of intelligence. In: Advances in infancy research (LP Lipsitt, Ed.). Vol. 2, ABLEX, 1983.

22. Goldberg R. From personal conversations with this cartoonist and from quotations in the press at his death.

23. Robinson HM. Clinical studies in reading. In: Supplemental Educational Monographs. Includes A.Gesell's, Vision and reading from the standpoint of child development. Chicago: University of Chicago Press, 1953.

24. Selye H. The stress of life. New York: McGraw-Hill, 1956.

25. Richards R. Visual skills appraisal. Novato, CA: Academic Therapy Publications, 1984.

26. Bachara GH, Zaba JN. Psychological effects of visual training. Acad Therapy, 1976, 12 (1):99-104.

27. Duke-Elder S. Ophthalmic optics and refraction, Vol. 5, Chapter 15. St. Louis, MO: C. V. Mosby, 1970.

28. Aoki C, Siekevitz P. Plasticity in brain development. Sci Am, December 1988.

29. Hayakawa SI. The revision of vision. In: The language of vision, G. Kepes. Chicago: Paul Theobald, 1944.

30. Staff Writers. Readin', 'ritin', and Ritalin. Freedom (Education Section), Los Angeles, CA, August 1988.

31. Peachy GT. Learning disabilities: reflections and perspectives. Symposium '86, K Adamson, Ed. Jeffersonville, PA, The Pathway School, 1987.

32. Halstead, WC. Brain and intelligence. Chicago: University of Chicago Press, 1947.

33. Getman GN, Henderson C, Marcus S. The visual recall test. Aptos, CA: Efficient Seeing Publications, 1985.

34. Meeker M, Meeker R. Structure of intellect learning abilities test, (SOI-LA), Los Angeles, CA: Western Psychological Services, 1985.

35. Lyons CV, Lyons EB. The power of optometric visual training, Parts I - V. J Am Optom Assoc, Dec. 1954, Nov. 1956, June 1957, June 1961, Aug 1967.

36. Western Psychological Services, 12031 Wilshire Blvd., Los Angeles, CA 90025.

37. SOI Systems, 45755 Goodpasture Road, Vida, OR 97488.

38. Hermon DB. The coordinated classroom. AIA File No. 35-B,, American Seating Co., Grand Rapids, MI, 1949.

39. Handwriting (special section). Acad Therapy 18 (4), 1983:389- 436.

40. Tadd JL. New methods in education. New York: Orange Judd Co., 1898 (Student's edition, 1901).

Other educational materials published by VisionExtension and the Optometric Extension Program Foundation on the subject of vision as it relates to behavior and learning:

BOOKS

Suddenly Successful Student by Hazel Richmond Dawkins, Ellis Edelman, O.D., and Constantine Forkiotis, O.D.

A parent and teachers guide to learning and behavior problems—how behavioral optometry helps.

Suddenly Successful by Hazel Richmond Dawkins, Ellis Edelman, O.D., and Constantine Forkiotis, O.D.

The expanded comprehensive companion to *Suddenly Successful Student* written for the whole population.

How to Develop Your Child's Intelligence by G.N. Getman, O.D.

Written to help parents and teachers understand the critical relationship between vision and intelligence. Discusses school readiness.

Vision and School Success by Lois Bing, O.D., Lillian Hinds, Ph.D., and George Spache, Ph.D.

A broad discussion of vision: its sensory, motor and central processing dimensions. Written to help educators understand the visual demands of the classroom and ways of alleviating visual stress.

PAMPHLETS

Educator's Guide to Classroom Vision Problems

Helps school personnel make observations of childrens' visual behavior that could interfere with academic progress.

Does Your Child Have a Learning-related Vision Problem?

Provides a simple-to-use checklist of signals to help parents and teachers recognize a child who is having learning-related vision difficulties.

VIDEOS

Vision and Learning

Produced by Sharon Luckhardt, O.D., and AT&T. Demonstrates signs and symptoms of learning-related vision problems as well as numerous vision therapy techniques.

Vision in the Classroom

Based on Educator's Guide. Outlines vision development and learning problems and the signs and symptoms of these problems.

For more information on these publications or a catalog please contact:
VisionExtension
2912 S. Daimler Street
Santa Ana, CA 92705-5811
(714) 250-0846